Extending the Limits
of Reliability Theory

EXTENDING THE LIMITS OF RELIABILITY THEORY

HAROLD GOLDBERG

Former Chief Weapons Engineer
U.S. Naval Sea Systems Command
Washington, D.C.

A WILEY-INTERSCIENCE PUBLICATION

JOHN WILEY & SONS,   New York • Chichester • Brisbane • Toronto

Library of Congress Cataloging in Publication Data:

Goldberg, Harold, 1914—
  Extending the limits of reliability theory.

  "A Wiley-Interscience publication."
  Includes index.
  1. Reliability (Engineering) I. Title.

TS173.G63   620′.00452   81-4534
ISBN 0-471-07799-2   AACR2

Printed in the United States of America

10 9 8 7 6 5 4 3 2 1

Preface

This book is not a rearrangement of the material that can be found in the many existing books on reliability theory; in fact, it presupposes a reader already familiar with that literature and its present application. This book is for those who view current theory and its application results with nagging doubts. Why do so many reliability predictions fall so far short of actual field experience? Why does the mean time between failures (MTBF), considered as unique a characteristic of a system as its physical dimensions, vary so substantially from individual to individual in a supposedly identical set of systems? Must one be satisfied with a theory based only on the exponential distribution, the law of chance failure, when everyone agrees it does not apply to mechanical systems? How well can we know the failure characteristics of the components we design and manufacture into systems? Are these components truly in that flat part of the "bathtub curve," where the failure rate can be considered constant and beyond "infant mortality"? Does the failure behavior of systems after failure and repair differ from the time to the first failure of the system? Does the average behavior of systems in the aggregate tell us very much about the behavior of individuals? What can redundancy really do for reliability? Is it always effective? This book is aimed at answering these and other questions. The fundamentals of reliability theory are examined broadly, not just confined to the narrow limits of the exponential distribution.

The first six chapters concentrate on the fundamental cornerstone of reliability theory, the time-to-failure distribution of a component, on the problems of determining this basic characteristic of any component, and on the impossibility of ever achieving precise determinations of this fundamental characteristic because of the "tyranny of large numbers" fundamental to probability. This part of the book also reviews current sources of component failure data such as MIL-HDBK-217C, whose modest claims to precision are overlooked by so many of its users.

Chapter 7 defines the mean time to first failure of a new system, the MTTFF, a system characteristic quite different from the MTBF. Chapter 8 examines the "survivor" behavior of new systems under a variety of time-to-failure distributions; Monte Carlo experiments are performed to show the relation of real world performance to theory. Chapter 9 takes the time to first failure of new systems into the world of redundancy and discovers some remarkable but not previously known behavior in such systems.

The remainder of the book is almost entirely devoted to a topic that is given little coverage in reliability texts: "renewal theory." This is the study of the behavior of systems that are not discarded after the first failure but are repaired after each failure. This is the true realm of the MTBF, but even here it is seen that the MTBF is not properly understood. The book makes major extensions to renewal theory and, in particular, makes extensive use of Monte Carlo experiments to demonstrate the behavior of individual systems under renewal. The Monte Carlo routines were carried out on a vest-pocket-size, card-programmable computer; the programs used are provided. The limitations of this modest computer have not prevented powerful insights into the behavior studied, many of which are quite surprising.

HAROLD GOLDBERG

Pembroke Pines, Florida
March 1981

Contents

Extending the Limits of Reliability Theory

CHAPTER ONE

Introduction

1.1 THE NATURE OF PHYSICAL THEORIES

One can adequately discuss this matter by considering the development of the theory of the motions of the heavenly bodies. The first mathematically inclined astronomers fitted the observed data to a set of curves (a mathematical model); these assumed the earth to be the center of reference (observer based) and required the considerable complication of epicyclic curves. This theory had splendid utility in predicting future positions of the heavenly bodies, a fortunate result of their basic periodicity, but could not explain the reasons for the observed motions nor predict the behavior of a body that was as yet unobserved. The Copernican modification of the theory, making the sun the reference point, enormously simplified the mathematics but provided no more insight.

The advent of the theory of gravitation, however, moved the astronomer from the macroscopic to the microscopic, in a sense. Gravity itself was an unexplained observable, but the motion of heavenly bodies could now be predicted and explained. This ability to predict the behavior of ballistic bodies was necessary to the space program; for example, reaching the moon by the cut-and-try method would have been impossible.

The purpose of the above discussion is to point out that until a theory has predictive powers in new situations, its utility is limited. In terms of man's scientific approach, a theory is a mathematical model of a phenomenon or a device. Being mathematical, there is no limit to the arithmetic precision possible, but as a description of something in the real world, the precision possible is not a matter of arithmetic, but a matter of how well the mathematical model predicts its real-world counterpart. Accordingly, and reliability theory is no exception, the precision appropriate to a prediction must be determined by the fit to the real world, not by the number of bits in one's computer. The author believes that current reliability practice has exceeded the predictive power of the theory and the limits of that theory need to be understood. Further, there is inadequate understanding of the renewal process, the successive cycles of failure and repair in a system, and the difficulties of getting good failure data on components.

1.2 SOME EXAMPLES OF CURRENT PRACTICE

The mean time between failures (MTBF) is undoubtedly the cornerstone of current reliability theory; it is specified, predicted, and demonstrated. The user of the output of the reliability community usually regards the MTBF of an equipment in the same sense that one regards its physical dimensions, that is, as constant within some reasonable tolerance band. Can the MTBF be interpreted in this sense? Let us look at Figure 1.1. This is a histogram of the MTBFs of 115 "identical" computers, measured over one year's operating time, plotted to the nearest 100 hours; note that the MTBFs range from 200 to 7200 hours. This is certainly far from a reasonably constant value. Incidentally, in connection with an improvement program the manufacturer and designer of this equipment predicted a MTBF of 1413 hours. Does this indicate a limitation of current reliability theory? As a matter of fact, we shall show later in this book that one cannot expect a constant MTBF in the above sense and behavior similar to that shown in Figure 1.1 is to be expected. If one predicates a spare-parts provisioning on a constant MTBF, it is clear that provisioning is unlikely to prove successful.

A not unusual example of reliability allocation comes from a reliability prediction submitted in connection with the design of a major weapon system; it specified a MTBF of 2,687,334 hours for a particular component. This number undoubtedly came out of a computerized prediction routine; is it justified? Can one order a component to such a requirement? Having received it, is it possible to verify that it meets that specification? We shall examine this problem very carefully in this book.

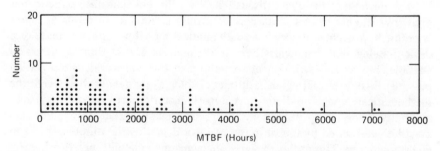

Figure 1.1 Histogram of the MTBFs of 115 identical computers, one year's operation.

Finally, in a report on CMOS life evaluation we find a predicted failure rate of 5.93×10^{-92} per hour at 50°C. This was calculated by applying the Arrhenius equation to failure rates measured at a higher temperature; this is an accepted procedure in reliability predictions. Since the above failure rate implies one failure in about 10^{91} hours, the "big bang" origin of the universe is supposed to have happened some 10^{14} hours ago, and the lives of the most stable elementary particles are now thought to be on the order of 10^{35} hours, it is fair to ask whether such calculations require some limitation.

The above examples reflect another problem in the current application of reliability theory, namely, the precision implied in numerical statements relative to failure rates, MTBFs, and so on, a problem not unique to the reliability community. In the case of the computers whose performances are portrayed in Figure 1.1, the procuring agency advised the user community that the computer MTBF was 1747 hours. The implication of such a statement is that the MTBF is known to the nearest hour, that it is not 1748 or 1746 hours. The implied precision is 1 part in 1747. The data of Figure 1.1, however, belies such precision. In fact, even a statement that the MTBF is 1700 hours is misleading if made without remarking that the range is 200 to 7200 hours. In the case of the failure rate allocation of 2,687,334 hours the implied precision is better than 1 part in 2 million. We shall see later that this order of precision is a practical impossibility when one is determining real failure rates. Even the relatively modest precision implied in the failure rate of 5.93×10^{-92}, 1 part in 593, will be questionable if the sample is insufficient.

1.3 HISTORICAL COMMENTS

While it is true that "reliability formalism" and "reliability theory" undoubtedly saw their flowering as a result of the horrendous unreliability of electronic weapon systems in the "electronic technology explosion" that started with World War II, to imply that reliability was not a concern, or was not understood, or was unattainable before that period is to deny a simple fact. Man's earliest preoccupation with reliability was undoubtedly related to weaponry and, soon after, to structures. In the structural world reliability meant structures that would not collapse; the ability to design and build reliable structures was quite far advanced by the Roman era. Initially, structural design was not a science, it was heuristic. If a bridge collapsed when tested with a team of elephants, a stouter bridge was built and tested again; this was the "test-fix-test" phase. Later, structural design became an engineering science and it became possible to design the necessary structural strength into new types of structures (prediction) without resorting to "test-fix-test." Except for some notable failures, the Tacoma Narrows Bridge, for example, we now have so much confidence in our ability to design structures that we do not ask for demonstrations and predictions. In fact, it would be economically disastrous should we have to do so.

"Structures" is a broad term; it includes steam engines, turbines, electrical generators, transformers, automobiles, and a wide variety of the items we take for granted. Very reliable representatives of these classes of items were designed and manufactured long before the advent of reliability formalism. Even in the electronic world Bell Telephone Laboratories managed to design and build highly reliable undersea telephone cables before this formalism became known and widely practiced. Many of these cables are operating reliably today; these are being replaced for economic reasons, not for lack of reliability. Despite the comments above, however, the reliability activities and formalisms that have developed since the 1940s are crucial to the enormously complex devices that we face today. To use them properly it is necessary that we thoroughly understand these tools.

1.4 A SHORT REVIEW OF CURRENT THEORY

Although the Preface stated that this was not a stand-alone book and it assumes the reader has considerable knowledge of the field and the literature, a short review of the basics of the current "law of chance failure" (exponential) theory follows.

Put N identical devices into operation at the same instant ($t = 0$) and operate these devices for some time t. If at time t the number of devices surviving is $s(t)$, the usual definition of the reliability of the devices is

$$R(t) = \frac{s(t)}{N} \tag{1.1}$$

where the interpretation of reliability is the fraction of devices surviving at time t. The fraction of devices failed at time t is obviously

$$F(t) = 1 - R(t) \tag{1.2}$$

Now consider N becoming large without limit; $R(t)$ and $F(t)$ have now become continuous functions of t. Define a failure density function $f(t)$,

$$f(t) = \frac{d}{dt} F(t) = \frac{-d}{dt} R(t) \tag{1.3}$$

One may also define the instantaneous failure rate, or hazard rate,

$$\lambda(t) = \frac{f(t)}{R(t)} \qquad (1.4)$$

$Nf(t)\,dt$ is interpreted as the number of devices failing in the interval dt, expressed as a fraction of the original number N under test, while $N\lambda(t)\,dt$ is the number of devices failing in the interval dt, expressed as a fraction of the number surviving at time t. The total function group has various properties

$$\int_0^\infty f(t)\,dt = 1$$

$$\int_0^\infty \lambda(t)\,dt \neq 1$$

$$\int_0^t f(t)\,dt = F(t) \qquad (1.5)$$

$$f(t) = \lambda(t)\exp\left[-\int_0^t \lambda(x)\,dx\right]$$

The mean time to failure (MTTF) of the devices under test can be calculated as

$$\text{MTTF} = \int_0^\infty tf(t)\,dt = \int_0^\infty R(t)\,dt \qquad (1.6)$$

Most of the reliability literature confuses the MTTF, the average time of failure of a number of devices put under test, with the MTBF, the mean time between failures of a single device as it goes through successive cycles of failure and repair (renewal).

The preceding discussion is concerned only with describing the results (outcome) of an experiment; nothing is said about predicting the results of an experiment about to be performed. To make that transition assume that the devices for the preceding experiment were picked at random from a very large population, large compared to N. This population has a time-to-failure probability density function $f(t)$. The predicted reliability function for a new experiment is now

$$R(t) = 1 - \int_0^t f(x)\,dx \qquad (1.7)$$

The correspondence between the prediction and the outcome of an experiment will depend on the size of N and the degree to which $f(t)$ is actually known. *It is important to understand that the reliability function describes what happens when a large number of devices are put into operation. It has no meaning applied to a single device, since one cannot talk about the fraction surviving of a single device.*

1.4.1 The "Bathtub Curve" and the "Law of Chance Failure"

Early in the development of reliability formalism it was observed that when large numbers of particular complex systems are tested, the instantaneous failure rate (hazard function) $\lambda(t)$ behaves in the general manner shown in Figure 1.2. The similarity of this curve to a bathtub's cross section gave it its name. The important observation is that this curve has a minimum, that is, a point of zero slope. In the neighborhood of this point $\lambda(t)$ is essentially constant. The mathematical properties of a system whose hazard function is constant are remarkable for their mathematical convenience and are widely studied in the literature. The probability density function $f(t)$ corresponding to a constant failure rate is

$$f(t) = \lambda e^{-\lambda t} \tag{1.8}$$

where λ is the constant failure rate. This mathematical model of a failure process is also called the "law of chance failure." The corresponding reliability function is

$$R(t) = e^{-\lambda t} \tag{1.9}$$

The MTTF of a large number of systems that fail according to this law is $1/\lambda$.

The present theoretical basis for most reliability analysis assumes that the exponential law corresponding to the constant hazard function describes a system's behavior throughout its service life. This leads to a most convenient

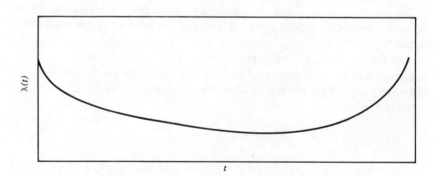

Figure 1.2 The bathtub curve.

reliability function for a system composed of different components, provided that any component failure constitutes a system failure and component failures are independent. Given a particular component type with hazard rate λ_j, the reliability function for a single component with that hazard rate is

$$e^{-\lambda_j t}$$

If there are M_j of these particular components in a system, the reliability function of the M_j components is the product of the component reliability functions

$$R_j(t) = e^{-M_j \lambda_j t}$$

Finally, if there are n different component types, the system reliability function is the product of the group reliability functions

$$R_s(t) = \exp\left(- \sum_{j=1}^{n} M_j \lambda_j t \right) \tag{1.10}$$

This result has compelling mathematical convenience but troublesome philosophical inferences. A large group of identical systems of this nature has the following interesting behavior. If a large number of new systems are put on test and the failures observed as they occur, the reliability function is seen to correspond to the function (1.10). Suppose that record keeping is stopped at some time t and the surviving systems are considered as the basis of a new experiment. The surviving systems are now operated with the clock restarted, failure times are recorded, and the reliability function determined. It is found that both reliability functions are the same. Thus the exponential law of failures seems to imply that the future is not influenced by the past; regardless of the previous history of the systems to be tested, their reliability function does not change.

This leads to the conclusion, for example, that the reliability function of a large number of 10 year old television sets is the same as the reliability function exhibited by these sets when new. This does not mean that an individual set is miraculously renewed when the clock is restarted; a used individual set has lost a part of whatever life it had when new. Nevertheless, in general, the inference remains and challenges experience. Experience can be satisfied, of course, by arguing that a constant hazard rate does not persist indefinitely.

The exponential time-to-failure distribution has another troublesome philosophical inference: the law of chance failure, that is, the exponential time-to-failure distribution describes a process in which failure occurs solely by chance and is not deterministic. Yet the same reliability community that uses this law fervently believes that failure is deterministic and is due to design flaws, poor workmanship, inadequate process control, handling damage, and a host of other factors. In fact, the advances in real reliability have come from stringent efforts to eliminate failure mechanisms, matériel and human, and not from reliability formalism. Thus there is a dichotomy between real world belief and reliability formalism; this is illustrated by the following thought experiment.

You have agreed to make a parachute jump, provided the parachute supplier can convince you that the parachute reliability exceeds .99. You may take the supplier's assurances, conduct your own examination, or test up to 1000 randomly sampled parachutes from an inventory of 50,000. How are your actions from this point dependent on whether you believe in chance or deterministic failure?

If you are a believer in chance failure, you will organize a reliability demonstration employing all 1000 chutes, since you are unwilling to entrust your life to small-sample theory. Test realism poses some problems: an aircraft is available for the test, but volunteers for the jumps are scarce. Dummies are substituted and the tests result in five failures. Statistical calculation shows that there is a 97.5% confidence that there are no more than 9 defectives per 1000. You agree that the chutemaker has met his end of the bargain, and the day of the jump arrives. You pick a chute at random from the remaining inventory and make the jump believing that:

All parachutes in the inventory are equally reliable.
The outcome of the jump will be determined by chance during the jump.
The chance of survival is better than .99, with a confidence of 97.5%.

If you believe that failure is causal, a different process is followed. If you are not a parachute expert, you hire one; he states that the parachute involved uses an aerodynamic design that is well proven and that given good materials and quality workmanship, the crucial determinant of proper function is packing. An inspection of a random sample of 1000 chutes shows proper material and excellent quality; five chutes are found to be improperly packed. The jump is made with a chute picked at random. Your thoughts are:

About 5 chutes in a 1000 are improperly packed.
My life depends on the chance that the chute I picked is improperly packed.
The chance of that is no more than 9 in a 1000, with a confidence of 97.5%.

The statistical conclusions about the chance of failure are the same; the procedures and philosophy are very different.

1.5   A PARABLE

In the days before reliability became a formal discipline, a mature design engineer was asked to design a reliable, expendable device for a service life of 1 hour. The device required about 100 components, all identical; a large stock of the required parts happened to be in inventory. The engineer was not a statistician, but he was a sensible designer with good business sense; naturally, his first thought was to use existing inventory, if possible. His preliminary design indicated the need for about an hour of manufacturing assembly and testing; thus at least 2 hours of reliable life were needed. To provide a 100% margin the engineer decided that 4 hours of failure-free life was necessary. To check the suitability of the inventory he withdrew 500 parts, taking them from various boxes (he didn't know about random sampling, but it seemed good common sense), and put them into operation under a simulation of the operational environment. Finding only one failure after 5 hours, he terminated the test, convinced that the parts in inventory were satisfactory. Ultimately, the company learned that the customer had been quite happy with the product. The moral to this parable is that one can design and build reliable equipment without reliability theory and its concepts. Further, if only two hours of reliable operation is required, it is not necessary to know what happens to the components over a longer period.

CHAPTER TWO

Probability and Statistics

2.1 THE OBJECTIVE VIEW OF PROBABILITY

Two apparently contradictory statements appeared in the discussion of the reliability function $R(t)$ in Section 1.4. While discussing $R(t)$ as a description of the outcome of an experiment, it was stated that $R(t)$ had no meaning when applied to a single device—how could one intepret the fraction surviving of a single device? Nevertheless, while discussing prediction, it was stated that $R(t)$ was the probability of survival of a single device at time t. (This is a universally accepted concept.)

Most of us freely use the notion of probability without really appreciating its meaning. The jargon of probability is so widespread that almost anyone will state that the probability of getting a head in a single toss of a coin is $\frac{1}{2}$. Nevertheless, if one had never heard about probability theory (another special mathematical model), the only honest statement one could make would be either, "I don't know" or, "It will either be a head or a tail." If we consider another thought experiment, rolling a fair die and asking the probability of rolling a one, probability theory tells us that the probability is $\frac{1}{6}$. Without knowledge of probability theory, one would still have to say, "I don't know" or, "A one will occur or it will not." Although these two situations have different probabilities, the statements made about the next event were identical. *The fact of the matter is that in the case of a single event,* probability theory or no, one can only say that this event or its null will occur. The attachment of a probability to the event means that *if one repeats the toss or roll an enormous number of times in the same environment, one would expect heads to occur on-half the time or a one to occur one-sixth of the time.* This is the objectivist definition of probability. *Thus the statement of the probability of a single event automatically refers to the massive repetition of that event.* Thus the apparent contradiction referred to at the beginning of this chapter is no contradiction at all. Nevertheless, it is customary for the laity, and even some members of the reliability community, to somehow derive meaning from applying $R(t)$ to a single device. As a matter of fact, that meaning can be thought of as the "personal" view of probability. In this school an event probability of .99 is translated into, "I'm very sure its going to happen the next time I try it." It can also cover, "There's a high probability that this planet has been visited by extraterrestrials."

To fix the lesson of the above discussion consider yourself to be at a crap table in a Las Vegas casino with just enough time for one bet. You are an expert at craps and know all of the probabilities, odds, and house advantages; what do you play? The "don't pass" bar gives the house the least advantage; however, the person rolling the dice has made 10 consecutive passes. If you are not swayed by hunches and really believe that knowledge of probabilities does not forecast the outcome of the next event, it would seem that the correct strategy is to make the bet with the highest payoff. Incidentally, the house does play probabilities and prospers; it deals with large numbers of events.

2.2 THE BINOMIAL DISTRIBUTION

The binomial distribution is a very basic probability model and an extremely important one for much of what comes later in this text. It is a discrete distribution and deals with binary events, that is, events that have only two possible outcomes. Given p, the probability of an event, and q equal to $1 - p$, the probability of the null event, then the probability that the event will occur exactly x (a positive integer) times in n trials is

$$P(x) = C_x^n \, p^x \, q^{n-x} \qquad (2.1)$$

where

$$C_x^n = \frac{n!}{x! \, (n - x)!} \qquad (2.2)$$

is the combination of n things taken x at a time. Now

$$\sum_{x=0}^{n} P(x) = 1 \qquad (2.3)$$

and $P(x)$ is a discrete probability density function, defined only for

$$x = 1, 2, \ldots, n.$$

This contrasts with the continuous probability density function that is defined for all values of its variable.

$$\sum_{x=0}^{j} P(x) \qquad (2.4)$$

is the cumulative probability that no more than j events have taken place, with $j \leq n$. It follows that the cumulative probability that no less than $j + 1$ events have taken place is

$$\sum_{x=j+1}^{n} P(x) = 1 - \sum_{x=0}^{j} P(x) \qquad (2.5)$$

As an illustration, compute the probability of exactly 5000 heads in 10,000 coin tosses. It is

$$p(5000) = \frac{10,000!}{(5000!)^2} (\tfrac{1}{2})^{10,000}$$

$$= .008 \qquad (2.6)$$

The above probability applies to a single event, 10,000 tosses of a coin; accordingly, heads would appear exactly 5000 times in 0.8% of a great many repetitions of the event, 10,000 tosses. In fact, if one calculated the probability of exactly 50,000 heads in 100,000 tosses, one would find that the probability was even smaller. This seemingly contradicts the definition of objective probability given in this chapter; it will be shown that the two agree in the mathematical sense of limits. In a trial in which the number of tosses may increase without limit it can be shown that the fraction of heads that do occur, even if not exactly one-half, approaches one-half as closely as one may desire.

To obtain an estimate of the number of tosses required for the actual fractional number of heads to fall within some given range about $\tfrac{1}{2}$, one needs some additional properties of the binomial distribution. These are

$$\text{Mean value} = np$$

$$(2.7)$$

$$\text{Standard deviation} = (npq)^{1/2}$$

If n is very large, it has been shown that 0.9987 (rounded to four significant digits) of the possible outcomes will lie within ± 3 standard deviations of the mean. Given 10,000 tosses, the mean is 5000 and the standard deviation is 50. The theory predicts, therefore, that whenever one tosses 10,000 coins, the number of heads that will occur will fall between 4850 and 5150 over 99% of the time that the experiment is repeated, that is, within $\pm 3\%$ of $\tfrac{1}{2}$. This calculation should impress one with the fact that precision in probability involves very large numbers of experiment iterations. For a result within $\pm 1\%$ of $\tfrac{1}{2}$ over 99% of the time, the number of trials is 90,000; for $\pm 0.1\%$, the number is 9×10^6. In other words, the precision increases as the square root of n.

2.3   USING PROBABILITY FOR PREDICTION

Probability models are used to predict events that are influenced by chance. The previous discussion of the binomial theorem applied such a model to predicting the result of coin tossing. Is it a correct model? In the early beginnings of probability theory even celebrated mathematicians did not accept it without experimental verification; they actually resorted to coin tossing. In the years since those early days there has been ample opportunity to test these models. In fact, the definition of statistics is in part the analysis of data stemming from probability models and in part the development of the probability models needed to treat problems.

The probability density function (p.d.f.) is the basis for predicting the behavior of any probabilistic situation, such as system reliability. Given the p.d.f., one can compute a reliability function, and the instantaneous failure rate if that is also desired. The study of reliability problems requires a special class of p.d.f.'s. These are functions of time and are zero for all negative values of the variable. These p.d.f.'s describe the time-to-failure behavior of components of systems.

Why should one believe that statistical analysis and probability models provide the means for prediction? The heuristic basis for such a belief lies in the assumption that if one randomly draws a large sample from a very large population with a known p.d.f., the sample will possess the same properties and behavior as the total population. Thus a device constructed with this sample will statistically behave in the manner described by an appropriate probability model using the p.d.f. of the original population. Implicit in this process is all the variability characteristic of statistical behavior, that is, the need for very large numbers if one is to achieve results close to the predicted values.

2.4   THE MEANING OF THE RELIABILITY (SURVIVOR) FUNCTION

The reliability function is

$$R(t) = 1 - \int_0^t f(x)\, dx \qquad (2.8)$$

where $f(t)$ is the time-to-failure p.d.f., also known as the time-to-failure distribution. It is the fraction of a large number of identical devices put into operation at time zero that survive in the interval $(0, t)$. When $R(t)$ is used in the predictive sense, the binomial distribution provides the estimate of the degree of correspondence to be expected between the actual fraction surviving in a real experiment and the value predicted by $R(t)$. Close correspondence requires the testing of very large numbers.

It is unfortunate that the term "reliability" has been linked to the above function. Many interpret $R(t)$ as applying to a single unit; it is doubtful that a term such as "fraction surviving" would be similarly applied, since "fraction" implies more than one. The temptation to link $R(t)$ with a single unit is even more persuasive to many if that unit is a complex of many components; yet this is completely irrelevant.

To illustrate, consider a component drawn from a time-to-failure distribution $\lambda e^{-\lambda t}$. The fraction surviving, $R(t)$, is $e^{-\lambda t}$. One such component by itself, however, assuming that components either perform properly or are otherwise considered failed, has a survival graph in time which is unity up to the time of failure and zero thereafter. This is true of any component, regardless of the time-to-failure distribution it is drawn from.

As a matter of fact, the term "reliability function" is not universally used. Cox (1962) refers to it as the "survivor function." From this point on, this text will also use the term "survivor function," symbolized $\underline{fs}(t)$ to represent

$$\underline{fs}(t) = 1 - \int_0^t f(x)\, dx \qquad (2.9)$$

The sole purpose of the name and symbol is to emphasize the true nature of the function and to discourage its misuse.

2.5 DISCRETE AND CONTINUOUS DISTRIBUTIONS

The time-to-failure distributions used in current reliability theory are generally continuous, $\lambda e^{-\lambda t}$ being a notable example. These distributions are defined everywhere in the interval $(0, \infty)$. A continuous, uniform time-to-failure distribution is shown in Figure 2.1. It has the constant value 1.25 in the interval $(0, 0.8)$, and is zero elsewhere. The cumulative failure distribution for this uniform distribution is shown in Figure 2.2; it is continuous and defined over the interval $(0, 0.8)$.

A discrete time-to-failure distribution is defined at discrete values of time t_n only in the interval $(0, \infty)$. The t_n are usually equally spaced, such as

$$t_n = n\underline{t}$$

but need not be. In general, a discrete time-to-failure distribution is written

$$f(t_n) \qquad t_n = t_0, t_1, \ldots \qquad (2.10)$$

where

$$t_0 = 0$$

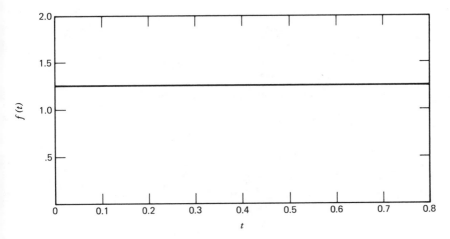

Figure 2.1   Continuous, uniform time-to-failure distribution.

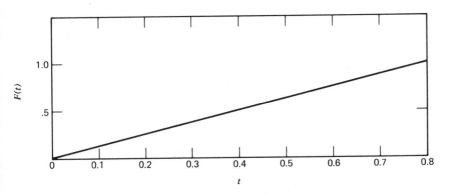

Figure 2.2   Cumulative, continuous, uniform time-to-failure distribution.

Figure 2.3 exhibits two discrete analogs of the continuous distribution shown in Figure 2.1. The solid dots portray one analog, the crosses, the other.

Continuous time-to-failure distributions have the following properties:

$$f(t) = 0 \qquad t < 0$$

$$f(t) \neq 0 \qquad 0 \leq t \leq L$$

$$f(t) = 0 \qquad L < t \leq \infty$$

L is called the "life" of the distribution and may be finite or infinite.

$$\int_0^L f(t)\, dt = \int_0^\infty f(t)\, dt = 1$$

$$\underline{fs}(t) = 1 - \int_0^t f(x)\, dx = 1 - F(t) = \int_t^\infty f(x)\, dx$$

defining $F(t)$, the cumulative time-to-failure distribution.

$$f(t) = \frac{-d}{dt}\, \underline{fs}(t)$$

$$\text{MTTF} = \int_0^L t\, f(t)\, dt = \int_0^L \underline{fs}(t)\, dt$$

or

$$\text{MTTF} = \int_0^\infty t\, f(t)\, dt = \int_0^\infty \underline{fs}(t)\, dt$$

The discrete time-to-failure distribution has the following properties:

$f(t_n)$ is defined only for $(0 \le n \le L)$ where t_L is defined as the life of the discrete distribution and may be finite or infinite. $f(0)$ is zero.

$$\sum_{n=1}^L f(t_n) = \sum_{n=1}^\infty f(t_n) = 1$$

$$(2.11)$$

$$\underline{fs}(t_j) = 1 - \sum_{n=1}^j f(t_n) = 1 - F(t_j)$$

defining $F(t_j)$, the cumulative discrete distribution.

$$\underline{fs}(t_0) = \underline{fs}(0) = 1 - \sum_{n=1}^0 f(t_n) = 1$$

defining the meaning of the above summation. (2.12)

$$f(t_j) = \underline{fs}(t_{j-1}) - \underline{fs}(t_j)$$

$$\text{MTTF} = \sum_{n=1}^L t_n f(t_n) = \sum_{n=0}^{L-1} (t_{n+1} - t_n)\underline{fs}(t_n)$$

If

$$(t_{n+1} - t_n) = \underline{t}$$

$$\text{MTTF} = \sum_{n=1}^L n\underline{t}\, f(t_n) = \underline{t} \sum_{n=0}^{L-1} \underline{fs}(t_n)$$

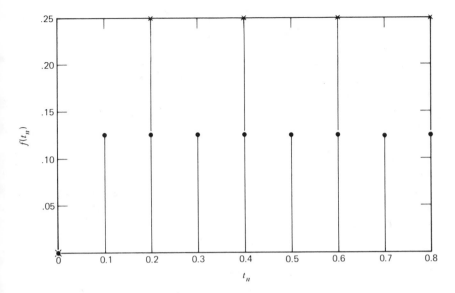

Figure 2.3 Discrete analogs of the continuous, uniform time-to-failure distribution.

There are significant additional differences between continuous and discrete time-to-failure distributions.

Figure 2.3 depicts two discrete analogs of the continuous distribution of Figure 2.1. One of these is the amplitude series, 0, .125, .125, ... at $t_n = 0$, 0.1, 0.2, 0.3, ... The other has amplitudes 0, .25, .25, .25, and .25 at $t_n = 0$, 0.2, 0.4, 0.6, and 0.8. These are not the only analogs; there are an infinite number possible, depending on the number and location of the t_n. The graphic convention employed in Figure 2.3 is not universally accepted, but is the one to be employed in this text. The vertical lines are merely visual aids, they have no other significance.

2.5.1 Graphic Representation of Discrete Cumulative Distributions

Recall that $F(t_n)$ is defined at the t_n only. In the case of a distribution such as the binomial distribution, $F(x)$, the cumulative binomial distribution, is defined for integer values of x only; the cumulative distribution has no meaning for noninteger values of x. In the case of a continuous process in time represented by a discrete p.d.f. of time the cumulative distribution represents a different problem. Although $F(t_n)$ is only defined at t_n, $F(t)$ has unknown but bounded values in the interval (t_{n-1}, t_n). In that interval

$$F(t_{n-1}) \leq F(t) \leq F(t_n)$$

A representation of the left-hand side of the inequality is shown in Figure 2.4. The straight line is the cumulative probability distribution for the continuous uniform distribution; the black dots are the cumulative discrete probability function representing one of the analogs of Figure 2.1. The staircase represents the lower bound of $F(t)$ as represented by the discrete cumulative distribution.

A representation of the complete inequality is shown in Figure 2.5. The straight line is the cumulative probability distribution for the uniform distribution; the crosses are the discrete values of $F(t_n)$ for the other discrete analog, and the boxes enclose the possible values of $F(t)$. While logical, this graphic method is too busy. Accordingly, the convention that will be used is the lower bound convention, that of Figure 2.4; it is widely accepted. Incidentally, when graphing a discrete survivor function, the same convention logically results in an upper bound, since

$$\underline{fs}(t_n) = 1 - F(t_n)$$

Additional insights are provided by Figures 2.6 and 2.7. The trapezoidal figure in Figure 2.6 is a continuous p.d.f.; the discrete function shown is one of its analogs. Figure 2.7 shows the cumulative probability distribution of the continuous distribution of Figure 2.6, accompanied by the lower bound convention of the discrete cumulative probability distribution for the analog shown in Figure 2.6.

The above examples portray the fundamental relationship between a continuous distribution and any of its discrete analogs. Each value $f(t_n)$ is the cumulative probability of the continuous distribution in the interval (t_n, t_{n-1}). Thus the discrete analog is a sort of pseudocumulative version of the continuous distribution.

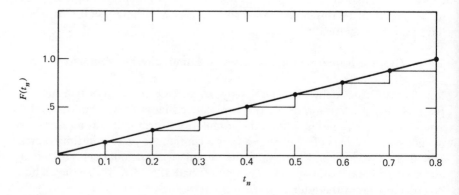

Figure 2.4 Properties of the cumulative distribution corresponding to the discrete, uniform, time-to-failure distribution.

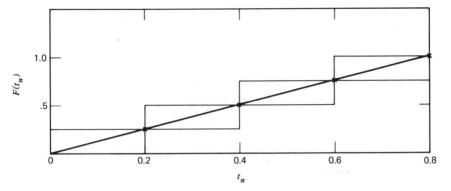

Figure 2.5 Other properties of the cumulative distribution corresponding to the discrete, uniform, time-to-failure distribution.

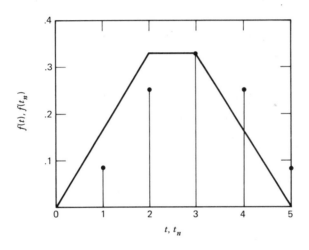

Figure 2.6 A continuous distribution and its discrete analog.

2.6 TIME-TO-FAILURE DISTRIBUTIONS

It has been noted before that a time-to-failure distribution is a single-valued function that may be a continuous or discrete function of time, is zero for time less than zero, and has the property

$$\int_0^\infty f(x)\, dx = 1 \quad \text{or} \quad \sum_{n=1}^\infty f(t_n) = 1 \qquad (2.13)$$

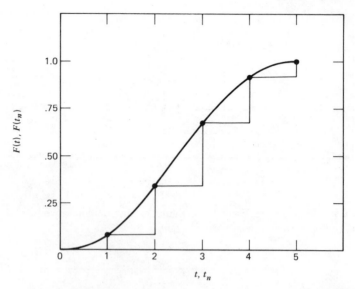

Figure 2.7   The cumulative distributions corresponding to the distributions of Figure 2.6.

Quite obviously, there are an unlimited number of mathematical functions that can serve this role. In fact, the restriction of equation (2.13) need not be explicit, it need only be implied or possible.

To illustrate this, consider the following function.

$$f(t) = 0 \qquad t < 0$$

$$f(t) = \frac{1}{L} \qquad t \geq 0 \tag{2.14}$$

As given above, the function violates condition (2.13). We can cure the violation by declaring $f(t)$ to be zero for t greater than L. If we stay within the interval $(0, L)$, however, our calculations of $F(t)$, $fs(t)$, and $\lambda(t)$ are absolutely correct, whether we declare the cure or not; it is sufficient that the cure exists and that we are mindful of the limits it imposes. In fact, it is unecessary to declare $f(t)$ to be zero for t less than 0; staying within the interval $(0, L)$ is sufficient. We can also construct time-to-failure distributions piecewise. Consider the function defined as

$$f(t) = \lambda e^{-\lambda t} \qquad 0 \leq t < L$$

$$f(L) = e^{-\lambda L} \delta(L) \qquad [\delta(L), \text{ a delta function}] \tag{2.15}$$

$$f(t) = 0 \qquad \text{for all other } t$$

This function satisfies all conditions for a time-to-failure distribution. It also has the same properties as the exponential distribution in the interval (0, *L*).

The probability and statistics literature contains many distributions and extensive analyses of their properties. The majority of the distributions are continuous and all are expressed in mathematically closed forms. Mathematical convenience and tractability are important characteristics, sometimes overshadowing the need for the best model for a particular problem. Many of these are found in the reliability literature. The exponential distribution was extensively studied in the statistical literature long before reliability theory was developed.

2.7 DISTRIBUTIONS FOUND IN THE RELIABILITY LITERATURE

2.7.1 The Exponential Distribution, $\lambda e^{-\lambda t}$

This distribution is universally used to model the behavior of components of systems having substantial electronic content. It is used to model not only the behavior of electronic parts of a system, but of mechanical parts as well. There is powerful argument for its use, wherever justified; reliability calculations based on this distribution are the simplest possible. Is its universal use based on reasons other than its mathematical convenience?

Now

$$f(t) = \lambda(t) \exp \left[- \int_0^t \lambda(x) \, dx \right]$$

In any interval in which $\lambda(t)$ is a constant, λ, $f(t) = \lambda e^{-\lambda t}$ in that same interval. There is no doubt that all new "unscreened" components exhibit a hazard function $\lambda(t)$ resembling the bathtub curve of Figure 1.2 generally but not in detail. Such functions have a minimum; in the neighborhood of a such a minimum, one may declare, to some approximation, that the function is constant. Subject to the degree of approximation, is this a sufficient condition to declare that the survivor function of a system composed of one or more of these components may be calculated using the exponential distribution? What is the situation in a system composed of many different kinds of components? Is it necessary that the flat portions of the components' respective hazard functions coincide or at least overlap? Further, if it is valid to apply the exponential distribution in the flat parts of the hazard function, how valid is the assumption that the results extend to the nonflat regions?

The above inquiries deserve serious consideration and their study forms a substantial portion of this book. The reliability literature has not given this matter sufficient attention; the limitations inherent in the above situation require understanding.

2.7.2 The Uniform Distribution

The distribution shown in Figure 2.1 is one example of a uniform p.d.f. suitable as a time-to-failure distribution. In general, such uniform distributions are characterized as

$$f(t) = \frac{1}{L} \qquad 0 \le t \le L$$

$$F(t) = \frac{t}{L}$$

$$\underline{fs}(t) = 1 - \frac{t}{L}$$

$$\lambda(t) = \frac{1/L}{1 - t/L}$$

(2.16)

Note the interesting property of the hazard function of a uniform distribution; its minimum is at zero time. This means, of course, that in the neighborhood of zero time *a uniform distribution can be approximated by the exponential distribution $(1/L)e^{-t/L}$*. Of course, for values of time in the neighborhood of zero,

$$\underline{fs}(t) \cong e^{-t/L}$$

This derives directly from the expression for $\underline{fs}(t)$.

2.7.3 The Weibull Distribution

This distribution, valid in the interval $(0, \infty)$, is derived by assuming the hazard function to have the form

$$\lambda(t) = Kt^m \qquad m > -1$$

$$f(t) = Kt^m \exp\frac{-Kt^{m+1}}{m+1}$$

(2.17)

$$\underline{fs}(t) = \exp\frac{-Kt^{m+1}}{m+1}$$

In the range of m, $(-1^+, 0^-)$, the Weibull distribution hazard function is a decreasing function of time. A zero value for m yields a constant hazard function, that is, the distribution is exponential. All values for m greater than one represent a rising hazard function. The Weibull distribution is not claimed to represent any particular physical process.

2.7.4 The Exponential Hazard Function

Another mathematical model is the distribution corresponding to an exponential hazard function. Thus

$$\lambda(t) = Ke^{at}$$

$$f(t) = Ke^{at} \exp\left[-\left(\frac{K}{a}\right)(e^{at} - 1) \right] \tag{2.18}$$

$$\underline{fs}(t) = \exp\left[-\left(\frac{K}{a}\right)(e^{at} - 1) \right]$$

2.7.5 The Normal Distribution

One would assume that the celebrated normal distribution needs no comment; such is not the case. *The normal distribution does not satisfy the conditions required for a time-to-failure distribution*! It violates the condition that

$$\int_0^\infty f(t) \, dt = 1$$

Instead

$$\int_{-\infty}^\infty n(t) \, dt = 1$$

where $\tag{2.19}$

$$n(t) = \frac{1}{\sigma(2\pi)^{1/2}} \exp \frac{-(t - \mu)^2}{2\sigma^2}$$

One can modify the normal distribution so as to fully satisfy the conditions for a time-to-failure distribution. The modified function is

$$f(t) = \frac{n(t)}{1 - \displaystyle\int_{-\infty}^0 n(t) \, dt} \qquad 0 \le t \le \infty \tag{2.20}$$

This is one possible modification; others can be proposed. $f(t)$ is no longer a normal distribution; its mean is no longer μ. If μ is positive, the modification above is very minor if μ/σ is large; it is major if that constraint is not present. The modified function above is analyzed in a later chapter.

2.7.6 Composite Distributions

One can form distributions as the sum of other distributions, provided that one takes care to satisfy the necessary constraints. For example, if

$$f_1(t) = \lambda e^{-\lambda t} \qquad \text{over the interval } (0, \infty) \tag{2.21}$$
$$f_2(t) = 1/L \qquad \text{in the interval } (0, L) \text{ and } 0 \text{ elsewhere}$$

then $\frac{1}{2} f_1(t) + \frac{1}{2} f_2(t)$ is a time-to-failure distribution in the interval $(0, \infty)$.

REFERENCES

Cox, D. R. *Renewal Theory*. Methuen, London 1962.

CHAPTER THREE

Determining the Time-to-Failure Distribution of a Component, Introduction

3.1 DEFINING SOME TERMS AND CONCEPTS

Component A nonrepairable device.

System A complex device consisting of one or more components of one or more types.

New component A component, not yet operated, randomly selected from a population with a known time-to-failure distribution.

New system A system with zero operating time, composed of new components.

These definitions involving the term "new" are very important. Whenever one makes a reliability prediction at any time, one must know the time-to-failure distributions representing the state of the components of systems at that time. At best, one has only the possibility of knowing these distributions at specific times and not at arbitrary times. For example, if one knows the time-to-failure distribution of a particular component at the time it is shipped from a vendor's factory, the parts may not correspond to that distribution after passing through incoming inspection and will certainly not when delivered as part of a new system by the system manufacturer. Depending on the product, the system may have undergone minimal or no testing by the time it reaches the shipping dock, or it may have seen more than 1000 hours of testing and have been repaired more than once. In the latter case, certainly, it is not valid to predict the survivor function of the shipped equipment based on component distributions, for example, as measured at the component vendor's plant. Accordingly, these considerations will continue to receive close scrutiny.

3.2 TIME-TO-FAILURE DISTRIBUTION OR HAZARD FUNCTION?

The p.d.f. is the fundamental building block of probability theory and, of course, is fundamental to reliability theory. Nevertheless, reliability literature makes great use of the hazard function, or instantaneous failure rate function. Mathematically, since one can be derived from the other, there is no reason to choose one or the other. They are substantially different; however, the hazard function is not a distribution, that is,

$$\int_0^\infty \lambda(x)\,dx \neq 1$$

Further, when t is equal to L, the life of the distribution, $f(L)$ is always finite or zero but $\lambda(L)$ is infinite.

A much more important aspect of their difference is the manner in which a distribution or a hazard function is determined. In theory, a time-to-failure distribution is determined by putting N components into operation and operating these to failure *without replacement*. The continuous distribution is determined by allowing N to increase without limit. (This entire process is explained in great detail in later sections of this chapter.) The hazard function can then be derived from

$$\lambda(t) = \frac{f(t)}{fs(t)}$$

As mentioned before, the time-to-failure distribution $f(t)$ can be interpreted in the following manner. $N f(t)\,dt$ is the probable number of failures in an interval dt about t. Expressed as a fraction of the number put under test, it is $f(t)\,dt$. Then the average rate of change of $f(t)\,dt$ in dt is obtained from $f(t)\,dt/dt$, or $f(t)$. Thus $f(t)$ is the "instantaneous failure rate" expressed fractionally in terms of the original number put into test. In the same interval dt about t, however, $N f(t)\,dt$ expressed as a fraction of the number surviving at time t is

$$\frac{N f(t)\,dt}{N fs(t)}$$

Dividing the above function by dt yields the average rate of change in dt about t. But this is $\lambda(t)$. Thus $\lambda(t)$ is the instantaneous failure rate expressed fractionally in terms of the number surviving at time t.

This interpretation for $\lambda(t)$ seems to suggest a method for determining $\lambda(t)$ directly, one that avoids determining $f(t)$. Since $\lambda(t)$ is based on the number surviving, it would seem that, equivalently, one could start with N components under test and *replace these as they fail.* The number of replacements per unit time would then be the desired hazard function. *The fact is that the outcome of such an experiment is not the hazard function except in one exceptional theoretical situation.* The process proposed above is an example of a "renewal process," a subject of considerable importance which is dealt with in later chapters.

Convenience is the reason usually given in the literature for concentrating on the hazard function rather than the time-to-failure distribution. Considering the almost universal commitment of the community to the exponential distribution, there is no doubt that the hazard function is convenient; what is simpler than a constant? Not only is the community and the literature overwhelmingly committed to a constant hazard function, but *essentially the entire available data base on component failure behavior is predicated on that assumption.* In fact, it is a matter of edict in the U.S. Department of Defense. Nevertheless, the validity of this assumption will be examined.

3.3 HOW MAY TIME-TO-FAILURE DISTRIBUTIONS BE OBTAINED?

It would seem that there are three sources from which time-to-failure distributions may be obtained: *a priori* knowledge, estimation, and test. Factually, there are only two, since *a priori* knowledge simply means using a previously existing estimation or test. The mechanical structures world is well endowed with *a priori* knowledge that is dependable and well coupled to design practices which do not use the reliability formalism typical of the electronics world. Industry discipline is such that handbook and vendor data may be trusted, except in the most critical situations. The electronics world also has a wealth of information available, but its dependability is quite inferior to that of the structures world.

The designer/manufacturer of equipment rarely embarks on internal programs of component testing on the scale required to yield an even moderately precise time-to-failure distribution. Even the Bell System, a very large integrated component and system manufacturer, will only perform a sufficient test program in critical situations. In most cases one depends on experience or the credibility of the component design and the quality capability of the vendor. In critical situations the purchaser will therefore resort to extensive vendor surveillance and critical incoming inspection methods, including dissection.

Estimation is an alternative to testing whenever there is a requirement for reliability over very long periods of time. Bell Laboratories carried out a 20 year design and test program before committing an undersea, electronic telephone cable to service; they no longer consider this economical, or even necessary. Ultimately, the only proof of an estimate is real time experience.

3.4 THE "HOW TO GET MORE OF THE SAME" PROBLEM

Assuming that the manufacturer has obtained satisfactory parts but now needs more, he is always faced with the problem of "how to get more of the same." To one experienced in the real world this is no trivial problem. In theory, one may avoid this problem by taking the following action:

Make a one-time purchase of each of the required components sufficient to support the test program for time-to-failure distribution determination, the design and manufacture of the requisite number of deliverables, and for the spare parts required to support these deliverables during the intended service life.

Incidentally, the environment for the distribution test program should faithfully conform to the environmental profile for each part, not only service use but all phases of manufacturing. Needless to say, the above conditions are rarely, if ever, met. Nevertheless, an investigation based on the above ideal is useful: it sets an upper bound to expected performance.

3.5 "EMPIRICAL DISTRIBUTIONS"

If one proceeds, without *a priori* assumptions, to determine an unknown time-to-failure distribution only by testing, one is attempting the determination of an "empirical distribution," according to the statistical literature. The literature has little to say about empirical distributions; many texts ignore the subject altogether. Rather, the thrust of most of the statistical literature is the fitting of an assumed continuous distribution to failure test results. This process can lead to rather ambiguous results when the data are few. For example, suppose one has a small number of failures grouped closely together in time. One now makes a best fit of the peak of a Weibull function to this data. Do the tails of the resulting Weibull function really represent the nonexistent failure data in those regions? How can one be sure of this without taking considerably more data? Nevertheless, there are cases in the literature where it is solemnly assumed that there is no need for further data taking, that is, the fitted function represents reality.

3.6 AN ALGORITHM FOR DETERMINING A DISCRETE EMPIRICAL DISTRIBUTION

The following sequence of steps will determine a discrete empirical distribution.

1 Put N components into operation under the specified environment; stop the operation when all components have failed or the intended service life has been exceeded. The magnitude of N should be based on statistical inferences and a guess as to the possible distribution.

2 Record failures and failure times to the accuracy and resolution deemed necessary and construct the histogram of the data.

3 Apply statistical tests to determine whether N was sufficiently large to determine all parts of the distribution to the desired precision and confidence. If N is found to be insufficient, use statistical inference to estimate an appropriate N based on the results and repeat step 1 on the additional sample indicated. Then repeat step 2 on the total data. If N is still found to be insufficient, repeat as necessary.

4 Obtain the discrete time-to-failure distribution by dividing the ordinates of the final histogram by the total number of components tested. To the precision and confidence statistically imputed for each ordinate of the final graph this is the "empirical," discrete time-to-failure distribution for the components tested.

The above procedure is straightforward except in two areas. It does not give specifics on how to choose N to satisfy desired precision and confidence. It is also vague with respect to the recording of failures and failure times and the construction of the histogram. These concerns can be clarified by running a real world experiment. Let us conduct the above procedure on a population with a known time-to-failure distribution and see how large N must be to determine this known underlying distribution to a particular precision and confidence. Fortunately, for some distributions the experiment can be carried out as a Monte Carlo simulation, a purely mathematical operation. This requires a method of obtaining random numbers; one can either use a computer—and the appendix of this book contains various programs for this purpose using the Texas Instruments TI-59 card programmable computer—or a published table—a good source is the CRC Press *Handbook of Tables for Probability and Statistics,* second edition.

3.7 A THOUGHT EXPERIMENT ON A UNIFORM DISTRIBUTION

The first phase of the following experiment is carried out in our imagination, a thought experiment. An infinitely large "bingo shuffler" is filled with an infinite number of balls, each imprinted with a number in the interval (0, 10^5). These numbers, representing failure times in that interval, uniformly cover the interval; no two are identical. The "shuffler" and the balls represent a population having the uniform time-to-failure distribution shown in Figure 3.1. To run an experiment on a sample size N of 100 it is only necessary that 100 balls be drawn from the shuffler, the numbers recorded, and a histogram constructed. Immediate difficulty surfaces, the numbers cannot be recorded.

3.7.1 Time Resolution in the Real World

In our thought experiment each of the infinite numbers printed on the balls must be of the form

$$I_1I_2I_3I_4I_5.D_1D_2D_3\ldots$$

where the I_n represent the numbers in the interval (00000, 99,999) and the D_n represent the decimal digits. There are, of course, an infinite number of D_n possible. Obviously, one cannot record an infinite number of digits in a finite time. *This is tantamount to the statement that one cannot record time with infinite resolution,* that is, time may only be recorded with finite precision.

To solve this problem the experiment must be reconstituted to provide finite time resolution. One method is to read only certain digits on each ball. For a time resolution of 10^{-5} of the life of the distribution it is only necessary to read the I_n, ignoring the D_n. Then any number falling in the interval (00000, 00001) would be read as 00001, any number in the interval (00001, 00002) would be read as 00002, and so on. (Alternatively, the first number

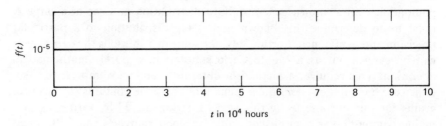

t in 10^4 hours

Figure 3.1 Uniform distribution for Section 3.7.

could be read as 00000, the second as 00001, etc.) This truncation has several consequences.

1   Certain data has been lost. The number of failures within the finite time of resolution are known, but not the times of occurence within that interval. Further, multiple failures within the resolution interval must be considered simultaneous.

2   The method of experimentation may now be revised. Instead of truncating readings, one may use truncated imprints. In this case imprints on the balls in the shuffler are repeated; appropriate care is required so that each number in the now finite set is equally represented.

3   With truncated imprints, a thought experiment is no longer necessary. The shuffler and its balls may be replaced by a random number generator and the experiment conducted in the real world. Parenthetically, the real world experiment conforms to the conditions of avoiding the "how to get more of the same" problem.

4   *It is no longer possible to discover a continuous distribution; the above process can only yield a discrete distribution to any desired degree of precision.* A continuous distribution can only be approximated by smoothing the discrete distribution.

3.7.2   An Experiment With the Random Number Population (00000, 99,999)

The population above can represent a uniform, discrete time-to-failure distribution with a time resolution of 10^{-5} of its life. The time value assigned to a resolution element is arbitrary: let us consider it to be 1 hour for this experiment; the life of the distribution is now approximately 11 years. The experiment requires a test conductor, an analyst, and a source of 100 random numbers. The source of these numbers is the first two columns of page 342 of the CRC Press *Handbook of Tables for Probability and Statistics,* second edition. This table provides 2800 five-digit numbers, that is, a sample of 2800 from the uniform distribution (00000, 99,999).

The conductor knows the source of the data, its parent distribution, and the time resolution; the analyst does not. The conductor arranges the 100 random numbers in ascending order and gives this data to the analyst along with the statement that 100 devices were tested. This data is given in Appendix A. The analyst scans the data and notes that there are 100 failure times listed; all devices were operated to failure. The indicated maximum life of 99,562 hours may or may not be indicative of the life of the distribution. The experiment has been ambitious and expensive; 100 costly devices have been expended over a 11 year period and failure times have been recorded to *the nearest hour*. Noting that the failure times are reasonably scattered over the total test time, it appears that about 5 million device hours were experienced.

The earliest failure is 358 hours. Does this imply zero failures in a shorter time for the distribution? The actual MTTF is 45,900 hours; it is obvious that many failures occur before the MTTF. Upon inquiring about the intended use of the device the analyst finds that it is for a guided missile that has a 10 minute flight time between launch and target but undergoes some 1000 hours of testing during manufacture.

The analyst's next thought is to construct a histogram from the data. The usual statistical approach is to base the histogram on the time resolution intervals; this poses an immediate, practical problem. Graph paper with 100,000 devisions along the abscissa is unavailable. Further, it is obvious that such a histogram would have 99,100 empty "time cells," or "class intervals." This histogram, if actually constructed, would have little significance; time cells would be empty or, at most, contain one event. Statistically, this is very little to work with. Perhaps some other form of data manipulation would be more rewarding.

3.7.3   Data Aggregation

Noting that a graph with 100 divisions along the abscissa is practical, the analyst decides to construct a histogram based on aggregating the failures between successive 1000 hour time intervals; that is, using 1000 hour time cells, or class intervals. Figure 3.2 is the result. (The graphing convention conforms to that used to depict discrete distributions as in Figures 2.3 and 2.6.) A little more insight is evident; the asymmetry in failure times, favoring early failure, conforms to the information already obtained from the calculation of the MTTF. (The reader knows, of course, that the underlying distribution is not asymmetric.) The histogram is still meager in a statistical sense; there are still 34 empty cells, the maximum frequency in any cell is five, and 41 cells represent one failure each.

Noting the apparent beneficial effect of the first attempt at aggregation, the analyst constructs a histogram based on aggregating the data in 10,000 hour time cells and obtains Figure 3.3. The maximum and minimum frequencies are now 17 and 5, respectively; these have some statistical strength. An overall look at the histogram, ignoring the time cell to the far right, suggests the possibility of an exponential distribution, particularly in view of the overwhelming tilt of current theory. Accordingly, the analyst decides to construct the hazard function from the data of Figure 3.3. An immediate problem arises: what convention should be used to calculate the discrete (in this case) hazard function? Is it calculated by dividing the failures in a particular time cell by the number surviving at the beginning or at the end of that cell?

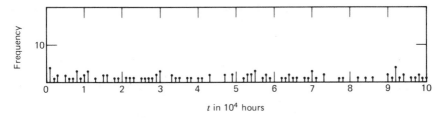

t in 10⁴ hours

Figure 3.2 Histogram of 100 samples from a discrete, uniform distribution, aggregated into 1000 hour time cells.

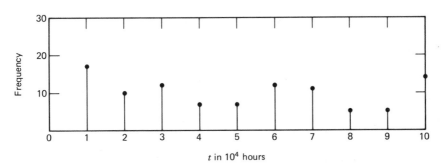

t in 10⁴ hours

Figure 3.3 Histogram of 100 samples from a discrete, uniform distribution, aggregated into 10,000 hour time cells.

This problem arises only in respect to discrete distributions; it gets worse as the time resolution becomes coarser. Shooman (1968) advocates the use of the number surviving at the start of the time cell, the author, the end. The author contends that his convention is correct because it results in an infinite discrete hazard function at the end of the last time cell of the function; this is in accord with the behavior of continuous hazard functions. The use of the number surviving at the beginning of a time cell does not result in an infinite last point. The hazard function shown in Figure 3.4 was constructed according to the author's convention from the data of Figure 3.3.

On viewing Figure 3.3, there is a strong temptation to assume a constant hazard function for the interval (00000, 50,000). Interestingly, if one assumes the constant failure rate to be the average of the first five points, 0.15×10^{-4}, the survivor function $\exp(-0.15 \times 10^{-4}t)$ is .47 when t is 50,000 hours. This happens to coincide with the actual data. Does this justify the conclusion that the first half of the distribution is exponential? After all, the reader knows that the distribution is not exponential. Further comparisons may be made by considering Figure 3.5. Figure 3.5 depicts the

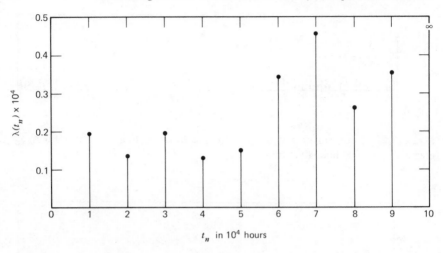

Figure 3.4   The hazard function corresponding to the distribution of Figure 3.3.

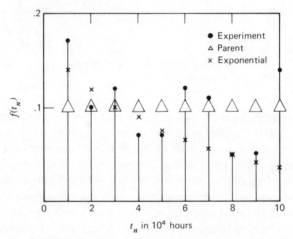

Figure 3.5   Experimental data (•), parent distribution (Δ), and exponential fit (×).

discrete distribution obtained by dividing the ordinates of Figure 3.3 by 100, and the discrete distributions equivalent to the continuous parent distribution and the continuous exponential distribution determined above. If one excepts the point t_{10}, it seems that either the exponential and uniform distributions are equally good fits to the experimentally derived distribution. In fact, calculating the respective chi-square statistics confirms the observation. If t_{10} is included, the parent distribution gives the better fit. It is clear, therefore, that a very large amount of data is necessary to elicit the true underlying distribution. To complete the data treatment the survivor functions of all three distributions are shown in Figure 3.6. The stepped function is the survivor function of the experimental data; for clarity the survivor functions of the other two distributions are shown in continuous form. The dotted points on the staircase are the values of the survivor function for the experimental data; these will ultimately fall on the straight line indicated if enough units are tested. As the data stands, however, these points fall very close to the exponential curve, at least for t_n less than 50,000 hours. It should be noted that plotting data in the survivor function format tends to visually suppress departures from the expected values; the relationship of actual data and the parent distribution seems much closer in this format than when plotted as time-to-failure distributions.

Finally, for illustration an aggregation is made on the basis of a 50,000 hour interval. The result is

$$f(50,000) = .53 \qquad f(100,000) = .47 \qquad (3.1)$$

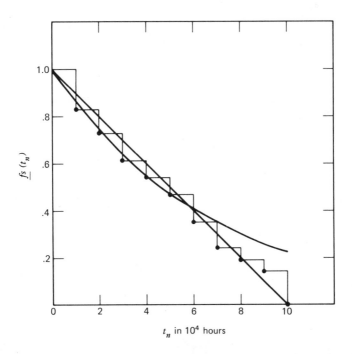

Figure 3.6 Survivor function for experimental data (stepped line), survivor function for parent distribution (straight line), and survivor function for fitted exponential distribution (curved line).

This tells us little that we did not already know. In fact, it tells us that aggregation may be carried too far.

It was found that the test of 100 components not only did not discover the true nature of the underlying distribution, but led the analyst into error. Does adding another 100 devices to the test help? Figures 3.7 and 3.8 are the analogs of Figures 3.2 and 3.3 for the test of 200. The histograms are naturally less sparse but still do not strongly suggest a uniform distribution. In the case of the 50,000 hour aggregation the surprising result is an identity to equation (3.1) when the histogram is reduced to a distribution.

The experiment and its analysis yields a message.

1   A real world experiment can only yield a discrete distribution. A continuous distribution derived from such an experiment is always an approximation; it presumes knowledge of the behavior of the distribution within the finite time cell, or class interval.

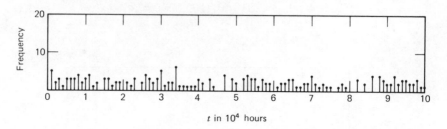

Figure 3.7   Histogram of 200 samples from a discrete, uniform distribution, aggregated into 1000 hour time cells.

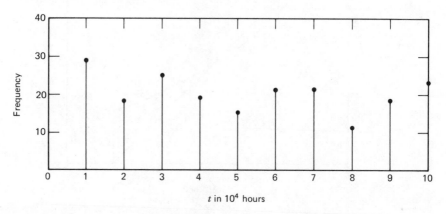

Figure 3.8   Histogram of 200 samples from a discrete, uniform distribution, aggregated into 10,000 hour time cells.

2   Having chosen a time cell (time resolution), the absence of an event in a time cell must be tentatively regarded as signifying an insufficient number put into test. If one requires that each time cell contain at least one event, a relationship has been established between the unknown distribution, the size of the time cell (resolution), and the lower bound on the number to be tested. Given this minimum requirement, it follows that the number under test increases without limit as the time cell decreases without limit. This automatically leads to the conclusion that no real experiment can directly lead to a continuous distribution.

The next step in our analysis, therefore, is to appeal to statistical theory to develop the relationship between the number of events in a time cell, the estimated probability of failure in that cell, the precision of that estimate, and the confidence that can be placed on the results. The statistical tools required are the binomial distribution and the notion of confidence limits. Before proceeding with this analysis, the importance of the discrete distribution to all subsequent work suggests that the properties and conventions relating to such distributions be carefully reviewed.

3.8   DISCRETE DISTRIBUTIONS: PROPERTIES AND CONVENTIONS

Section 2.5 provided an introduction to discrete distributions but gave no reasoning supporting the statements made. The following discussion does not concern naturally discrete distributions such as the binomial, but the discrete results of attempts to discover underlying continuous time-to-failure distributions.

The experiment discussed in Section 3.7 provided an hourly examination for failures occurring during the previous hour. No information was available concerning the exact time those failures took place. The aggregation technique used was the equivalent of an experiment with less frequent observations. Equivalently, Figure 3.2 represented an experiment in which observations took place every 1000 hours, Figure 3.3, every 10,000 hours. Had the test conductor aggregated the data, the analyst would have had to accept the data as truly representing the test conditions.

Figure 3.9 depicts four conventions. Figures 3.9 *a* and *b* have been used in the literature to depict the binomial distribution, a distribution defined only for values 0, 1, ..., *n* of the argument, where *n* is the number of trials. Figure 3.9*b* is easily understood; it shows the discrete nature of the distribution. Figure 3.9*a*, on the other hand, shows the same distribution as continuous; the area of the rectangle surrounding each value of the argument is

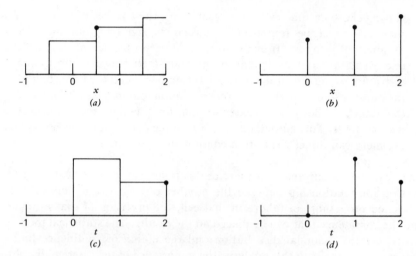

Figure 3.9 Some discrete conventions.

the probability for that argument. This leads to the interesting anomaly of a value of $P(x)$ for negative values of x.

Figures 3.9c and d are candidates for depicting discrete time-to-failure distributions. Figure 3.9d is the author's preference. The ordinate at $t = 0$ is zero; the ordinate at $t = 1$ is the probability of failure in the interval (0, 1). Similarly, the ordinate at $t = 2$ is the probability of failure in the interval (1, 2). Figure 3.9c portrays the probability of failure in the interval (0, 1) as the area of the rectangle in that interval; the rectangle in the interval (1, 2) is the probability of failure in that interval. This implies that the failures are uniformly distributed in each interval. In reality, despite its steplike appearance, Figure 3.9c is a *continuous distribution*. In this manner knowledge is implied that simply does not exist. If it is necessary that finer detail be known, finer resolution is required; this entails larger test numbers.

Even given the author's preference, further interpretation is required. First consider the matter of $f(0)$. Section 2.5 stated this quantity to be zero in every case. The rationale is simple: $f(0)$ represents the probability of failure prior to time zero; this is zero by the definition of a time-to-failure distribution. $F(L)$, the cumulative probability of failure at end of life, must have the value one. Since

$$F(L) = \sum_{n=0}^{L} f(t_n) = 1 \tag{3.2}$$

this implies

$$f(L) \neq 0 \quad \text{and} \quad F(0) = 0$$

Accordingly, $fs(0)$ is equal to one and $fs(L)$ is equal to zero, as they should. The correctly consistent hazard function is defined as (see Section 3.7.3)

$$\lambda(t_d) = \frac{f(t_d)}{1 - \sum_{n=1}^{d} f(t_n)} \qquad (3.3)$$

3.9 INFINITE DISTRIBUTIONS

Reliability and statistics literature not only makes routine use of continuous distributions, but many such distributions covering an infinite time interval. It is impossible to empirically determine such distributions, since that would require infinite time. The use of such infinite distributions in reliability applications requires justification inasmuch as reliability analyses always apply to finite time intervals, at most, the intended service life of equipment.

REFERENCES

Handbook of Tables for Probability and Statistics, 2nd ed. CRC Press, Boca Raton, FL, 1968.
Shooman, M. L. *Probabilistic Reliability: An Engineering Approach,* McGraw-Hill, New York, 1968.

CHAPTER 4

Precision, Confidence, and Numbers Tested

4.1 THE "UNBIASED ESTIMATOR" FOR THE TIME CELL

The process of discovering the underlying distribution from test failure data is one of determining the probability of failure in each time cell. In any given time cell the first step is to obtain the "unbiased estimator" (commonly known as the "point estimate") for the cell. The unbiased estimator for the probability of failure in any given time cell is the ratio of the number of failures in that cell to the total number under test.

The original data in the uniform distribution experiment exhibited 100 single failures in as many time cells and 99,900 cells with no failures. Thus the estimator was either 0 or .01, far from the known value of .000 01. The problem, of course, was that there were too few components under test compared to the attempted resolution. Had only 10 components been tested, the result would have been even more ludicrous. The experiment corresponding to a time resolution of 1000 hours yielded a range of 0 to .04, compared to a true .01, an improvement, but still very imprecise. The 10,000 hour resolution provided a range of .05 to .17 versus the true .1; matters were improved. Finally, the 50,000 hour resolution provided .47 and .53, compared to the true .5. It is apparent that increasing the number of failures per unit time cell increases the validity of the failure probability determination. There is theoretical basis for the behavior noted; it can be found in the binomial distribution.

4.2 APPLYING THE BINOMIAL DISTRIBUTION

Figure 4.1 graphs the binomial distribution for n equal to 100 and p equal to .53; this is the case of the first interval for the 50,000 hour resolution. The figure does not show the entire distribution, only that occurring between the

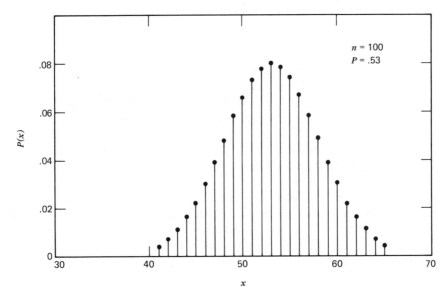

Figure 4.1 A portion of a binomial distribution with $n = 100$ and $p = .53$.

values of x for which the cumulative distribution lies between .01 and .99. The cumulative binomial distribution is shown in Figure 4.2. (The stair-step visual aid convention has been used.) The mean value of x, 53, the value of np, is also seen to provide the maximum value of $P(x)$. This is always the case when np is an integer; the mean value of x will fall between the adjacent integer values of x when np is not an integer. Thus np, rounded to the nearest integer, is the most likely number of failures in a time cell, where p is obtained from the underlying distribution. Therefore even to get the likelihood of just one failure in a time cell requires that np equal one; this was the case in the experiment depicted in Figure 3.2. Note, however, that despite one failure per time cell being most likely, 34 time cells showed no failures. For further insight into what is required for better insurance of at least one failure per time cell, that is, insurance against zero failures in any of the time cells in the experimentally determined histogram, observe the following interpretation of the binomial distribution:

$$\sum_{x=0}^{n} P(x) = 1$$

Then

$$n \sum_{x=0}^{n} P(x) = n \tag{4.1}$$

$$nP(0) + n \sum_{x=1}^{n} P(x) = n \qquad (4.2)$$

Equation (4.2) may be interpreted to be the number of time cells exhibiting no failures plus the total number of failures. Thus for the case of Figure 3.2, $np(0)$ is $n(1 - p)^n$, or 37, compared to an actual 34. Requiring $nP(0)$ to be less than one, therefore, should determine a lower bound to the number tested, one that at least assures one failure per time cell. To further illustrate this interpretation consider the case of a pack of 100 cards, labeled 1 through 100. Consider a shuffle of an infinite set of such packs. Draw 100 cards, draw another 100 cards, and so on. Record after each draw the number of missing numbers; this is equivalent to the number of time cells without failures. The interpretation previously developed is that the average number of missing numbers in each of the draws is $nP(0)$, that is, $100(0.99)^{100}$.

This lower-bound case can be computed by solving

$$n(1 - p)^n < 1 \qquad (4.3)$$

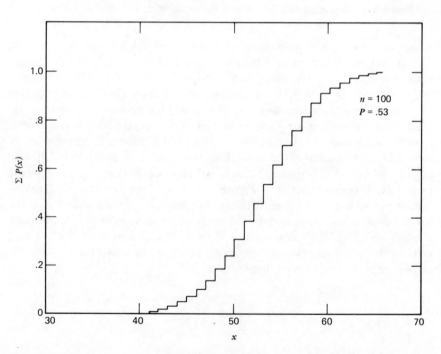

Figure 4.2 The cumulative distribution corresponding to the binomial distribution of Figure 4.1.

or

$$\ln n + n \ln(1 - p) < 0$$

$\ln(1 - p)$ can be approximated by $-p$; thus

$$\ln n - np < 0 \qquad (4.4)$$

is the equation to be solved. A solution can be easily effected as follows: replace the equation above by

$$n = \frac{(1.001)(\ln n)}{p} \qquad (4.5)$$

This equation certainly satisfies condition (4.4). Now convert this equation to the recursion formula

$$n_j = \frac{(1.001)(\ln n_{j-1})}{p} \qquad (4.6)$$

It is found that repeated iterations of equation (4.6) converge to the solution of equation (4.5). The convergence is quite rapid if one starts with $5/p$ for n_0. In the case corresponding to Figure 3.2 one obtains 500, 622, 644, 647, 648, 648, ... This is the test number that virtually assures non-empty time cells. The analogous number in the one hour resolution situation is 1,420,000! This result can be used in another manner: given a component with a failure rate of 10^{-9} per hour, a highly reliable microcircuit, for example, what test number is required to virtually insure at least one failure in 1000 hours? It is 16,600,000! This interesting result, however, is still not the last word on the test numbers required to attain a particular precision in a distribution discovery process.

4.3 CONFIDENCE STATEMENTS, INTERVALS, LIMITS, AND COEFFICIENTS

The notions of "confidence statements, intervals, limits, and coefficients" combined with the properties of the binomial distribution provide the final information. The base experimental information required is the test number n and the number of failures F in the time cell under investigation. Instead of determining an estimator, the above notions attempt to bracket the true underlying probability between limits. These limits are called "confidence limits," the interval between the limits is the "confidence interval." The "confidence statement" is typically "the true probability lies in the interval

(p_L, p_U), with a confidence of y percent"; y percent expressed in decimal form is the "confidence coefficient." Naturally, one also talks about a "y percent confidence interval." The confidence limits are defined as

$$p_L \leq p \leq p_U \qquad (4.7)$$

where p is the true underlying probability of failure. These limits are defined by the solutions to the following equations:

For the upper limit p_U $\qquad \sum_{x=0}^{F} P(x) = \dfrac{\alpha}{2}$

$$(4.8)$$

For the lower limit p_L $\qquad \sum_{x=F}^{n} P(x) = \dfrac{\alpha}{2}$

where $1 - \alpha$ is the confidence coefficient. It is sometimes convenient to transform these equations to

For p_U $\qquad \sum_{x=F+1}^{n} P(x) = 1 - \dfrac{\alpha}{2}$

$$(4.9)$$

For p_L $\qquad \sum_{x=0}^{F-1} P(x) = 1 - \dfrac{\alpha}{2}$

The above definitions and equations define the "two-sided" limits and intervals. There are also "one-sided" limits and intervals. In this case

$$0 \leq p \leq p_U \qquad p_L \leq p \leq 1 \qquad (4.10)$$

The corresponding confidence intervals are

$$(0, p_U) \qquad \text{and} \qquad (p_L, 1)$$

The equations required to solve for the one-sided values of p_U and p_L are (4.8) and (4.9), with the division by two eliminated. The confidence coefficient is still $1 - \alpha$.

What is the meaning of the confidence statement? To the non-statistician the word "confidence" implies the dictionary definition "a feeling of assurance." In that sense what does 50% confidence mean? How much better is 90%? Is this concept so precise that one should differentiate between 90 and 95%? Is the statistician comfortable with the meaning he assigns? Additional development of the topic is required before these questions can be addressed.

Solutions to the equations above can be obtained from tables of the cumulative binomial distribution, the equivalent in programmed computers, or from graphs called "confidence belts for proportions." Very elaborate tables of the cumulative distribution are available; almost every book on statistics contains reproductions of the confidence belts.

4.3.1 Confidence Limits Applied to the Experiment

Applying the equations to the first interval of the 50,000 hour aggregation of the uniform distribution data, 53 failures in a test of 100, for a confidence coefficient of 90% ($\alpha = 0.1$) yields

$$.443 \leq p \leq .616 \tag{4.11}$$

correct to three decimal places. How many decimal places should the calculation cover? Any number are mathematically available. One of the objectives of this book is to explore the limitations on precision. Suppose the number of failures had been 52. The corresponding solutions are now

$$.433 \leq p \leq .606$$

A change in the number of failures cannot be less than one; in this case such a change was significant in the second decimal place. If the confidence coefficient is changed to 91%, the solutions for 53 failures are

$$.441 \leq p \leq .618$$

Thus a change from 90 to 91% appears in the third decimal place only; but what is significant about that change? Finally, we see that the ratio p_U/p_L is 1.39! Roughly speaking, the underlying probability has been placed in a $\pm 20\%$ range (at 90% confidence); this does not justify two decimal places.

Let us make additional calculations. As we saw in the experiment, the second interval had 47 failures. The 90% confidence interval for this case is

$$.384 \leq p \leq .557 \tag{4.12}$$

This could just as well have been the result for the first interval: in fact, Figure 4.1 indicates a wide range of likely failure numbers; all will give different 90% confidence intervals. Finally, let us see the 99% confidence interval for 53 failures:

$$.40 \leq p \leq .66$$

a range of 1.65; and for 50% confidence,

$$.49 \leq p \leq .57$$

Clearly, the higher the confidence, the lower the precision.

Returning to the statistician's meaning of a confidence statement, the literature says that "confidence of y percent," as applied to a confidence statement, means that "the statement is correct y percent of the time." In talking about "y percent of the time," the literature obviously refers to repeated experiments in which n components are tested to failure and the calculation of confidence limits for a given time cell in each experiment. It has been seen that repeated experiments are not likely to repeat the same number of failures in a given time cell. Accordingly, the sequence will lead to a succession of disparate confidence limits. Which of these disparate statements is correct y percent of the time? Can all be correct y percent of time?

4.3.2 Paradoxes in the Confidence Limit Equations

The 100% confidence, with a two-sided or one-sided upper limit ($\alpha = 0$), poses a problem. The equation to be solved,

$$\sum_{x=0}^{F} P(x) = 0$$

cannot be solved in the case of $F = n$, since the summation is not zero, but one. A similar situation is obtained with respect to the lower limit if F is zero, yet it is reasonable to expect that the confidence interval should be (0, 1) with 100% confidence, regardless of the number tested or the number of failures.

The 0% confidence case, two-sided, presents another dilemma. In this instance the equations to be solved are

$$\sum_{x=0}^{F} P(x) = .5 \qquad \sum_{x=F}^{n} P(x) = .5$$

This also presents a paradox, since the sum of the left sides of the above equations is greater than one. All of these paradoxes become less constraining as the number of trials n approaches infinity, that is, as the discrete binomial distribution approaches continuity.

4.3.3 Confidence and the Time Cell

The entire discussion to this point was introduced by the experiment on the uniform distribution. This was only a crutch, however, since the discussion only concerned the happenings in a given time cell, regardless of the distribution that generated the recorded failures. The point is that the number of failures in a particular cell is a function of both n and the underlying distribution; the study of the implications of a given number of failures in a time cell depends only on n.

4.4 THE "TYRANNY OF LARGE NUMBERS"

In further pursuing the study of the relationship between confidence coefficients, test numbers, and precision, one finds that the equations do not have great utility. Fortunately, there are more convenient treatments in the case where the number of failures is large. Reconsider the computation of the 90% confidence limits for 53 failures in a test of 100. Examine Figure 4.2, the cumulative binomial distribution for $p = .53$ (the estimator). The cumulative distribution is .044 at $x = 44$ and is .956 at $x = 61$, a good approximation to .95, which is $(1 - \alpha/2)$ in the p_U equation (4.9). Similarly, .044 approximates $\alpha/2$, .05 in the p_L equation (4.8). Dividing 44 and 61 by n, 100, yields .44 and .61. These are very nearly the results found from the equations, .443 and .616. It is even moot as to whether these suffer in accuracy relative to the results immediately above; the difference is only in the third decimal place. The approximate method just employed may be formalized as follows. The upper and lower confidence limits F_U/n and F_L/n are obtained by solving

$$\sum_{x=0}^{F_U} P(x) \cong 1 - \frac{\alpha}{2}$$

$$\sum_{x=0}^{F_L} P(x) \cong \frac{\alpha}{2}$$

(4.13)

for F_U and F_L, where $P(x)$ is computed for p equal to the estimator F/n. Note that F_U and F_L can only be integers. Note too that the estimator F/n will always fall between the confidence limits so obtained.

For very large test numbers and numbers of failures an even more convenient approximation is possible. It happens that the normal distribution is the limiting form of the binomial distribution for large n, the number of trials (test number). The limiting form is obtained by substitution from the normal distribution

$$n(x) = \frac{1}{\sigma(2\pi)^{1/2}} \exp\frac{-(x - \mu)^2}{2\sigma^2}$$

(4.14)

For μ, the mean of $n(x)$, one may substitute np, the mean of the binomial distribution; for the standard deviation σ one may substitute the standard deviation of the binomial distribution, $(npq)^{1/2}$. Thus the limiting form becomes

$$P(x) = \frac{1}{(2\pi npq)^{1/2}} \exp\frac{-(x - np)^2}{2npq} \tag{4.15}$$

The upper and lower confidence limits x_U/n and x_L/n are obtained by solving

$$\int_{-\infty}^{x_U} P(x)\,dx = 1 - \frac{\alpha}{2} \quad \text{and} \quad \int_{-\infty}^{x_L} P(x)\,dx = \frac{\alpha}{2} \tag{4.16}$$

for x_U and x_L. These are easily obtained from the extensive tabulation of the normal distribution in the literature. In fact,

$$x_{U,L} = np \pm k(npq)^{1/2} \tag{4.17}$$

where k equals 1.96, 1.65, 1.28, and 0.842 for two-sided confidence limits of 95, 90, 80, and 60%, respectively. For one-sided upper or lower limits the same values of k yield 97.5, 95, 90, and 80%, respectively. The confidence limits are found by dividing expression (4.17) by n:

$$\frac{x_{U,L}}{n} = p \pm k\left(\frac{pq}{n}\right)^{1/2} \tag{4.18}$$

Applying these relationships to the first interval of the 50,000 hour aggregation of the uniform distribution data, 53 failures in a test of 100 for a confidence coefficient of 90%, yields (.612, .448) if p, .53, is taken to be the unbiased estimator. This differs from the solutions of equations (4.8) or (4.9) in the third decimal place only.

Dividing equation (4.18) by p converts it to the "fractional tolerance" form

$$\frac{x_{U,L}}{np} = 1 \pm k\left(\frac{q}{np}\right)^{1/2} \tag{4.19}$$

Thus confidence limits that are $\pm1\%$ from the mean of the confidence interval correspond to $k(q/np)^{1/2}$ equal to 0.01; for $\pm10\%$, $k(q/np)^{1/2}$ must equal 0.1, and so on. Symbolizing the fractional tolerance by δ, one has

$$k\left(\frac{q}{np}\right)^{1/2} = \delta \tag{4.20}$$

Solving for n,

$$n = \frac{k^2 q}{\delta^2 p} \qquad (4.21)$$

The above is the desired relationship between the underlying failure probability in the time cell, the confidence coefficient, the desired discovery precision, and the required test number.

It is now possible to explore the consequences of this relationship. For a first case, return to the familiar uniform distribution experiment, with 50,000 hour time cells and 53 failures. The unbiased estimator may be used for p, or the *a priori* knowledge that p is .5. To discover p in that time cell to a tolerance of $\pm 1\%$ with a 95% confidence requires a test number of 38,000. Reducing the demand to $\pm 10\%$ at 60% confidence requires a test number of 71. A tolerance of $\pm 3\%$ at 60% confidence requires 790.

The above examples are modest. Consider a moderately reliable electronic device with a failure rate of 10^{-6} per hour. To prove this failure probability for the first hour of operation to a tolerance of $\pm 10\%$ to the modest confidence of 60% requires the testing of 71 million devices. Increasing the time cell to the first 1000 hours, a time cell failure probability of 10^{-3} with the same precision and confidence as above requires testing 71,000 devices. Finally, consider the failure rates claimed for some of the most reliable microcircuits available, 10^{-9} per hour. These are used in commercial spacecraft; the life requirement of these spacecraft is on the order of 100,000 hours. Over such a period, given that the failure probability is that claimed, the probability of failure would be 10^{-4}. To prove this failure probability to $\pm 10\%$ with a confidence of 60% requires testing 710,000 microcircuits for 100,000 hours! A 95% confidence would require 3,800,000. Numbers such as these are the reason for the title of this section, "The Tyranny of Large Numbers." Clearly, no tests of such magnitude are likely.

4.5 THE "MINIMUM TYRANNY OF LARGE NUMBERS"

Since numbers under test become larger as more and more failures are desired in the time cell, the minimum test numbers should correspond to zero failures per time cell. Section 4.3.2 has shown that no lower confidence limit is possible in this case, only an upper confidence limit. The situation of zero failures in a time cell, therefore, allows a one-sided upper confidence limit only. Fortunately, this is quite satisfactory in the study of reliability, since the primary concern is to establish an upper limit to the possible failure probability.

Thus for the zero failure, one-sided case, P_U is the solution of

$$P(0) = (1 - p_U)^n = \alpha \qquad (4.22)$$

$$p_U = 1 - \alpha^{1/n} \qquad (4.23)$$

relating the upper confidence limit, the confidence coefficient, and the test number. A more convenient approximate solution, quite accurate for n greater than 50, is

$$p_U = \frac{-\ln\alpha}{n} \quad \text{from} \quad n \ln(1 - p_U) = \ln\alpha \qquad (4.24)$$

Thus p_U is $0.9/n$ for 60% confidence, $2.3/n$ for 90% confidence, and $4.6/n$ for 99% confidence.

The degree to which this has reduced the test numbers required may be appreciated by returning to the uniform distribution experiment. The probability of failure for the underlying distribution was 10^{-5} on a per hour basis. To establish an upper limit on the probability of failure in a 1 hour time cell that is only 2.3 times the true failure probability with a 90% confidence requires testing 100,000 parts. Increasing the time cell to 1000 hours provides the same ratio of the upper limit to the underlying probability at 90% confidence with only 100 parts in test. The "tyranny" has been reduced, but is still "tyranny." To come within a factor of two of being right, even on the minimum basis, still requires large numbers and/or time.

4.5.1 Confidence Limits for Small Numbers of Failures

Equations (4.8) and (4.9) may be used for this purpose, but a more convenient approach is available in reliability studies because test numbers are moderately large and the probability of failure small. The use of the Poisson distribution, an approximation to the binomial distribution, is the approach. The Poisson distribution is

$$P_{np}(x) = \frac{(np)^x e^{-np}}{x!} \qquad (4.25)$$

and may be substituted for $P(x)$ in equations (4.8) and (4.9). The convenience of this substitution lies in the fact that the solution of the equations yields np_U and np_L as functions of the confidence coefficient. This avoids the problem of separately specifying n each time a solution is required. The above solutions are universal in that given $np_{U,L}$, one immediately has the confidence limits, given any n. The literature provides extensive tables of the cumulative Poisson distribution and confidence limits based on that distribution. Table 4.1 is provided for illustrative purposes.

Table 4.1 Confidence limits using the Poisson distribution

	90% (95%)		60% (80%)	
x	np_U	np_L	np_U	np_L
1	4.7	0.051	3.0	0.22
2	6.3	0.35	4.3	0.82
3	7.8	0.82	5.5	1.5
4	9.2	1.4	6.7	2.3
5	10.5	2.0	7.9	3.1
6	11.8	2.6	9.0	3.9
7	13.1	3.3	10.2	4.7
8	14.4	3.9	11.4	5.6
9	15.7	4.7	12.5	6.4
10	16.9	5.4	13.6	7.3

The table may be used in two ways, two sided, using 90 and 60%, or one sided, using 95 and 80%. Inasmuch as conservatism should be the goal in reliability prediction, the use of a one-sided upper limit is indicated, since this tends to set an upper bound on the failure probability. The use of the table may be made clear by example. Given that a single failure occurs in a particular time cell, at 90% confidence np_U is 4.7. If the number under test is 100, the upper confidence limit of the failure probability is .047; if 1000, .0047. The corresponding lower confidence limits are .000 51 and .000 051.

Can one justify the use of three significant digits in the table? The maximum number of failures per time cell in the table is 10, a modest number. Further, the ratio of p_U to the unbiased estimator x/n at that maximum is 1.7 for a one-sided 95% confidence. This is a considerable spread. The inescapable conclusion is that three significant digits are not justified.

4.6 A MONTE CARLO EXPERIMENT ON A NORMAL DISTRIBUTION

In the finite range (00000, 99,999) 100 random normal numbers were generated with a mean of 50,000 and a standard deviation of 1000. The histogram of Figure 4.3 represents an aggregation of the data into 1000 hour time cells. An additional feature of Figure 4.3 is the plot of the 95% upper confidence limits for each time cell; these are the short horizontal marks. To be consistent with the histogram, these are also the numbers of failures, $100p_U$.

Assume that the above data were taken in order to determine an empirical distribution, that is, the experimenter had no *a priori* knowledge concern-

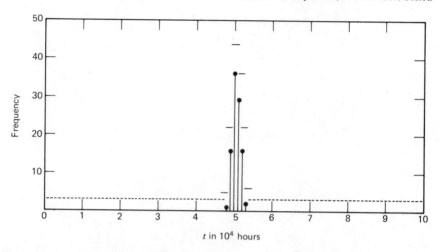

t in 10^4 hours

Figure 4.3 Monte Carlo experiment with 100 samples normally distributed: mean, 50,000; standard deviation, 1000.

ing the underlying distribution. Assume further that the experimenter wished to conduct the subsequent analysis with a continuous distribution. While a normal distribution is a possible choice as a fit, a Weibull distribution provides the asymmetry evident in Figure 4.3. Either choice will provide a good fit in the region (4.8, 5.3), and if this is the only region of interest, it is immaterial which assumption is used, unless one is a devotee of excessive precision.

In one approach to mechanical reliability, however, the needed information about the underlying distribution is in the region far from the available data, that is, in the empty time cells. Since the accumulation of sufficient test data to adequately characterize the distribution in this area is out of the question, the protagonists of this theory of mechanical reliability must assume that a distribution that fits the data over a narrow interval is valid in the regions where no data is available; the upper confidence limit for empty time cells is of no use in their approach. Thus, despite the intellectual appeal of this particular approach to mechanical reliability, it rests on the question of the validity of the above assumption.

4.7 DISCOVERING EMPIRICAL DISTRIBUTIONS

Despite extensive discussion here and in Chapter Four, many nuances involved in determining empirical distributions still require illumination. Consider a time cell in Figure 3.2 containing a single failure. The estimator for the failure probability is .01 *for a 1000 hour interval,* or 10^{-5} expressed on a per hour basis. This just happens to match the underlying distribution. Returning to the original data taken with a 1 hour resolution, the estimator is .01 *for a one hour interval!* Thus on a per hour basis one has 10^{-5} failures per hour as the estimator derived from the 1000 hour aggregation, 10^{-5} failures per hour from the underlying distribution, and an estimator of 10^{-2} failures per hour for the 1 hour aggregation, a ratio of 1000 to one. What is the problem?

4.7.1 Choice of Class Intervals or Time Cells

The preceding discussion has assumed equal time cells or class intervals. An examination of estimators derived from aggregations greater than 1000 hours show them all to be in the general neighborhood of 10^{-5} failures per hour (1.7×10^{-5} to 0.5×10^{-5}). It would seem, therefore, that too little aggregation gives misleading results when using equal time cells. This problem has been investigated in the literature. Sturges (1926) has shown that the optimum number of class intervals K is

$$K = 1 + 3.3 \log n \qquad (4.26)$$

Thus for a test number of 100 the optimum number is 7.6. The original data had 100,000 class intervals or time cells; Figure 3.2, 100; Figure 3.3, 10; and the 50,000 hour aggregation, 2. Figure 3.3 gave the best picture of the underlying distribution; the number of time cells was close to the optimum calculated from equation (4.26). The important conclusion is that too little aggregation must be avoided when using equal time cells.

Now consider using unequal time cells. The rule is that all time cells shall contain one and only one failure, each time cell is bounded by an adjacent pair of failure times, and the failure time for each cell is the upper time boundary. This yields a histogram that appears uniform except that the time intervals vary. The estimators for each time cell are uniformly $1/n$. The estimators expressed on a per unit time basis are not. Figure 4.4 shows the result of this process when applied to the first 20 failures of the original uniform distribution experimental data (1 hour resolution). The import of this scheme is that it avoids the problem that occurs when the number tested is too small for the time cell resolution chosen. Despite this advantage it is clear from Figure 4.4 that this is not a particularly attractive way to discover the underlying distribution. There are times, however, when this approach is viable.

Consider the following hypothetical situation. A test involves 1000 devices. To the nearest hour single failures occur at the 900th, 1100th, and 2900th hour, at which time the test is truncated. If one uses the variable time cell approach and the 95% confidence, one-sided limit analysis, the per hour

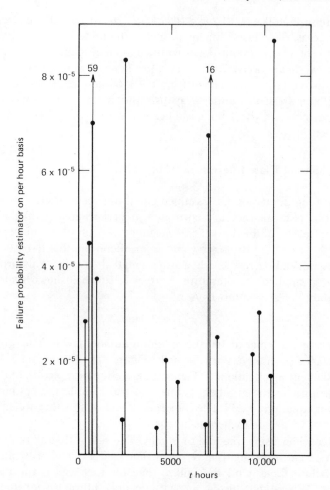

Figure 4.4   Allocating data into unequal time cells.

failure probability plot results in Figure 4.5. If equal 1000 hour time cells are used, the result is that of Figure 4.6; the optimum number of time cells is 10.9. Unfortunately, the test truncation has denied the possibility of determining the time required for all 1000 devices to fail; as a result it is impossible to determine the optimum time cell. Considering the data, however, time cells smaller than 1000 hours will result in empty time cells, longer time cells may simply confuse the issue. What is an analyst to report concerning the failure behavior of these devices? For an initial 3000 hour period he can assume a uniform distribution with a failure rate of about 5×10^{-6} per hour, based on the assumption of Figure 4.6, or he can try to make sense out of

Failure probability, per-hour basis, 95% confidence

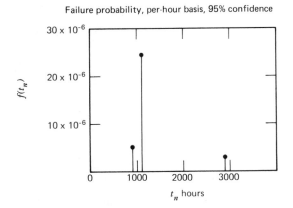

Figure 4.5   Analysis in a hypothetical situation using unequal time cells.

Failure probability, per-hour basis, 95% confidence

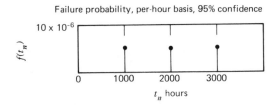

Figure 4.6   Analysis in a hypothetical situation using equal time cells.

Figure 4.5. It seems reasonable, although only two examples have been considered, that the equal time cell approach is preferable.

4.8   THE SIGNIFICANCE OF "DEVICE HOURS"

In the test of the previous section, considering the entire test time of 3000 hours as one time cell, the estimator is $3/1000$. Assuming that the true underlying distribution for the first 3000 hours is uniform, the magnitude of $f(t_n)$, the time-to-failure discrete p.d.f., based on 1 hour time cells is $3/1000/3000$. Rearranged it is $3/(1000 \times 3000)$, that is, F/nT, where T is the test time. Now nT is the product of the test time and the test number; in most real situations, where the number of failures F is very small compared to the number under test, *nT can be taken to be the "device hours."* Thus on the *assumption of a uniform distribution* the unbiased estimator of the p.d.f. of time-to-failure, on a per hour basis, is the *ratio of test failures to device hours.*

Suppose, however, that the assumed distribution is exponential. Then the governing equation is

$$1 - e^{-\lambda T} = \frac{F}{n}$$

$$\lambda = \frac{-\ln(1 - F/n)}{T}$$

$$\lambda \cong \frac{F}{nT} \tag{4.27}$$

This is identical to the result obtained for the assumption of a uniform distribution. This chance happening is not peculiar to the uniform and exponential distributions. The definition of $\lambda(t)$ is

$$\lambda(t) = \frac{f(t)}{1 - F(t)}$$

As long as $F(t)$, the cumulative failure probability, is small compared to one, $\lambda(t)$ and $f(t)$ are substantially identical. The test time T for which that equivalence holds is obviously determined by the nature of $f(t)$.

The above relationship, although attractive, must be used with great care. The current, universal belief in the applicability of the exponential distribution unfortunately results in the assumption that once λ has been determined by some test of length T, the distribution is known for all t greater than T. Further, it is common to treat device hours as a universal parameter, regardless of the time involved in the test. It must be made clear that the statistical inferences depend not only on device hours, but on the test time during which the device hours accumulate.

4.9 JUSTIFIABLE PRECISION IN EMPIRICAL DISTRIBUTIONS

As an introduction to justifiable precision in empirical distributions, consider the following situation. A set of data is 2, 4, 7, 9, 11, 13, and 15. To the limit of the calculator used for the computation the mean and standard deviation are 8.714 285 714 and 4.715 728 495 respectively. It is mathematically correct to report those numbers, but the real world situation is that the data are the ages of a group of children. Now, yearly age is an approximation, thus reason would indicate that the mean and standard deviations be given as nine and five years, respectively. The moral of this story is that arithmetic must be tempered by reality.

The preceding discussions have indicated the impractical test numbers and test times needed to achieve even moderate precision in the determination of empirical distributions. Table 4.1 tells the story. A test that results in 10 failures can only determine the underlying failure probability in the test interval to a precision of $\pm 30\%$ with a 60% confidence; this is modest precision. If the component in question is one of moderate reliability, 10^{-6} failures per hour, the above test requires 10^7 device hours! A very reliable device, 10^{-9} failures per hour (one "fit"), requires 10^{10} device hours! These figures are so staggering that it is not surprising the community has turned to accelerated test methods. These realities, therefore, strongly suggest that *not more than two significant digits should be used to express failure rates.* Examination of MIL-HDBK-217, discussed in Chapter Five, supports this point of view not only in its basic data, but in its example of "how to use 217." This has not deterred users of 217 from applying its formulas to produce many more than two significant digits.

4.10 CONTINUOUS VERSUS DISCRETE DISTRIBUTIONS

Continuous p.d.f.'s are very convenient, mathematically, and appeal to reason in that it is expected that failure time is a continuum. Previous discussions have indicated that the real world does not permit the determination of continuous distributions; these may be inferred as approximations of discrete distributions only. The problem not only has to do with the fact that no event may be determined instantaneously, but that approaching closer and closer to a continuous distribution by continuously shortening time cells involves astronomical numbers of components under test, even with only modest precision and confidence. As an example, consider a component having a presumed failure rate of 10^{-9} per hour. To determine its empirical distribution in *1 minute time cells* to a precision of $\pm 10\%$ with a 60% confidence requires testing 4×10^{12} components! On a per hour basis this reduces to 7×10^{10}, hardly a relief.

Another interesting aspect of the conflict is that "Monte Carlo" experiments can only be conducted with discrete distributions. This is because of the fact that Monte Carlo experiments are conducted with random numbers; these too are discrete. Finally, it will be demonstrated later that there are important differences in the behaviors of systems, depending on whether their components are characterized by continuous or discrete distributions.

REFERENCES

Sturges, H. A. "The Choice of a Class Interval," *Journal of the American Statistical Association*, **21**, 65–66 (1926).

CHAPTER FIVE

Sources of Component Failure Data

5.1 MIL-HDBK-217C, APRIL 9, 1979

MIL-HDBK-217C is the Military Standardization Handbook for the Reliability Prediction of Electronic Equipment. It is sponsored by the U.S. Department of Defense and must be employed in all reliability predictions done under contract for that agency. It is a live document that is periodically updated to stay abreast of the rapidly changing electronic field. While primarily intended for Defense Department application, commercial organizations find it invaluable as well. Undoubtedly it is used throughout the world. The organization responsible for its issuance and continuing improvement is Rome Air Development Center.

The handbook covers the following types of components:

Microelectronic devices

Discrete semiconductors

Electronic vacuum tubes

Lasers

Resistors

Capacitors

Inductive devices

Rotating devices

Relays

Switches

Connectors

Printed wiring boards

Connections

Miscellaneous parts

Section 3.0, the final section of the handbook, contains instructions for "Parts Count Reliability Prediction." The method is based on the constant hazard rate assumption (exponential distribution).

5.1.1 Excerpts; Introduction, MIL-HDBK-217C

It is unfortunate that many users of this excellent document have failed to read its introduction, particularly Section 1.3, "Limitations of Reliability Predictions." The importance of the handbook and its widespread use justify the inclusion of excerpts from Section 1.

1.1 The Reliability Problem

When it is proposed to design an electronic system to perform a complex and demanding job, it is assumed that the required investment will be justified according to the perfection by which the job is performed or by the large number of times which the system can do the job. This assumption cannot be justified when a system fails to perform upon demand or fails to perform repeatedly. Thus, it is not enough simply to show that a chasm can be spanned by a bridge; the bridge must continue to span the chasm for a long time to come while carrying useful loads.

In the design of complex electronic systems, such an assumption as mentioned above, is, in fact, not accepted. Instead, considerable effort is made to obtain reliable system performance. Unlike bridge building and other evolving technologies, it is recognized that the electronics art, especially complex military systems, is often in revolution. It is sometimes referred to as an exploding technology. Without time for orderly evolution of systems, applications of electronics suffer most from unreliability. The ratio of new to tried and true portions of electronic systems is relatively high; therefore, until the new becomes tried and true, its reliability must be suspect. As an inevitable but not surprising result, it can be concluded that reliability remains a special problem in electronics and will remain so as long as the technology is in revolution rather than evolution. . . .

1.2 The Role of Reliability Prediction in Engineering

To be of value, *a prediction must be timely.* However, the earlier it is needed the more difficulties will be encountered. It is certainly true that the earlier a prediction has to be made about the unknown nature of a future event, the more difficult it is to make a meaningful prediction. As an example, it can be seen that the reliability of an electronic equipment is known with certainty after it has been used in the field until it is worn out and its failure history has been faithfully recorded. But for purposes of doing anything about the reliability of this equipment, this knowledge has no value. Before this point, reliability cannot be known with certainty; but a great deal of knowledge about reliability can be accumulated over a short early period in the equipments' useful life. Even though the degree of certainty of knowledge is less, there is some opportunity to do something to influence the reliability of the remaining life portion.

Similarly, considering the various stages back through installation, shipment, test, production, test design, development, procurement, etc., less and less can be known with certainty about reliability. However, what is known or predicted becomes more and more valuable as a basis for taking action. After all, there is no value in simply knowing that a certain failure will occur at some specific time in the future. The value comes in having the opportunity to do something to prevent the failure from occurring. Once this is done the future is changed from what was predicted with certainty. Thus, prediction becomes a part of a process of "designing the future."

An early prediction is made on the basis of very little knowledge in order to form a rational basis for doing something about changing the basis of the prediction. The process, in order to have any meaning at all, requires predicting, acting, measuring (or gaining new knowledge), then reprediction, acting again and remeasuring continually throughout a program of development. The two trends in the prediction are (1) to gain better records of class characteristics in more usable and realistic forms and (2) to develop improved techniques for applying the consequent knowledge to predictions in appropriate confidence settings. The current state-of-art in reliability prediction rests at the level of development of these data and techniques. Much room remains for advancing the state-of-the-art.

1.3 Limitations of Reliability Predictions

The art of predicting the reliability of electronic equipment has practical limitations such as those depending on data gathering and technique complexity. Considerable effort is required to generate sufficient data on a part class to report a statistically valid reliability figure for that class. Casual data gathering on a part class occasionally accumulates data more slowly than the advance of technology in that class; consequently, a valid level of data is never attained. In the case of many part classes, the number of people participating in data gathering all over the industry is rather large with consequent varying methods and conditions which prevent exact coordination and correlation. Also part reliability in the field use of equipment is difficult to examine due to the lack of suitable data being acquired. Thus it can be seen that derivation of failure rates (being mean values) is empirically difficult and obtaining of valid confidence values is practically precluded because of lack of correlation.

The use of failure rate data, obtained from field use of past systems, is applicable on future concepts depending on the degree of similarity existing both in the hardware design and in the anticipated environments. Data obtained on a system used in one environment may not be applicable to use in a different environment, especially if the new environment substantially exceeds the design capabilities. Other variants that can affect the stated failure rate of a given system are: different uses, different operators, different maintenance practices, different measurement techniques or definitions of failure. When considering the comparison between similar but unlike systems, the possible variations are obviously even greater.

Thus, a fundamental limitation on reliability prediction is the ability to accumulate data of known validity for the new application. Another fundamental limitation is the complexity of prediction techniques. Very simple techniques omit a great deal of distinguishing detail and the prediction suffers inaccuracy. More detailed techniques can become so bogged down in detail that the prediction becomes costly and may actually lag the principal hardware development effort.

The failure rates and their associated adjustment factors presented herein are based upon evaluation and analysis of the best available data at the time of issue.

5.1.2 Failure Rate Model

A typical model for a discrete semiconductor, a model typical of most components other than microelectronic devices, is

$$\lambda_p = \lambda_b (\pi_E \pi_A \pi_{S_2} \pi_C \pi_Q) \tag{5.1}$$

where λ_b is the base (generic) failure rate expressed by a model relating the influence of electrical and temperature stresses on the part. π_E and the other factors modify the base failure rate: π_E is an environmental multiplier (there are 11 different environments); π_A is an application multiplier and has to do with circuit function; π_{S_2} is a multiplier accounting for voltage stress; π_C accounts for component complexity; and π_Q is a measure of the vendor quality level. (More than one quality level is acceptable.) The resulting total product is a constant failure rate that is plugged into the prediction model.

MIL-HDBK-217C does not, except for the remarks made in the introduction, particularly Section 1.3, detail the process by which the voluminous contents are generated, nor does it identify a confidence level associated with the data. Private discussion with the sponsoring agency revealed that 60% confidence is the goal! No statements are made as to whether component data actually conform to the constant failure rate portion of the "bathtub curve" or where this occurs in the life cycle. The document recognizes the validity problem in the data and in the main *expresses failure rates in no more than two significant digits.* Illustrations of the application of the document *round the product of the several factors to two significant digits!* Many users, however, unmindful of the document's caveats, persist in retaining as many significant digits as their computational aids generate.

None of the remarks concerning MIL-HDBK-217 should be construed as critical in any way. This is an invaluable document and the electronics community would be in dire straits without it. It addresses an extremely difficult data gathering and reduction problem and the sponsors deserve nothing but praise for their efforts. Despite possible disagreement with both approach and data, *it does tell the equipment designer where the "reliability ball park" is located.* Using the information provided, the designer can judge whether a demanded reliability is physically possible or hopelessly out of reach. The customer, therefore, can face dilemmas early, rather than experiencing catastrophe when it is too late. *Everyone must understand that predictions made with 217 data are "ball park"; they are not guarantees.*

5.2 "STORAGE RELIABILITY OF MISSILE MATERIEL PROGRAM"

The Defense Department has a particular problem in that many weapon systems must be put into storage for long periods of time, pending possible employment. An assessment of the effects of storage on the expected reliability after storage is necessary; getting valid statistical data for the storage phase of system life is even more difficult than getting the data contained in MIL-HDBK-217. An example of one such study is "Storage Reliability of Missile Materiel Program" by the U.S. Army Missile R&D Command.

The abstract states:

> This report summarizes analyses on the non-operating reliability of missile materiel. Long term non-operating data has been analyzed together with accelerated storage life test data. Reliability prediction models have been developed for various classes of devices.
>
> This report is a result of a program whose objective is the development of non-operating (storage) reliability prediction and assurance techniques for missile materiel. The analysis results will be used by U.S. Army personnel and contractors in evaluating current missile programs and in the design of future missile systems.
>
> The storage reliability research program consists of a country wide data survey and collection effort, accelerated testing, special test programs and development of a non-operating reliability data bank at the U.S. Army Missile R&D Command, Redstone Arsenal, Alabama. The Army plans a continuing effort to maintain the data bank and analysis reports.

From Section 1.5 of the report, "Limitations of Reliability Prediction":

Practical limitations are placed on any reliability analysis effort in gathering and analyzing data. Field data is generated at various levels of detail and reported in varying manners. Often data on environments, applications, part classes and part construction are not available. Even more often, failure analyses are non-existent. Data on low use devices and new technology devices is also difficult to obtain. Finally, in the storage environment, the very low occurrence of failures in many devices requires extensive storage time to generate any meaningful statistics.

These difficulties lead to prediction of conservative or pessimistic failure rates. The user may review the existing data in the backup analyses reports in any case where design or program decision is necessary.

Another limitation not previously mentioned concerns the use of data, such as provided by the above study, not for decision making relative to the missiles surveyed, but *for estimating storage reliability of systems yet to be built.* In the latter case it is almost certain that much of the information gathered on the storage behavior of materiel concerns components *that will not be used in new systems* because of the rapid advance in technology. The information available from studying systems in storage, therefore, has general utility in respect to environmental conditions encountered, but specificity in respect to the behavior of new components will be guesswork and certainly not precise.

5.2.1 Content

The report covers the gamut of MIL-HDBK-217 items and much more, even in the electronics field. Volume One covers electronics; four other volumes cover electromechanical devices, hydraulic and pneumatic devices, ordnance devices, and optical and electro-optical devices. The mechanical, hydraulic, pneumatic, and ordnance fields are not normally considered to behave exponentially, yet the reporting is obviously tied to the constant hazard rate, or exponential distribution assumption.

The precision with which failure rates are expressed in these volumes is not consistent, statistically, with the data from which these are derived. For example, 58 CW Klystrons are listed as having been stored an average of seven months; six failed in this time. A total of 280,000 device hours is indicated, the failure rate is given as 21.429×10^{-6} per hour! Note that F/nT, 6/280,000, is 21.4286×10^{-6}; thus one digit was rounded off. Table 4.1 of Chapter 4 shows that even at 60% confidence the estimate is good only to $\pm40\%$; at 90 percent, $\pm64\%$. Nevertheless, even six significant digits are observed in some tables. While most tables give estimators only, others also provide the 90% confidence, one-sided upper limit. Some of the extreme precision noted is even more questionable when one observes the use of single-digit environmental multipliers (π_E). The single digit recognizes the difficulty of assigning meaningful multipliers to environmental factors. Not all tables exhibit this disregard of the verities; it must be concluded, therefore, that more than one analyst was responsible for the various tables, and they had different notions as to what precision was appropriate.

While the above remarks are critical—and they are meant to be, particularly in the light of the stated limits in Section 1.5 of the report,—the report is of immense value as a valiant attempt at a very difficult problem. In particular, as an examination of the storage environment and its effects the guidance available for future designs is priceless. While designers of new equipment suffer from the problem of galloping technology in the semiconductor arena, which makes lessons learned on equipment in storage only useful by similarity, it is the best there is and can be. It is certainly far better than no information at all.

5.3   OTHER SOURCES OF ELECTRONIC DATA

5.3.1   Government-Industry Data Exchange Program (GIDEP)

The Government-Industry Data Exchange Program (GIDEP) was established by the Joint Military Logistics Commanders of the Army, Navy, Airforce Logistics Command, Air Force Systems Command, NASA, and the Canadian Military Electronics Standards Agency and is participated in by the AEC, FAA, Small Business Administration, Defense Supply Agency, and other federal department and/or agencies. GIDEP was originally established to minimize the duplicate testing of parts and materials through the interchange of environmental test data and technical information among contractors and government agencies involved in design, development, and fabrication of government-funded equipment. Information contained within the GIDEP storage and retrieval system includes environmental test reports and procedures, reliability specifications, failure analysis data, failure rate data, calibration procedures, and other technical assurance and testing of parts and related materials. To enable immediate data access all information is computer indexed and recorded on microfilm. GIDEP provides the only comprehensive service of this type available without charge to the users. Of particular interest are the Failure Rate Data Bank and the Failure Experience Data Bank. This last bank includes ALERTs, used to warn all participants whenever significant problems are identified on parts and materials.

5.3.2   Long-Life Assurance Study for Manned Spacecraft

The objective of the above study was the development of design, process, test, and application guidelines for achieving reliable spacecraft hardware with a life of 10 years or more. The study approach consisted of an intensive review of technical data performed concurrently with a comprehensive survey of the aerospace industry.

5.4   MECHANICAL STRUCTURES AND MECHANICAL RELIABILITY

The reliability formalism that has arisen since World War II, whose practice is addressed by this book, is essentially only applied to electronic components and systems. It excludes the purely mechanical world, except for the unavoidable inclusion of electromechanical devices such as switches, relays, connectors, rotating electrical machinery, etc; these are treated in the same manner as electronic components. The structures world has developed very successfully over thousands of years without appeal to probabilistic methods: as it developed into an engineering science, it has involved the examination of the properties of materials such as yield strength, fatigue strength, elastic limit, shear strength, stiffness, corrosion resistance, etc. Reliability has been served by establishing factors of safety relative to these various properties, and by excellent discipline on the part of the community, both material user and material producer. The largest factors of safety are applied to the most critical situations, except where weight is a governing element; the smallest are found in unmanned air- and spacecraft. A probabilistic approach to mechanical reliability has developed in the past 20 years. It is based on the probability that the "failure governing strength" exceeds the "failure governing stress"; that probability is defined as the "reliability." This is, of course, quite a departure from the "survivor function" (reliability) of the electronic formalism.

The calculation of the reliability in the above formalism involves the determination of the p.d.f.'s of failure governing strength and failure governing stress. The former must be application oriented, the latter is material oriented. In addition to all of the problems involved in the determination of an empirical distribution (these usually are empirical distributions) the calculation of the reliability involves the interaction of the tails of these distributions. The tails, of course, are the most difficult parts of the distribution to determine. The final goal of this approach is to determine equivalence between the probabilistic definition and the commonly used "factor of safety."

5.4.1 Materials Properties and Procurement

The mechanical world long ago realized the pressing need for standardization and discipline; compared to the electronics world, it is extremely well organized. The material properties reported in handbooks for an enormous variety of standardized materials, fasteners, and so on, are almost always realized in routine purchases from reputable suppliers. Only in the most critical cases is it necessary to check received material to see that the handbook properties are indeed exhibited. In other words, "how to get more of the same" is not a problem, generally, in the mechanical world. The electronics world is an unfortunate contrast, even in the world of Defense Department-controlled material.

REFERENCES

Burrows, R. W., *Long Life Assurance Study for Manned Spacecraft*. Martin Marietta Corp., Denver, Colorado, December 1972.

GIDEP, MIL-STD-1556 (U.S.A.F.), 14 June 1974.

Military Standardization Handbook, MIL-HDBK-217C, 9 April 1979, Commander, Rome Air Development Center, ATTN. RBRT, Griffiss Air Force Base, N.Y.

U.S. Army Missile Research and Development Command, Storage Reliability of Missile Materiel Program, January 1978, Commander, U.S. Army Research and Development Command, ATTN: DRDMI-QS, Redstone Arsenal, Alabama.

CHAPTER SIX

The Real World of Electronic Component Procurement

6.1 STANDARDIZATION

Prior to World War II the U.S. world of electronics was the commercial world of radio, communications, and the beginning of commercial television, including color television. Unlike the professional societies and industrial organizations of the mechanical world and their preoccupation with materials specification and control, the electronic world (commercial telephony excluded) was primarily system oriented. Industry and professional organizations were primarily concerned with system standards rather than component standards. Preferred number series had been established for resistor and capacitor values; one company tried to stem the growing proliferation of electron tube types by advocating preferred tube types, but component standards and reliability were entirely up to the individual company. The entry of the United States into the war, with its explosive proliferation of electronics application, quickly demonstrated the need for standardization. The Defense Department, as the major buyer for such goods, took on the task; they are still the major standardizing agency in the electronics component area in the United States. The role of commercial and professional organizations outside of their involvement with the Federal government has not changed.

6.2 PURCHASING SPECIFICATIONS

One may purchase to military specifications, federal specifications, NASA specifications, industry specifications, internal specifications, or any combination of these. *However, purchasing to any industry or government specification modified is purchasing to one's own specification.* Insofar as the Defense Department and NASA are concerned straight commercial parts have the poorest reliability ratings (by orders of magnitude, possibly), even though they come from vendors of approved parts and may be from the very parts production from which the approved parts are culled. This category includes "nonstandard" parts, parts that can be used in government-procured equipment only by acceptably demonstrating their suitability and reliability.

6.3 U.S. MILITARY SPECIFICATIONS

Commercial grade, military grade and military ER (Established Reliability), and JAN grade components are physically and functionally identical, except for failure rate levels that may vary by orders of magnitude. ER and JAN grade components have been screened (culled) per military test standards as required by specific component specifications and they are made by manufacturers qualified and certified to these specifications by government inspectors. These inspectors monitor and periodically survey and requalify these manufacturers to assure that the high reliability levels of the components are maintained.

In addition to the military grade ER and JAN components there are various so-called "vendor equivalents." These devices have been subjected to screening tests similar to those required by ER or JAN specifications, but they do not meet the full requirements nor are they carried out under government supervision. These may be more reliable than straight commercial grades and non-ER and non-JAN military grades.

6.3.1 ER Active/Passive Electrical Components

ER components are procurable to various failure rate levels from manufacturers qualified and certified to these levels by government inspectors. Such manufacturers are listed on Qualified Parts Lists (QPLs); their parts are so labeled. ER components provide the minimum known levels of reliability (maximum failure rates) *demonstrated* under controlled test conditions. The failure rate levels *usually* provided for by ER specifications are listed in Table 6.1.

Components procured to ER specifications are subjected to special process controls, lot acceptance testing, screening, and extended life tests. Failure rate levels of ER components are statistically established during life testing at 60 or 90% confidence levels as required by component specifications. These rates conform to *rated* electrical stress; for other stress levels MIL-HDBK-217 provides appropriate modifiers. Level P or higher is recommended for military equipments when available.

Table 6.1   ER specification failure rates

MIL symbol	Failures per 10^6 hours
L	2000
M	1000
P	100
R	10
S	1
T	0.1

6.3.2   JAN, JANTX, and JANTXV Semiconductors

Military grade, high reliability semiconductors are procured to MIL-S-19500 and designated as above. These designations are quality levels indicating the screening process involved. The prefix "JAN" on a semiconductor type designation refers to the standardization program for the device. JAN is the minimum level of MIL-S-19500. "TX" indicates JAN processing plus "Testing Extra"; the "plus" refers to specific process and power conditioning on a 100% basis. "TXV" devices pass all JAN and TX requirements plus an internal, visual PRECAP inspection. These devices are not accepted unless they pass the appropriate Lot Tolerance Percent Defective (LTPD) criterion. MIL-HDBK-217, Section 2.2, provides failure rate data. The relative failure rates for JAN, JANTX, and JANTXV are 1.0, 0.2, and 0.1, respectively.

6.3.3   High Quality/Reliability Level Microcircuits

The above circuits are purchased to MIL-M-38510. This specification establishes the design, quality, reliability assurance, and vendor qualification and certification requirements for monolithic, multichip, and hybrid microcircuits. There are three classes of screening, JAN Class S, B, and C; S (space) is the highest class. The JAN designation may be applied only to devices procured to MIL-M-38510. The screening tests are described in MIL-STD-883.

A current misconception is that "procurement to 883" is equivalent to "procurement to MIL-M-38510." Procurement to 883 only means that the devices have been subjected to the tests described in 883; they have not been subject to the in-process controls required by 38510 and have higher failure rates. There are also "vendor equivalents" and "vendor classes," which are claimed by vendors to be identical to 38510. Government procurement officers do not recognize these as being equivalent.

6.4   CONFORMANCE TO SPECIFICATIONS

To the uninitiated it would seem that ordering to government specifications guarantees the receipt of devices performing to the requirements of these specifications. Unfortunately, this is not the case. The agencies with very critical space applications, NASA and the Air Force, for example, have gone to the extraordinary lengths of establishing "captive lines" at chosen manufacturers. These lines are under continuous surveillance by the contracting agency. In other cases where complete captive lines could not be economically justified, the procuring agency has placed full-time representatives at "certified vendors," despite the government involvement guaranteed by the word "certified."

Unfortunately, good parts are obtained only by the exercise of extreme suspicion and cynicism concerning not only suppliers, but of one's own employees. With respect to suppliers, particularly of semiconductor devices, "economic clout" is the best guarantor of satisfactory performance. The purchase of a small number of parts will not get the same attention as a large order, unless it comes from a large user. The U.S. Government finds itself in trouble, because its total demand is small compared to the commercial consumption of semiconductor devices. The automobile industry will soon dwarf all other users; a large black box full of microcircuits in 10 million cars each year will impact all other users. The automobile industry will be the most exacting customer the semiconductor manufacturers will have faced, barring none. General Motors, for example, has designed its own microcircuits and specifies all phases of their manufacture. They will have full-time representatives at all of their suppliers; the production of their devices will result in *de facto* captive lines.

Controls, however, are designed only to cope with human frailty; they cannot provide statistical validity where conditions make it impossible. Reality says that even the two-digit characterization of failure rates may be a hopeless illusion and the remaining digit may be very much in doubt, as well as the power of 10 with which it is associated.

6.5   CONTROLS ON SUPPLIERS

The minimum control, of course, is no controls at all; simply place an order and wait. The maximum is almost tantamount to taking over part of the supplier's operation. A typical approach is high reliability parts procurement involves a detailed vendor survey covering all manufacturing operations, quality system, and so on, made in concert by purchasing, quality assurance, reliability, and engineering. Generally, unanimous approval is required for a potential vendor to be eligible for further negotiation. Once an order is placed and its manufacture is in process, either full-time or visiting representatives are provided to watch the supplier for conformance to purchase requirements.

6.6 CONTROLS AT THE USER'S FACILITY

The entry point at the user's facility is incoming inspection. Unless this operation has adequate instructions and facilities on hand to determine that the received material conforms to the purchase order at the time the material is received, the system is inadequate. Incoming inspection may range from a mere verification of parts count to very elaborate sampling and test procedures including destructive tests and examinations. The latter is the rule in extremely high reliability applications such as commercial spacecraft; these are usually specified to a .98 probability of survival in 10 years. In such applications parts serialization is routine so that defects discovered in inspection and during manufacture can be traced back to the source. High reliability does not come from "an act of faith" but from exquisite attention to the most minute detail; this equally applies to the control of workmanship and parts handling during manufacture.

6.7 "ADVERTENT SCREENING"

The term "screening" is a byword in component procurement for reliable equipment; what is the intent of "advertent"? It is used here to denote "purposeful" screening, screening specifically performed to cull defective parts from a production run. Section 6.8 will discuss "inadvertent screening." Screening employs nondestructive, deteriorative, and destructive methods. Nondestructive methods (inspection is generally nondestructive screening) are preferred for the obvious reason that the survivors of the process have not been affected. One must be careful in the definition of nondestructive methods. Many inspections of this type are thought to be nondestructive but are actually harmful when closely examined. The author's term, "deteriorative," refers to all methods that stress parts and cause deterioration but are not catastrophically destructive. These include "burn in," centrifuging, vibration for particle detection, x ray, temperature cycling, and so on. Some argue that these are nondestructive, but all result in deterioration. Destructive tests must obviously be sample tests; nondestructive tests may also be sampled.

Explosive devices have long been candidates for destructive testing; no operational nondestructive test is possible. In critical applications, however, these tests are supported by nondestructive tests. Dissection of components to provide a detailed examination of internal structure and workmanship is universal in very high reliability applications. A very obvious destructive test, not usually thought of in this regard, is the determination of the time-to-failure p.d.f. of a component.

Nondestructive and deteriorative testing are the major tools for parts screening. The rationale is the assumption that the output of a production process consists of two distinct populations: "main" (good parts) and "freak" (bad parts); these are separable by a process of "screening." The terms "nondestructive" and "destructive" are not as descriptive of the screening process as are "operating" and "nonoperating" testing.

Most nonoperating screens are nondestructive or, at most, mildly deteriorative; the exception is dissection. The nonoperating screens are the first line of defense against freaks, since they result in the least damage to the main population, the desirable output of the manufacturing process. These are totally aimed at the discovery of poor workmanship and process control, defects which are known or suspected to be the cause of failures not inherent in the design. These cover a broad spectrum of disciplines.

The operating screen is the last resort for separating the freak from the main population. It must cover faults overlooked in the nonoperating inspections and those not discoverable by nonoperating methods. This screen is operation in a specified environment and application for a given length of time. The crucial assumption is that the time-to-failure p.d.f. of the freak population is clearly separable from that of the main population. Obviously, it is also necessary that the "life" of the freak population be short compared to that of the main population. To establish both the separability and the time required to fail the freak population requires detailed and continuing knowledge of the underlying time-to-failure p.d.f. The required time may be impractically long even for moderately reliable components; hence the search for accelerated methods. The most obvious mode of acceleration is increased stress, particularly that of temperature. With increased stress there is always the burden of proof of correlation with the effects of normal stress and the proof that the increased stress does not irreparably damage the main population.

The effort to control product quality can become quite elaborate when high reliability is desired. For example, listed below are the product assurance steps required for MIL-M-38510 Class S Microcircuits.

Qualification
  General
  Class B certification
  Class S certification
Qualification (Groups A, B, C, and D)

Wafer lot acceptance
Traceability
Inspection during manufacturing
Screening
    Internal visual (precap)
    Stabilization bake
    Temperature cycling and/or thermal shock
    Constant acceleration
    Particle impact noise detection
    Seal
    Serialization
    Interim electrical
    Burn in (240 hours)
    Interim electrical
    Reverse bias burn in (72 hours)
    Interim electrical
    Seal
    Final Electrical
    Radiographic
    External visual
Quality conformance inspection
    Group A (each lot and sublot)
    Group B (each lot)
    Group C (periodic, every 3 months, die related)
    Group D (periodic, every 6 months, package related)

Despite the elaborate nature of these product assurance steps, considerable difference of opinion exists concerning the adequacy of this standardized set of tests, in particular, the burn in times and the temperature at which the burn in takes place. Quite clearly, it is not self-evident that one particular test protocol would suffice for different designs and semiconductor technologies. The time involved in determining the underlying distribution at normal stress is out of the question, even though this distribution must be known in order to determine the screening protocol. The present alternative is testing at elevated temperatures, using the Arrhenius equation to infer operation at normal temperatures from failure data at elevated temperature. Even this approach requires thousands of hours of testing.

    A typical transformation of the Arrhenius model used in the investigation of semiconductor accelerated testing is

$$\ln t_{50\%} = c + E_A/k\,T \qquad (6.1)$$

where $t_{50\%}$ is the time required for 50% of the test population to fail, c is a constant, E_A is the experimentally determined activation energy in electron volts, k is Boltzmann's constant, and T is the junction temperature in degrees Kelvin. Having determined the value of c by a test at some elevated temperature, $t_{50\%}$ can be calculated for any other temperature. The use of high temperature testing and the prediction of failure rates at ordinary temperatures through the use of equation (6.1) gave rise to the failure rate of 5.93×10^{-92} per hour mentioned in Section 1.2.

Although the reliability community is well aware of high temperature screening (burn in), there is one implication not generally appreciated. Peck and Zierdt (1974) point out in their paper that

Although the intent of a burn in is to remove freak units, it also has an equivalent effect on the main population. For example, a 20 hour burn in at 300°C on a conventional silicon transistor has the effect of nearly 10 million hours at 80°C so that this would represent the beginning of service life.

Now 10 years of service life represents only an addition of one hundreth of the "life" already passed, providing an essentially constant failure rate.

In other words, the separation of the freak population would have required operation of all delivered components for 10 million years at ordinary temperatures; this is such an enormous span of life that an additional 10 years of service life could not result in an appreciable change in hazard rate (an assumption); therefore the hazard rate could be assumed constant during that additional 10 years. The important impact of the above studies and statements is that *most systems are in a state of infant mortality and never reach the minimum of the bathtub curve.*

6.8 INADVERTENT DAMAGE

The personnel who handle and test components during their progress from raw material to finished systems seem oblivious to the damaging effects many of these procedures inflict on the product. Electronic test equipment often damages the components being tested; burn in racks often do not suppress parasitic oscillations that take place at frequencies unsuspected by the user. Mechanical feeding systems required to align and feed large numbers of semiconductor devices to test equipment deliver thousands of high g shocks to the devices, yet this fact goes unremarked by the industry. The basic alignment and feed device is generically known as a vibratory feeder; this is used in all industries for the alignment and feeding of small parts. It shakes the parts being fed at a 60 hz rate; the shocks are high g and uncontrolled. Nevertheless, some manufacturers of systems required to have high reliability follow a practice of discarding semiconductor devices that have dropped to a hard surface from a height of more than 3 inches!

There are other types of inadvertent damage, but an exaustive discussion of this topic is not appropriate here. The important matter is that there exists a certain blindness in the organizations that provide components and assemble them into systems, in which certain damage mechanisms are overlooked on a national scale. One might say that certain of these are "part of the woodwork" and are not questioned because they seem a permanent part of the industrial scene. The author has found time and time again that a question about some of these procedures and machines elicits total unawareness and shock. Nevertheless, these situations represent a dangerous leak in supposedly high reliability procedures.

6.9 CONCLUSIONS

Be eternally suspicious, take nothing for granted, investigate everything. Reliability is obtained only by enormous attention to detail *everywhere.* Despite the extraordinary efforts of the U.S. Department of Defense, component procurement in the electronic world is quicksand, not a bedrock foundation.

REFERENCES

Peck, D. S., and Zierdt, C. H., Jr. "The Reliability of Semiconductor Devices in the Bell System," *Proceedings of the IEEEE.* **62**(2), 185–211, (1974).

CHAPTER SEVEN

The Time to First
Failure for New Systems

7.1 DEFINITIONS, COMPONENTS, AND SYSTEMS

Section 3.1 defined component, system, new component, and new system. These terms require further discussion in order that the subtleties involved are fully appreciated.

Component   A nonrepairable device. This is not an absolute definition in the sense "once a component, always a component." One person's component may be another person's system. Thus the definition is contextual and is made in the framework of a particular discussion.

System   A complex of one or more components of one or more types. This is also a contextual definition, since it depends on the definition of component.

New component   A component whose life has not been affected in any way (by operation or other agencies) since its random selection from a population with a known time-to-failure distribution. *This does not necessarily mean a component with zero operating time or other handling; it means that the component's life has not been affected in any way since selection from a known population.* For example, the population may be a quantity of 38510 Class S Microcircuits. These have been screened in accordance with the description provided in Section 6.7. These components will be considered new by definition when delivered to receiving inspection if and only if the time-to-failure distribution is known *for the parts as received!*

New System   A system composed of new components. This definition sounds straightforward but has semantic traps. By way of illustration, consider a system manufactured from components meeting the "new" definition as received in incoming inspection. By the time the system has reached the shipping dock, its components have been handled, soldered, temperature cycled, operated, and tested in many ways if it is a complex electronic equipment. In fact, most complex electronic systems will have also undergone more than one repair during the manufacturing cycle. Unless the time-to-failure distributions of the components are known for the state reached at the time of system shipment, *the components are no longer new nor is the system!* On the other hand, many everyday household appliances are assembled and shipped without test; the effect on component life is most likely minimal in this instance.

7.2 MEAN TIME TO FIRST FAILURE (MTTFF)

Consider an experiment in which a large number of identical new systems are put into operation and the test continued until all have failed. In this instance "identical" means that the components for all the systems have been drawn from the same parent population. By making the test number large enough, the underlying time-to-failure distribution of these systems (as single entities) will have been discovered by the methods already discussed. (This is no different than determining the time-to-failure distribution for a component.) In the usual way, therefore, the MTTF (mean time to failure) of these systems can be computed as

$$MTTF = \int_0^\infty t f_s(t)\, dt \tag{7.1}$$

where $f_s(t)$ denotes the time-to-failure p.d.f. for systems as entities and the distribution has been approximated as a continuous function. If the discovered distribution is kept in its discrete form, the MTTF is

$$MTTF = \sum_{n=1}^{L} t_n f_s(t_n) \tag{7.1}$$

At this point the author chooses to call the above the mean time to first failure (MTTFF). First this calls to attention the fact that the systems are *new* and the system failures are the first failures. Second, and most important, this has been done to emphasize the difference between this function and the mean time between failures (MTBF)! The latter, the cornerstone of present theory, is almost universally confused with the MTTFF, even though they are fundamentally different. The MTBF refers to the time between failures of identical systems undergoing repeated cycles of failure and repair, that is, a "renewal" process; the MTTFF has nothing to do with renewal. It is true, however, that in the case of systems composed entirely of components obeying the continuous exponential distribution, the theoretical magnitude of the MTBF is the same as the MTTFF. *This is true of no other distribution!*

Thus far the result seems trivial. It is, however, the opening attack on predicting the MTTFF from a knowledge of the time-to-failure distributions of the components comprising a system. The mechanism involves the recall of two more relations:

$$\text{MTTF} = \int_0^\infty \underline{fs}(t) \, dt$$

$$\text{MTTF} = \sum_{n=0}^{L-1} (t_{n+1} - t_n) \underline{fs}(t_n)$$

(7.2)

The first relation above is derived from the first relation in equation (7.1) upon integration by parts after observing that

$$f(t) = \frac{-d}{dt} \underline{fs}(t)$$

The discrete relationship is derived by applying the equation

$$f(t_n) = \underline{fs}(t_{n-1}) - \underline{fs}(t_n)$$

to the discrete definition of MTTF, the second relation in equation (7.1). These are universal relationships and hold for any distribution. The reason for recalling these relationships is that it happens to be easier to calculate the survivor function from the distributions comprising the system than to directly calculate $f_s(t)$ or its discrete counterpart from these same distributions. Once the survivor function is available the MTTFF may be calculated directly from the survivor function. In fact, the system time-to-failure distribution $f_s(t)$ may also be determined from the survivor function.

7.3   THE STANDARD DEVIATION ABOUT THE MTTFF

The MTTFF by itself is insufficient information about the behavior of the failure times of the systems; the spread of failures about the mean is also necessary. This is determined by calculating the standard deviation about the MTTFF. A small standard deviation relative to the mean indicates a well-behaved failure pattern; that is, the time to first failure is essentially the same for all systems, the MTTFF. A large standard deviation relative to the mean indicates a badly behaved failure pattern, failure times vary considerably from system to system. It is most interesting to note, as will be shown later, that the standard deviation about the MTTFF is equal to the MTTFF for systems comprised of parts obeying the exponential distribution; this is not a happy state of affairs.

By definition, the standard deviation about the MTTFF, for both continuous and discrete distributions, is

$$\sigma_s = \left[\int_0^\infty t^2 f_s(t) \, dt - \text{MTTFF}^2 \right]^{1/2}$$

$$\sigma_s = \left[\sum_{n=0}^{L} t_n^2 f_s(t_n) - \text{MTTFF}^2 \right]^{1/2}$$

(7.3)

These may be transformed into functions of the survivor function to give

$$\sigma_s = \left[2 \int_0^\infty t \, \underline{fs}_s(t) \, dt - \text{MTTFF}^2 \right]^{1/2}$$

$$\sigma_s = \left[\sum_{n=0}^{L-1} (t_{n+1}^2 - t_n^2) \, \underline{fs}_s(t_n) - \text{MTTFF}^2 \right]^{1/2}$$

(7.4)

7.4 MTTFF OF NEW SERIES SYSTEMS: ONE COMPONENT TYPE

The term "new" has been defined; it means that the time-to-failure distributions of the system components are known at the moment the systems are turned on for the first time. "Series" indicates a system organization in which the failure of a single component is defined as a system failure. "One component type" refers to a system comprised of components having identical underlying time-to-failure distributions. This does not necessarily mean that the components are physically and functionally identical; these may differ as long as the underlying distributions are identical. This is not just a theoretical notion: for example, there exist microcircuits that differ functionally but, as far as can be determined, have identical underlying time-to-failure distributions.

Given the time-to-failure distribution $f(t)$ of a component, the cumulative probability of failure of that component in time t is

$$F(t) = \int_0^t f(x) \, dx \qquad \text{(continuous distribution)} \qquad (7.5)$$

Recalling the binomial distribution (Section 2.1), given the probability p of an event, the probability of its non-occurrence in M trials is

$$P(0) = (1 - p)^M \qquad (7.6)$$

Operating a system with M components is equivalent to M binomial trials; identifying $F(t)$ with p of the binomial distribution, the probability that none of the M components will have failed in the interval $(0, t)$, is

$$[1 - F(t)]^M = \left[1 - \int_0^t f(x)\, dx \right]^M = \left[\int_t^\infty f(x)\, dx \right]^M$$

But the survivor function is the probability that no failure will have occurred in the interval $(0, t)$; therefore the survivor function for the system is

$$\underline{fs}_s(t) = [1 - F(t)]^M \qquad (7.7)$$

The corresponding system time-to-failure distribution is

$$\frac{-d}{dt} \underline{fs}_s(t) = f_s(t) = M f(t)[1 - F(t)]^{M-1} \qquad (7.8)$$

Expression (7.8) could have been written directly. The probability that a component will fail in an interval dt about t is $f(t)\, dt$. The probability that no failures will have occurred in $M - 1$ components in the interval $(0, t)$ is $[1 - F(t)]^{M-1}$. The product of the two probabilities is the probability that both events will have occurred. Now, there are M ways in which this can happen. Thus multiplying by M and dividing by dt yields expression (7.8). Now

$$\text{MTTFF} = \int_0^\infty [1 - F(t)]^M\, dt \qquad (7.9)$$

$$\sigma_s = \left[2 \int_0^\infty t[1 - F(t)]^M\, dt - \text{MTTFF}^2 \right]^{1/2} \qquad (7.10)$$

The equivalent expressions for discrete distributions are

$$\underline{fs}_s(t_n) = \left[1 - \sum_{j=1}^n f(t_j) \right]^M = [1 - F(t_n)]^M \qquad (7.11)$$

$$f_s(t_n) = [1 - F(t_{n-1})]^M - [1 - F(t_n)]^M \qquad (7.12)$$

Note the difference between expression (7.12) and equation (7.8).

$$\text{MTTFF} = \sum_{n=0}^{L-1} (t_{n+1} - t_n)[1 - F(t_n)]^M \tag{7.13}$$

$$\sigma_s = \left[\sum_{n=0}^{L-1} (t_{n+1}^2 - t_n^2)[1 - F(t_n)]^M - \text{MTTFF}^2 \right]^{1/2} \tag{7.14}$$

In the case of the expressions based on continuous distributions, an interesting approximation is possible for $\underline{fs}_s(t)$ when t is in the neighborhood of zero. Taking the first two terms of a Maclaurin's expansion of the system survivor function yields

$$\underline{fs}_s(t) \cong 1 - M f(0) t \tag{7.15}$$

This result holds regardless of the underlying distribution. It should not be a surprising result: the initial behavior of the survivor function should obviously depend on the nature of the underlying distribution at time zero.

7.4.1 Behavior When $f(t)$ Is $\lambda e^{-\lambda t}$

The cumulative failure probability per component is

$$F(t) = 1 - e^{-\lambda t} \tag{7.16}$$

The system survivor function is

$$\underline{fs}_s(t) = (e^{-\lambda t})^M = e^{-M\lambda t}$$

The system time-to-failure p.d.f. is

$$f_s(t) = M\lambda e^{-M\lambda t}$$

$$\text{MTTFF} = \frac{1}{\lambda M}$$

$$\sigma_s = \left[\frac{2}{(\lambda M)^2} - \frac{1}{(\lambda M)^2} \right]^{1/2}$$

$$\sigma_s = \frac{1}{\lambda M} = \text{MTTFF}$$

From the result immediately above it is seen that MTTFF $\pm$ σ_s runs from zero to two MTTFF, a wide range of failure times. The point of stressing this result is that few reliability texts or practitioners bother to highlight this aspect of the behavior of the exponential law. As a result, lay customers of the community unfortunately tend to regard the MTTFF (mislabeled MTBF in the case of new systems) as a guaranteed minimum failure time.

7.5 MTTFF OF NEW SERIES SYSTEMS: MULTIPLE COMPONENT TYPES

All of the introductory remarks of Section 7.4 apply, except that more than one component type comprises the system, that is, more than one underlying time-to-failure distribution. Assuming all component failures to be independent, the system survivor function is the product of the survivor functions of the individual component types. It is important at this point to state that the use of the term "series" does not exclude systems employing redundant elements. Any redundant element can be resolved into an equivalent single element having a time-to-failure distribution appropriate to the redundant element and derived from the individual distributions of the components making up the element.

The system survivor function is

$$\underline{fs}_s(t) = \prod_{j=1}^{m} [1 - F_j(t)]^{M_j} \tag{7.17}$$

where there are M_j each of m component types, each having the distribution $f_j(t)$. The system time-to-failure distribution is quite complex:

$$f_s(t) = \sum_{j=1}^{m} \left\{ M_j f_j(t)[1 - F_j(t)]^{M_j-1} \prod_{\substack{i=1 \\ i \neq j}}^{m} [1 - F_i(t)]^{M_i} \right\}$$

$$f_s(t) = \underline{fs}_s(t) \sum_{j=1}^{m} M_j f_j(t)[1 - F_j(t)]^{-1} \tag{7.18}$$

All of the other functions can be written out but they would only clutter the text. What is needed is some simpler approximation, if possible. Returning to the system survivor function and noting that

$$1 - z \cong e^{-z} \tag{7.19}$$

when z is small compared to one, the system survivor function may be approximated

$$\underline{fs}_s(t) \cong \prod_{j=1}^{m} \{\exp[-F_j(t)]\}^{M_j} \qquad (7.20)$$

as long as the interval $(0, t)$ is restricted such that all of the $F_j(t)$ are small compared to one. Let us see if this constraint is as onerous as it might seem at first glance. Consider the component having the worst failure behavior, that is, its $F(t)$ exceeds those of all the others. Assume further that there can be no practical interest in a survivor function that is less than .01. Assume that interest ceases when the worst case $[1 - F_j(t)]^{M_j}$ reaches .01; at this point the system survivor function is much less than .01, unless the system uses only one component type. This yields

$$[1 - F_j(t)]^{M_j} = .01$$

$$-M_j F_j(t) \cong \ln(.01) = -4.6$$

$$F_j(t) \cong 4.6/M_j \qquad (7.21)$$

Taking t equal to 10,000 hours and M_j equal to 1000 (very reliable equipment and 1000 of the least reliable parts) gives

$$F_j(10,000) \cong 4.6 \times 10^{-3}$$

Assuming a uniform distribution, this translates to a failure rate of 4.6×10^{-7} per hour, a moderately reliable electronic part. Thus for the time to first failure the constraint is negligible in a typical real world situation. Rewriting expression (7.20) provides

$$\underline{fs}_s(t) \cong \exp\left[\sum_{j=1}^{m} - M_j \int_0^t f_j(t)\, dt\right]$$

$$\cong \exp\left\{-\int_0^t \left[\sum_{j=1}^{m} M_j f_j(t)\right] dt\right\} \qquad (7.22)$$

Consider for a moment a system composed of M of one component type only and having its survivor function approximated in the same manner as above. This would give

$$\underline{fs}_s(t) = \exp\left[-\int_0^t M f(t)\, dt\right]$$

The expression above will be identical to expression (7.22) if

$$Mf(t) = \sum_{j=1}^{m} M_j f_j(t)$$

$$f(t) = \frac{1}{M} \sum_{j=1}^{m} M_j f_j(t) \tag{7.23}$$

If M is now considered the total number of components in the system, that is,

$$M = \sum_{j=1}^{m} M_j$$

then for the first time to failure the multiple component type new system may be considered to be a single component type system whose component time-to-failure distribution is that given in equation (7.23) and whose component count is that of the total number of components in the system. This approximation reduces the complexity of the multiple component type system to that of the single component type system *only for the time to first failure calculation.* This approach applies to discrete distributions as well.

7.5.1   Behavior When $f_j(t)$ is $\lambda_j e^{-\lambda_j t}$

The evident complexity in the immediate discussion vanishes in the instance above, proving once again the remarkable mathematical convenience of the exponential distribution. The system survivor function is

$$\underline{fs}_s(t) = \prod_{j=1}^{m} [\exp(-\lambda_j t)]^{M_j}$$

$$= \exp\left(-t \sum_{j=1}^{m} M_j \lambda_j\right) \tag{7.24}$$

The system time-to-failure distribution is

$$f_s(t) = \left(\sum_{j=1}^{m} M_j \lambda_j\right) \exp\left(-t \sum_{j=1}^{m} M_j \lambda_j\right) \tag{7.25}$$

Expression (7.25) is an exponential distribution with failure rate

$$f_s(t) = \sum_{j=1}^{m} M_j \lambda_j \qquad (7.26)$$

Thus the multiple component system behaves like a single component exponential system, with the failure rate of equation (7.26). By analogy, the MTTFF of the multiple component exponential system is the reciprocal of equation (7.26), as is the standard deviation.

CHAPTER EIGHT

System Survivor Functions for Certain Component Distributions

8.1 PARAMETRIC REPRESENTATION OF SURVIVOR FUNCTIONS

The purpose of this chapter is to show how survivor functions of systems composed of a single component type vary with the nature of the underlying component distribution. In fact, the startling result of this analysis is that underlying component distributions may vary considerably without having a substantial effect on the survivor function. Certain aspects of the comparison of survivor functions are best shown graphically, employing a parametric representation of the survivor function, that is, graphing the survivor function as a function of t/T rather than as a function of t. In particular, T may chosen such that survivor functions of different underlying distributions have the same value at $t/T = 1$. This parametric choice is useful for visually comparing shapes of survivor functions and is used in the following material. A further convenience of the parametric method is that it allows a single computer program to cover both parametric and nonparametric computation, since the nonparametric case can be subsumed into the parametric formulation. The computer programs used to calculate the survivor functions shown in this chapter are provided in the Appendix.

The development of the parametric approach below is given for continuous distributions only, but applies equally to discrete distributions. The parameter T is defined as the solution of

$$F(T) = \int_0^T f(t)\, dt = \frac{\gamma}{M} \tag{8.1}$$

where $f(t)$ is the time-to-failure distribution of the component and M is the number of components in the system. Consequently,

$$\underline{fs}_s(T) = \left(1 - \frac{\gamma}{M}\right)^M \tag{8.2}$$

If γ/M is less than 0.1,

$$\underline{fs}_s(T) \cong e^{-\gamma} \tag{8.3}$$

The least value of interest for $\underline{fs}_s(T)$ is surely 0.01; this corresponds to a value of 4.6 for γ. This, therefore, is the largest value of interest for γ. To satisfy the condition for approximation (8.3) M must exceed 46. Accordingly, the approximation is good for any real situation. The values of γ for $\underline{fs}_s(T)$ equal to 0.05, 0.1, $1/e$, 0.9, 0.95, and 0.99 are 3, 2.3, 1, 0.1, 0.05, and 0.01, respectively. The corresponding T's are designated T_{05}, T_{10}, and so on.

Use of the parametric representation above always converts $\underline{fs}_s(t)$ into a function of t/T only. Computation of survival functions in this form, therefore, are carried out with t/T as the variable.

Computation of the MTTFF is based on

$$\text{MTTFF} = \int_0^\infty \underline{fs}_s(t)dt = T \int_0^\infty \underline{fs}_s(t)d(t/T)$$

or

$$\text{MTTFF}/T = \int_0^\infty \underline{fs}_s(t)d(t/T) \tag{8.4}$$

The right side of equation (8.4) has an integrand that is a function of t/T only; the integral may be numerically evaluated as the parametric form of $\underline{fs}_s(t)$ is computed. The quantity MTTFF/T correctly positions the MTTFF on the graph of $\underline{fs}_s(t)$ plotted against t/T. Similarly,

$$\sigma_s/T = [2\int_0^\infty (t/T)\underline{fs}_s(t)d(t/T) - (\text{MTTFF}/T)^2]^{1/2} \tag{8.5}$$

The above quantity can also be evaluated as the computation of $\underline{fs}_s(t)$ proceeds. This quantity correctly locates the positions of MTTFF $\pm$ $n\sigma_s$ *on the graph of* $\underline{fs}_s(t)$ *plotted against* t/T.

8.2 THE GENERALIZED EXPONENTIAL DISTRIBUTION $ae^{\delta at}$

The generalized exponential distribution is a versatile one. When $\delta = -1$ the distribution is the "law of chance failure." When δ is zero the distribution is uniform. The system survivor function is

$$\underline{fs}_s(t) = \left[1 - \frac{1}{\delta}(e^{\delta at} - 1) \right]^M \tag{8.6}$$

When δ is greater than -1 the life of the distribution cannot be infinite but must be finite. That life is defined by

$$F(L) = \int_0^L f(t)\, dt = \frac{1}{\delta}(e^{\delta aL} - 1) = 1 \tag{8.7}$$

$$L = \frac{1}{\delta a}\ln(1 + \delta) \tag{8.8}$$

Then

$$f(L) = a(1 + \delta) \tag{8.9}$$

As can be seen, $f(L) = $ zero when $\delta = -1$; it is a when $\delta = $ zero and becomes increasingly large with increasing δ. L itself is a decreasing function of increasing δ. *Regardless of the magnitude of δ, however, f(0) is the same. Thus, as pointed out in equation (7.15), the initial behavior of the survivor function is independent of δ.*

8.2.1   Behavior for Moderate Values of $\delta > -1$

Is there a condition on δ such that the survivor function is independent of δ over the entire practical range of the survivor function? The answer is yes. To find the range on δ consider the survivor function, equation (8.6). From the discussion on parametric representation,

$$\underline{fs}_s(T_{05}) = [1 - (1/\delta)(e^{\delta aT_{05}} - 1)]^M = .05 \tag{8.10}$$

If $\delta a T_{05}$ is less than 0.2, the above equation may be approximated by

$$\underline{fs}_s(T_{05}) \cong (1 - aT_{05})^M = .05$$

independent of δ. From this one obtains

$$aT_{05} \cong 1 - .05^{1/M}$$

Then

$$\delta \leq \frac{0.2}{(1 - .05^{1/M})} \tag{8.11}$$

Thus in the range $(1, .05)$ the survivor function of the generalized exponential time-to-failure distribution is essentially independent of δ for M equal to

10,000, 1000, and 100, and δ less than 700, 70, and 7, respectively. Figure 8.1 displays the survivor functions for ae^{-at} and ae^{700at} when M is 10,000; the correspondence is remarkable. It follows, therefore, that over any practical time interval the survivor functions for ae^{-at} and the uniform distribution are virtually indistinguishable.

8.2.2 Monte Carlo Simulation, Uniform Distribution, and Survivor Functions for 100 Component Systems

The simulation is based on the random number set (00000, 99,999) representing the underlying distribution of the components. The simulation used is the generation of sets of 100 random numbers; this is system manufacture. As each set of 100 is generated, the least number of the set is determined; this is the time of failure. There were 100 systems simulated, requiring the generation of 10,000 random numbers. Survivor functions for 20 systems and for 100 systems were calculated from the failure data. The results are shown in Figures 8.2 and 8.3. Each figure also contains the theoretical continuous system survivor function (smooth line) derived from the equivalent continuous component time-to-failure distribution. That survivor function is

$$\underline{fs}_s(t) = (1 - at)^M$$

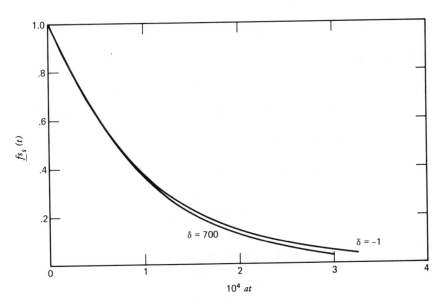

Figure 8.1 Survivor functions of the distribution $a\,e^{\delta at}$, $M = 10^4$, with $\delta = 1$ and $\delta = 700$.

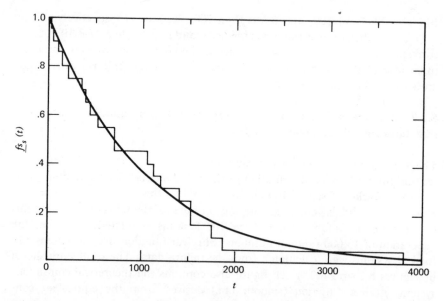

Figure 8.2 Monte Carlo simulation of 20 systems of 100 components each, from a discrete, uniform distribution: actual survivor function compared to theoretical survivor function; actual MTTFF, 944, compared to theoretical 990.

Figure 8.2 displays the survivor function for 20 systems. Note that while it tends to follow the theoretical curve, the departures from the curve are extensive. Figure 8.3, the survivor function for 100 systems, follows the theoretical curve with more fidelity but still has some departures from it. The lesson is twofold: the law of large numbers still holds and there is little reason to predict system behavior in the real world to more than two significant digits.

8.2.3 Behavior for $\delta < -1$

Returning to the cumulative probability distribution

$$F(t) = \int_0^t ae^{\delta at}\, dt = \frac{1}{\delta}(e^{\delta at} - 1)$$

$$(1/\delta)(ae^{\delta aL} - 1) = 1$$

(where L is the life), but

$$e^{\delta aL} = (1/a)(\delta + 1) \geq 0 \tag{8.12}$$

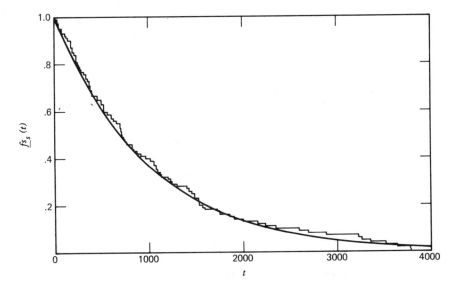

Figure 8.3 Monte Carlo simulation of 100 systems of 100 components each, from a discrete, uniform distribution: actual survivor function compared to theoretical survivor function; actual MTTFF, 1024, compared to theoretical 990.

since an exponential can never be negative. Consequently, since a is always positive,

$$\delta + 1 \geq 0$$

$$\delta \geq -1 \tag{8.13}$$

It seems, therefore, that δ can never be less than -1. However, this is only apparent, rather than real, and is due to the constraint that $F(L)$ must equal one. This must be true if the entire distribution is $ae^{\delta at}$. There is no reason, however, why the total distribution cannot be

$$f(t) = ae^{\delta at} + \phi(t) \tag{8.14}$$

where $ae^{\delta at}$ is defined only in the interval $(0, T)$ and $\phi(t)$ is defined only in the interval (T, ∞). The requirement that $f(t)$ be a p.d.f. is now satisfied by

$$\int_0^T ae^{\delta at} \, dt + \int_T^\infty \phi(t) \, dt = 1 \tag{8.15}$$

If $\int_T^\infty \phi(t) \, dt$ is unity, for example,

$$\int_0^T ae^{\delta at} \, dt = 0$$

It is easily seen that δ is $-\infty$ in the above instance. However, this is a trivial case. A realistic case is one in which the interval $(0, T)$ is $(0, T_{05})$, for example. In accordance with the parametric definitions, one has

$$\frac{1}{\delta}(e^{\delta a T_{05}} - 1) = \frac{3}{M} \tag{8.16}$$

The cumulative probability of $\phi(t)$ in the interval (T_{05}, ∞) is then $1 - 3/M$. This leads to the result

$$\delta \geq \frac{-M}{3} \tag{8.17}$$

If T_{10} had been used, the result would have been $-M/2.3$.

8.2.4 Parametric Representation of $ae^{\delta at}$

From

$$\int_0^T ae^{\delta at} \, dt = \frac{1}{\delta}(e^{\delta a T} - 1) = \frac{\gamma}{M}$$

$$a = \left(\frac{1}{T\delta}\right) \ln\left(1 + \frac{\gamma\delta}{M}\right)$$

$$\underline{fs_s}(t) = \left\{1 - \frac{1}{\delta}\left[\left(1 + \frac{\gamma\delta}{M}\right)^{t/T} - 1\right]\right\}^M \tag{8.18}$$

a function of t/T. For T_{05}, $\gamma = 3$; for $T_{1/e}$, $\gamma = 1$. For $T = 1/Ma$,

$$\gamma_{1/Ma} = \frac{M}{\delta}(e^{\delta/M} - 1) \tag{8.19}$$

For $T = 1/a$, that is, for expressing the functions in their original form as functions of at,

$$\gamma_{1/a} = \frac{M}{\delta}(e^{\delta} - 1) \tag{8.20}$$

Although result (8.20) may seem silly, and it would be if calculating the expressions in their original form was to be the only such calculation, it does provide for calculating a variety of forms with a single computer program. The data for Figure 8.1 was obtained using the program and the value of γ determined from equation (8.19).

Figure 8.4 is a graph of the survivor functions of $ae^{\delta at}$, $M = 10^4$, parametric in T_{05} and δ having the values -3333, -1, 10^4, 10^5, 10^7, 10^9, and ∞. Since the functions are parametric in T_{05}, all cross at the value .05. The filled in circles on the curves are the positions of the respective MTTFFs; the open circles are the respective positions of the MTTFF $\pm\ \sigma_s$. Now while the time scale is linear and the slopes and points of inflection are correct for each function, the relative positions of the functions in time are distorted. This is clearly seen in Figure 8.5, where the same functions are plotted parametrically in $1/10^4 a$. The time scale is now the same for all functions and the relative positions in time are shown correctly. In this graphic context, however, it is impossible to show all of the survivor functions as clearly as in Figure 8.4. The functions for δ equal to 10^7, 10^9, and ∞ become spikes at or near time zero; the delineation of the shapes of the functions for δ equal to 10^4 and 10^5 is poor. Further, the relative positions of the MTTFFs and MT-

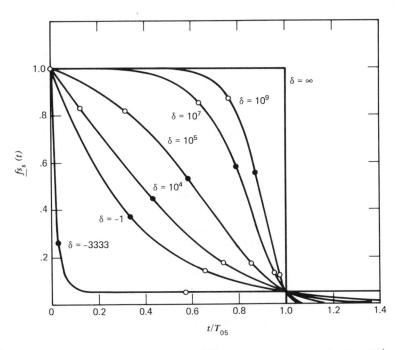

Figure 8.4 Survivor functions of $a\,e^{\delta at}$, parametric in T_{05}, with $M = 10^4$.

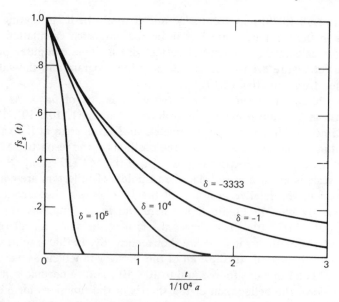

Figure 8.5   Survivor functions of $a\,e^{\delta at}$, parametric in $1/10^4 a$, with $M = 10^4$, linear plot.

TFF $\pm\ \sigma_s$ cannot be adequately depicted. Figure 8.6 provides still another representational graph: the time scale is the same for all functions, as in Figure 8.5, but time is plotted logarithmically on semilog paper. Thus it really takes two different graphic modes to fully compare the survivor functions corresponding to different values of δ. The parametric representation in T_{xy} provides the shape of each function and the locations of the MTTFF and MTTFF $\pm\ \sigma_s$ relative to the respective functions; the nonparametric representation on semilog paper provides the true time relationships between the survivor functions.

The survivor function for $\delta = \infty$ requires special mention. The survivor function for an ideally reliable system is one that looks like the function for $\delta = \infty$ in Figure 8.4; it is the survivor function of a system composed of components with a single failure time, that is, a time-to-failure distribution that is a delta function at a specific time. This is the survivor function of the "one hoss shay" in the famous poem by an early reliability theorist, Oliver Wendell Holmes. In the poem the shay operated without flaw until the instant that all parts failed at once. $ae^{\infty at}$ qualifies as such a distribution, except, unfortunately, the single time of failure is time zero. Nevertheless, the representation of Figure 8.4 is correct inasmuch as all T_{xy}, including T_{05}, occur at the time of system failure. In short, a system comprised of components

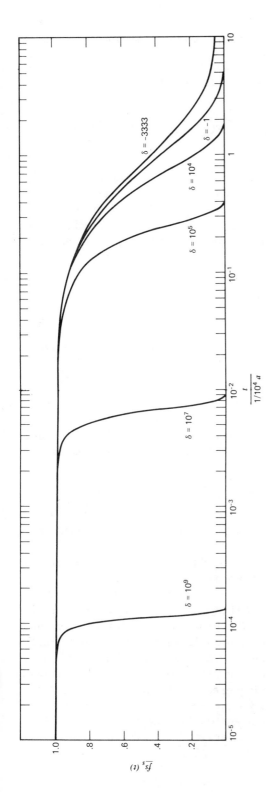

Figure 8.6   Survivor functions of $a\,e^{\delta a t}$, parametric in $1/10^4 a$, with $M = 10^4$.

characterized by the time-to-failure distribution $ae^{\infty at}$ experiences simultaneous failure of all components the instant it is turned on.

8.3 THE GENERALIZED POWER FUNCTION DISTRIBUTION $a(at)^\delta$

The generalized power function distribution in the interval $(0, L)$ has three modes of behavior depending on the value of δ. When δ is positive and not zero, the distribution is zero at time zero. For δ equal to zero the distribution is uniform. For δ in the range $(-1^+, 0^-)$ $f(0)$ is infinite; nevertheless, the cumulative probability exists, as does the survivor function. In parametric form the survivor function is

$$\underline{fs}_s(t) = \left[1 - \left(\frac{\gamma}{M}\right)\left(\frac{t}{T}\right)^{\delta+1} \right]^M$$

$$\gamma_{1/a} = \frac{M}{\delta + 1} \qquad (8.21)$$

$$aL = (\delta + 1)^{1/(\delta+1)}$$

A system whose components are characterized by a distribution for which $f(0)$ is zero has a unique property compared to those for which $f(0)$ is finite. Equation (7.15) demonstrated that in the immediate neighborhood of time zero

$$\underline{fs}_s(t) \cong 1 - M f(0) \, t$$

The slope of the survivor function in this same time region is $f(0)$. If $f(0)$ is zero, the survivor function has zero slope at time zero. This is a highly desirable characteristic for a survival function, since it denotes a very high initial survivability. In fact, to achieve this same characteristic with components for which $f(0)$ is finite parallel redundancy must be invoked.

Figure 8.7 graphs several survivor functions for 10,000 component systems parametric in T_{05}. The MTTFFs and the $\pm\sigma_s$ values are shown by filled in and open circles. Figure 8.8 plots the same survivor functions to a common time scale on semilog paper. The values of δ used are -0.9, -0.25, 0, 1, 3, 5, 20, and ∞. At first glance it might seem that Figures 8.4 and 8.7 are very similar. In fact, the functions for 0 would be identical in both figures. The graph for $\delta = 10^7$ in Figure 8.4 is quite similar to that for $\delta = 5$ in Figure 8.7. A look at Figures 8.6 and 8.8 however, tell a very different story. While the functions for zero δ are still the same, the time relationships for higher and lower values of δ are reversed. This is the consequence of the

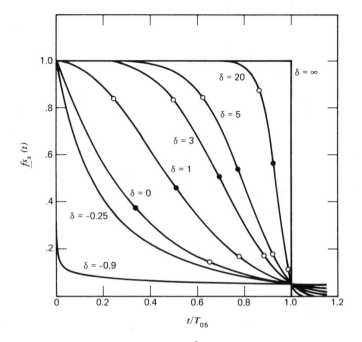

Figure 8.7 Survivor functions of $a(a\ t)^\delta$ parametric in T_{05}, with $M = 10^4$.

radically different behaviors of the two distributions for at less than one. For positive values of δ, $ae^{\delta at}$ starts at a at time zero and increases with increasing at; $a(at)^\delta$ starts out at zero and does not reach a until at becomes one. In fact, the rate of rise from zero becomes slower and slower as δ increases.

For an infinite value of δ the survivor functions look the same in Figures 8.4 and 8.7. They are markedly different in Figures 8.6 and 8.8. The survivor function for $ae^{\infty at}$ does not even appear in Figure 8.6 because it is compressed into a zero interval at time zero. In Figure 8.8 the survivor function for $a(at)^\infty$ is the rectangular plot extending to $at = 1$, a true "one hoss shay" survivor function in which no system failures occur until the simultaneous failure of all components when at reaches one. The reason for this, of course, may be seen by examining the behavior of the distribution: it is zero everywhere except at $at = 1$, where it is a delta function.

8.4 THE MODIFIED NORMAL DISTRIBUTION

Section 2.7.5 explained why the normal distribution could not be used as a time-to-failure distribution without modification. This was required because a time-to-failure distribution must be zero for negative time; the normal

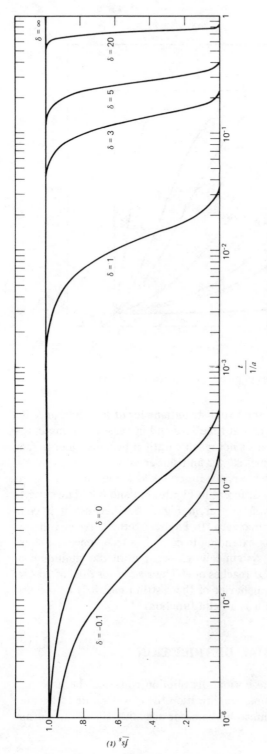

Figure 8.8 Survivor functions of $a(a\,t)^{\delta}$, parametric in $1/a$, with $M = 10^4$.

distribution does not satisfy that requirement. Additionally, if values of the normal distribution for negative time are ignored, its cumulative distribution for all positive values of time will no longer be one. One solution to this problem is to define a time-to-failure distribution based on the normal distribution as

$$f(t) = \frac{n(t)}{1 - \displaystyle\int_{-\infty}^{0} n(t)\, dt} \qquad 0 \leq t \leq \infty$$

where (8.22)

$$n(t) = \frac{1}{\sigma(2\pi)^{1/2}} \exp \frac{-(t - \mu)^2}{2\sigma^2}$$

It is easily demonstrated that

$$\int_{0}^{\infty} f(t)\, dt = 1$$

as defined above. The above form for $f(t)$ is not convenient in terms of published tables or calculator outputs; these normally provide

$$E(y) = \frac{\exp(-y^2/2)}{(2\pi)^{1/2}} \qquad \text{and} \qquad \int_{t}^{\infty} E(y)\, dy \qquad (8.23)$$

Using transformations

$$y = -(x - \mu)/\sigma \qquad \text{and} \qquad dy = -dx/\sigma$$

one sees that

$$\int_{0}^{t} f(x)\, dx = \frac{\displaystyle\int_{0}^{t} n(x)\, dx}{1 - \displaystyle\int_{-\infty}^{0} n(x)\, dx}$$

and

$$\int_{-\infty}^{0} n(x)\, dx = -\int_{\infty}^{\mu/\sigma} \frac{\exp(-y^2/2)\, dy}{(2\pi)^{1/2}} = -\int_{\infty}^{\mu/\sigma} E(y)\, dy$$

$$= \int_{\mu/\sigma}^{\infty} E(y)\, dy = \psi \qquad (8.24)$$

$$\int_0^t n(x)dx = -\int_{\mu/\sigma}^{(\mu-t)/\sigma} E(y)\, dy$$

$$= \int_{(\mu-t)/\sigma}^{\infty} E(y)\, dy - \int_{\mu/\sigma}^{\infty} E(y)\, dy$$

Then

$$\int_0^t f(t)\, dt = \frac{1}{1-\psi}\left[\int_{(\mu-t)/\sigma}^{\infty} E(y)\, dy - \psi\right] \tag{8.25}$$

While it is well known that the mean value of the normal distribution is μ in $n(t)$ as given in (8.22) the MTTF of $f(t)$ is not. It is calculated as

$$\text{MTTF} = \int_0^{\infty} tf(t)\, dt$$

Making use of the property of $f(t)$ [equation (8.22)] that

$$\frac{d}{dt}f(t) = \frac{-(t-\mu)f(t)}{\sigma^2}$$

such that

$$t\, f(t) = \mu\, f(t) - \sigma^2 \frac{d}{dt} f(t)$$

then

$$\int_0^{\infty} t\, f(t)\, dt = \mu \int_0^{\infty} f(t)\, dt - \sigma^2 \int_0^{\infty} \frac{d\, f(t)}{dt}\, dt$$

$$\text{MTTF} = \mu - \sigma^2[\,f(\infty) - f(0)\,]$$

$$= \mu + \sigma^2 f(0)$$

$$= \mu + \frac{\sigma \exp(-\mu^2/2\sigma^2)}{(2\pi)^{1/2}(1-\psi)} \tag{8.26}$$

This is quite different from the mean of the unmodified normal distribution unless μ is positive and very large; negative values of μ are not precluded in the modified normal distribution. Note that ψ, defined in equation (8.24), is a function of μ/σ.

8.4.1 Equivalence Between the Modified Normal Distribution and $ae^{\delta at}$

Returning to $f(t)$, equation (8.22), and rewriting

$$f(t) = \frac{\exp(-\mu^2/2\sigma^2)\,|\exp[(t/2\sigma^2)(2\mu - t)]}{(2\pi)^{1/2}\sigma(1 - \psi)}$$

$$\cong \frac{\exp(-\mu^2/2\sigma^2)\exp(\mu t/\sigma^2)}{(2\pi\sigma)^{1/2}(1 - \psi)} \qquad t \ll 2\mu \qquad (8.27)$$

This is of the form $ae^{\delta at}$, where

$$\delta a = \frac{\mu}{\sigma^2} \qquad a = \frac{\exp(-\mu^2/2\sigma^2)}{(2\pi)^{1/2}\,\sigma(1 - \psi)}$$

$$\delta = (\mu/\sigma)\sqrt{2\pi}(1 - \psi)\exp(\mu^2/2\sigma^2) \qquad (8.28)$$

The condition on t in equation (8.27) precludes the zero value for μ. This constraint is easily avoided, however, by making σ large without limit. Table 8.1 relates μ/σ and the equivalent δ. Some comments are now appropriate:

1 Distributions corresponding to values of μ less than three do not conform to the typical mental picture of the normal distribution. A zero value for μ yields a distribution that looks like the right half only of the conventional normal distribution; negative values correspond to only a portion of the right half.

2 The modified normal distribution can come close to approximating ae^{-at}; the minimum value of the equivalent δ is -0.98.

3 The survival functions generated by the modified normal distribution will closely resemble those of $ae^{\delta at}$ over a practical range, provided that the number of components is sufficiently large such that the condition t much less than 2μ is satisfied.

Table 8.1   Relation between μ/σ and δ

μ/σ	δ
-7	-0.76
-6	-0.98
-1	-0.66
0	0
1	3.5
2	36
3	680
4	3.0×10^4
5	3.4×10^6
6	9.9×10^8
10	1.3×10^{23}
15	2.7×10^{50}

8.4.2   Parametric Representation of the Modified Normal Distribution

By definition,

$$\int_0^T f(t)\, dt = \frac{1}{1-\psi}\left[\int_{(\mu-T)/\sigma}^\infty E(y)\, dy - \psi\right] = \frac{\gamma}{M}$$

$$\int_{(\mu-T)/\sigma}^\infty E(y)\, dy = \int_\beta^\infty E(y)\, dy = \frac{\gamma}{M} + \left(1 - \frac{\gamma}{M}\right)\psi$$

(8.29)

defining

$$\beta = (\mu - T)/\sigma \qquad (8.30)$$

The integral equation (8.29) can be solved for β as a function of μ, σ, and γ/M using tables of the integral of the normal distribution or a computer.

To compute $\int_0^t f(t)\, dt$, however, it is necessary to derive $(\mu - t)/\sigma$ from β. Equation (8.30) provides

$$T = \mu - \beta\sigma$$

$$t = (\mu - \beta\sigma)(t/T)$$

$$(\mu - t)/\sigma = \mu/\sigma - (\mu/\sigma - \beta)(t/T) \qquad (8.31)$$

Note that μ and σ appear only as μ/σ; this is also true of

$$\psi = \int_{\mu/\sigma}^{\infty} E(y)\, dy$$

Defining ϕ as μ/σ, the cumulative distribution in parametric form becomes

$$\int_0^t f(t)\, dt = \frac{1}{(1-\psi)}\left[\int_{\phi-(\phi-\beta)(t/T)}^{\infty} E(y)\, dy - \psi\right] \qquad (8.32)$$

Although the Appendix provides a computer program to calculate β for any T_{xy}, Table 8.2 provides a listing of values of β_{05} as a function of ϕ. M is equal to 10^4.

In plotting the survivor function of $ae^{\delta at}$ to a common base on semilog paper, the plot was really parametric in $1/Ma$. Now a is $f(0)$ for $ae^{\delta at}$; thus a similar treatment for the modified normal distribution is to plot the survivor functions parametric in $1/[Mf(0)]$. To compute β for this case,

$$T = \frac{1}{M f(0)} = \frac{(1-\psi)(2\pi)^{1/2}\sigma e}{M}$$

Table 8.2 β_{05} *as a function of* ϕ, $M = 10^4$

ϕ	β_{05}
0	$-0.000\ 375\ 989\ 2$
1	$0.998\ 957\ 426\ 3$
2	$1.994\ 599\ 171\ 0$
3	$2.938\ 411\ 523\ 0$
4	$3.404\ 336\ 238\ 0$
5	$3.431\ 399\ 559\ 0$
6	$3.431\ 658\ 062\ 0$
7	$3.431\ 658\ 956\ 0$
8	$3.431\ 658\ 957\ 0$
9	$3.431\ 658\ 957\ 0$
10	$3.431\ 658\ 957\ 0$
.	.
.	.
.	.

[see equation (8.22)]. Then from equation (8.30)

$$T = (\phi - \beta)\sigma$$

Therefore

$$\beta_{1/M f(0)} = \phi - \frac{(2\pi)^{1/2}(1 - \psi)\exp(\phi^2/2)}{M} \tag{8.33}$$

Table 8.3 lists $\beta_{1/Mf(0)}$ as a function of ϕ with M equal to 10^4. Considering all of the previous remarks about extreme precision, the reader may at this point wonder at the number of significant digits in the last two tables. It happens that specific calculations with respect to the modified normal distribution are very sensitive to the precision in β, hence the increase. However, none of this is meant to imply that the calculated survivor functions have more significance than previously indicated.

8.4.3 Survivor Functions and the Modified Normal Distribution

Figure 8.9 depicts the survivor functions parametric in T_{05} for several values of ϕ (μ/σ) and $M = 10^4$. Figure 8.10 graphs the same survivor functions parametric in $1/10^4 f(0)$, on semilog paper. The plotting conventions are identical to those used for the survivor functions of $ae^{\delta at}$ shown in Figures 8.4 and 8.6. The similarity of these two sets of figures is not fortuitous, it is real. A computation of the survivor function for $ae^{3 \times 10^4 at}$, parametric in T_{05},

Table 8.3 $\beta_{1/Mf(0)}$ *as a function of* ϕ, $M = 10^4$

ϕ	$\beta_{1/Mf(0)}$
0	$-1.253\ 333\ 3 \times 10^{-4}$
1	$0.999\ 652\ 3$
2	$1.998\ 189\ 9$
3	$2.977\ 466\ 2$
4	$3.252\ 796\ 9$
5	$-6.226\ 319\ 2 \times 10$
6	$-1.645\ 276\ 5 \times 10^4$
7	$-1.094\ 740\ 3 \times 10^7$
8	$-1.979\ 338\ 1 \times 10^{10}$
9	$-9.727\ 998\ 6 \times 10^{13}$
10	$-1.299\ 632\ 9 \times 10^{18}$
15	$-1.808\ 113\ 9 \times 10^{45}$

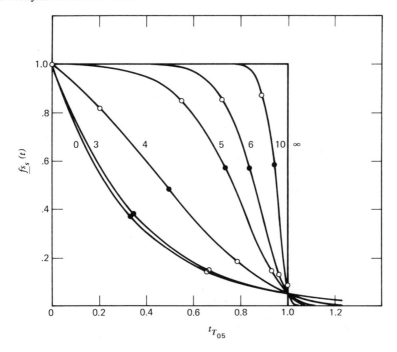

Figure 8.9 Survivor functions of the modified normal distribution parametric in T_{05}, with $M = 10^4$.

should, according to Table 8.1, closely approximate that for $\mu/\sigma = 4$. As a matter of fact, the two survivor functions agree, point by point, to better than 2%. Accordingly, the entire discussion of the survivor functions for $ae^{\delta at}$ applies to those of the modified normal distribution, except for values of δ less than minus one. A word of caution is necessary, however; this close correspondence is dependent on the condition that t be quite small compared to 2μ. The time range over which this obtains is a function of the number of components in the system.

8.4.4 A Monte Carlo Experiment with the Normal Distribution

A total of 200 systems containing 100 components each were manufactured by drawing sets of 100 random normal numbers from the distribution with mean 5×10^4 and standard deviation $5 \times 10^4/3$. The failure time of each system is the least random normal number of the set of 100. The program by which this was computed is given in the Appendix. The data was separated into two groups of 100 systems and the survivor functions were calculated for

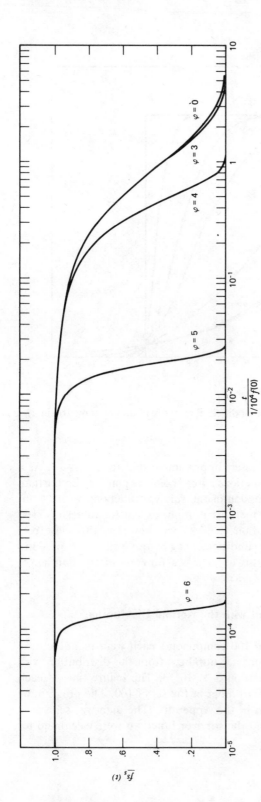

Figure 8.10 Survivor functions of the modified normal distribution, parametric in $1/10^4 f(0)$, with $M = 10^4$.

each group. Figures 8.11 and 8.12 show the results plotted against a theoretical curve based on the continuous modified normal distribution with ϕ equal to three.

The theoretical curve calculation using the parametric representation (this is the easiest computing approach) to obtain the survivor function as a function of t only requires that T be set equal to one. This yields t/T equal to $t/1$, which is t. Given relationship (8.33),

$$T = (\phi - \beta)\sigma$$

Setting T equal to one,

$$1 = (\phi - \beta)\sigma$$

$$\beta = \phi - 1/\sigma$$

In the specific case of Figures 8.11 and 8.12 β is 2.999 94. Seeing this figure, one is tempted to round it to three. This may not be done; the small difference is of fundamental importance. Setting β equal to three requires σ to

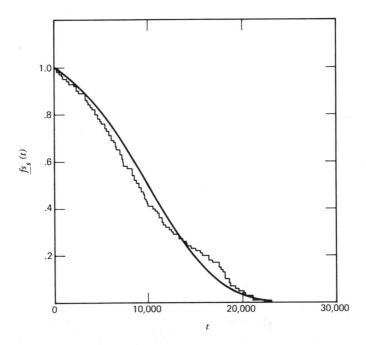

Figure 8.11   One hundred systems of 100 components each, from a discrete, normal distribution with mean 50,000 and standard deviation, 50,000/3; actual survivor function compared to theoretical survivor function.

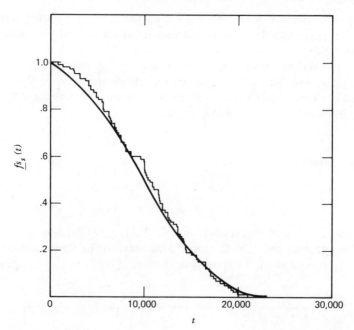

Figure 8.12   Identical to Figure 8.11 except that it is based on a separate sequence of random normal numbers.

be infinite; this violates the assumptions of the calculation. In fact, it is the difference between 3 and 2.999 94, 0.000 06, that is important. This last number has only one significant digit.

Returning to Figures 8.11 and 8.12, it is seen that the correspondence is reasonable, provided that the expectation is based on the realities of the "tyranny of large numbers." Note that the survivor functions are essentially complete in the interval (0, 20,000), while the peak of the component distribution occurs at 50,000.

8.5   CONCLUSIONS

This chapter has by no means exhausted the stock of available distributions. The author does believe, however, that the distributions chosen develop the necessary insights into the effect of distributions on the survival of new systems. One of the most crucial characteristics affecting the survivor function was $f(0)$, the magnitude of the component distribution at time zero. It was also seen that with a high component count the entire time of interest of the survivor function is small compared to such characteristics of the component distribution as its MTTF; for a large component count the system MTTFF is small compared to the component MTTF.

With respect to such apparently diverse distributions as $ae^{\delta at}$ and the normal distribution, it was seen that with a large component count the two distributions generated essentially identical survivor functions, given that $f(0)$ was the same, and the derived equivalence between δ and μ/σ was taken into consideration. Finally, Monte Carlo simulations continued to show the tyranny of large numbers and the futility of precise survival calculations.

Chapter Nine

Redundancy and Survivor Functions of Systems

9.1 INTRODUCTORY REMARKS AND SOME DEFINITIONS

The submarine telephone cable is a commercial system requiring extreme reliability for both service and economic reasons. The following extract from a paper by Miller (1974) of Bell Laboratories is an extremely good introduction to the subject of redundancy.

> The development of these systems of gradually increasing message capacity has been evolutionary in nature, paced primarily by the state of the art of electronic component technology and growth in traffic demand. The initial systems, which used vacuum tubes as the amplifying elements, achieved the necessary system reliability by conservative design philosophy and in one design, the use of redundancy in the repeater amplifier design. The more modern higher capacity systems which use semiconductor devices also use conservative design philosophy but have abandoned the provision of redundancy in the repeater amplifiers. The decision to eliminate redundancy in the amplifier circuits of the semiconductor versions of submarine-cable repeater was made in the early 1960s, near the inception of development of the first semiconductor repeater. This decision was made to exploit the better reliability which was anticipated for new semiconductor components. Studies during that period indicated that redundancy in broader band semiconductor repeaters would be difficult to achieve. Moreover, if the projected component failure rates were achieved, use of redundancy in repeater design, which would require more components per repeater, could result in a higher system failure than would occur if repeaters were designed without redundancy!

What is "redundancy"? It is the use of additional components or systems beyond the number minimally required to perform a required function (series system) solely to improve reliability; it is not intended to change any of the other system performance characteristics. The redundancy under discussion is *parallel redundancy,* the addition of series redundancy degrades reliability.

The minimum parallel redundancy requires two components or systems instead of one and some additional switching and/or interconnection apparatus. Thus the minimum application of redundancy more than doubles the amount of equipment needed to perform the tasks required of the original system. This in turn means more than double the number of service failures per unit time, and more than double the volume, weight, and power required for the system. The doubling of maintenance (repair of failures) and its economic consequences are of concern only if the equipment is intended to be used over many repair cycles; in one-use equipment, such as spacecraft, this is of no consequence, but even in this case the other penalties are severe. In many cases, however, the redundancy goes beyond the simple doubling; triply redundant, two-out-of-three voting systems are used for example. The penalties are now more than triple, since the voting equipment is not trivial in component count or complexity. It must never be forgotten that the extra components and added heat may more than destroy the presumed value of the redundancy.

Parallel redundancy is of two kinds: "operating" and "standby" (see Fig. 9.1). In the operating mode both elements are permanently connected and operating. Ideally, the operating parallel system is transparent to the failure of one of the two elements.

"Transparency" signifies performance that is invariant under the failure of one of the two elements of the couple. Generally, it is difficult to impossible to obtain true transparency, but it is possible to obtain semitransparency, that is, satisfactory system performance with one failure even though it is different than the performance without failure. A major problem in all operating redundancy is the difficulty of recognizing failure; failure is not always catastrophic, it may merely be incorrect operation. This is considered to be a major problem in digital systems; how to recognize which of two elements is operating correctly? The two-out-of-three voting system has been used as an answer to this problem; it is based on the assumption that agreement between two systems indicates that these, at least, are operating correctly. On the assumption of perfect reliability of the voting system, agreement of at least two outputs is considered proper operation.

Standby redundancy is very straightforward: only one element of the couple is used for system operation at any time; the other is disconnected and may or may not be operating in some fashion. When failure of the system in use is recognized it is switched out of the system and the standby element switched in. Regardless of the type of parallel redundancy, whether

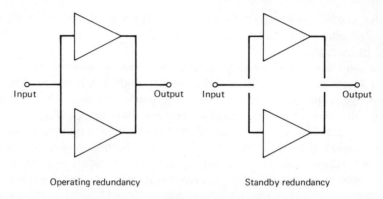

Operating redundancy   Standby redundancy

Figure 9.1 Forms of parallel redundancy.

operating or standby, "common mode" failure must be avoided. Common mode failure may be due to a design characteristic that permits an environmental condition that can fail both elements simultaneously, or one for which failure of one element causes failure of the other. It is obvious, of course, that the possibility of common mode failure severely degrades whatever advantages parallel redundancy is expected to provide.

9.2 IDEAL REDUNDANT SURVIVOR FUNCTIONS AND THEIR UNDERLYING DISTRIBUTIONS

For operating parallel redundancy of two identical single elements the survivor function is

$$\underline{fs}_p(t) = 1 - F(t)^2 \tag{9.1}$$

where $F(t)$ is the cumulative probability of failure of either element, $\int_0^t f(x)\,dx$. It is simply the complement of the probability that both elements will fail in the interval $(0, t)$. This may be put into another form by using

$$\underline{fs}(t) = 1 - F(t)$$

and substituting to get

$$\underline{fs}_p(t) = 1 - [1 - \underline{fs}(t)]^2 = \underline{fs}(t)[2 - \underline{fs}(t)] \tag{9.2}$$

Expression (9.2) shows that the redundant couple survivor function is no different than for a single element at time zero; however, as time progresses the redundant couple survivor function decreases at a slower rate than that for a single element and finally becomes $2\,\underline{fs}(t)$ to a close approximation. The distribution underlying the continuous operating redundancy survivor function is

$$\frac{-d}{dt}\,\underline{fs}_p(t) = 2f(t)\,F(t) \tag{9.3}$$

Expression (9.3) is zero at time zero, since $F(0)$ is zero regardless of the nature of the distribution $f(t)$. Accordingly, the slope of the redundant survivor function is zero at time zero rather than being $-f(0)$. If $f(t)$ happens to be a distribution that is zero at time zero, no redundancy is necessary to achieve a zero slope for the survivor function at time zero; if such distributions are paralleled, both the first and second derivatives of the survivor function are zero at time zero.

The continuous survivor function for the standby redundancy system is

$$\underline{fs}_p(t) = 1 - \int_0^t F(t - x)\,f(x)\,dx = 1 - \int_0^t F(x)f(t - x)\,dx \tag{9.4}$$

A general statement about the behavior of expression (9.4) cannot be made as it was for the survivor function for operating redundancy. The underlying distribution, however, is

$$\frac{-d}{dt}\,\underline{fs}_p(t) = \int_0^t f(t - x)f(x)\,dx \tag{9.5}$$

Distribution (9.5) is zero at time zero; thus the survivor function for standby redundancy also has zero slope at time zero. Despite the absence of an obvious mathematical statement as to the relative behavior of the two forms of parallel redundancy, a quantitative statement is possible. If two components or systems are drawn from identical distributions, these will generally have different failure times, even though they may have identical survivor functions (the survivor function and the time of survival of an individual component or system are quite different). If the two components or systems are associated in operating redundancy, the first failure time of the combination is that of the longest lived element; if they are associated in standby redundancy, the failure time of the combination is the ***sum of the two failure times***. The sum will always exceed the individual longest failure time unless one of the two elements fails at time zero. Thus the survival of any pair of elements associated in standby is equal to or better than the ***same two*** associated in operating redundancy.

The survivor function for a two-out-of-three voting system is

$$\underline{fs}_{23}(t) = \underline{fs}^2(t)\,[3 - 2\,\underline{fs}\,(t)] \tag{9.6}$$

The underlying distribution

$$\frac{-d}{dt}\, \underline{fs}_{23}(t) \;=\; 6\, \underline{fs}\,(t)\,f(t)\,[1-\,\underline{fs}\,(t)] \tag{9.7}$$

is zero at time zero; thus $\underline{fs}_{23}(t)$ has zero slope at time zero.

Figure 9.2 shows the comparative behavior of a single element, an operating redundant pair, and a two-out-of-three voting system. The survivor functions are plotted against the element survivor function. Figure 9.3 shows the comparative behavior of a single element, an operating redundant pair, a standby redundant pair, and a two-out-of-three voting system when the element time-to-failure distribution is $\lambda e^{-\lambda t}$.

9.2.1 Comments on Ideal Redundant Survivor Functions

The expressions provided in Section 9.1 assumed identity in the elements comprising the redundant system. Expressions may be written for dissimilar elements; for example, the operating parallel system survivor function becomes

$$\underline{fs}_p(t) \;=\; \underline{fs}_1(t) + \underline{fs}_2(t) - \underline{fs}_1(t)\,\underline{fs}_2(t) \tag{9.8}$$

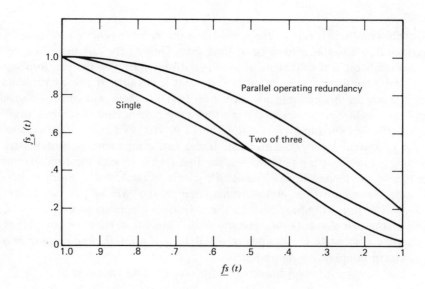

Figure 9.2 Comparative survivor functions.

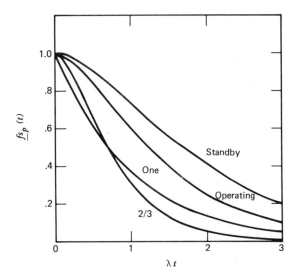

Figure 9.3 Comparative survivor functions of exponentially distributed systems: various redundancies.

In the real world elements are rarely identical. Even with one-use equipment (spacecraft, large missiles, and so forth) the components that are parallelled are substantial systems that have undergone considerable testing and some repair before use. In reusable equipment the parallel elements are subject to many cycles of failure and repair.

By way of illustration, consider an operating parallel redundant pair to have survivor functions fs (t) and fs^2 (t) for the two elements. Figure 9.4 displays the survivor function for this pair, the survivor function for another pair whose element survivor functions are fs (t), and the survivor function of a single element, fs (t). These are plotted against fs (t), as was done in Figure 9.2. The figure shows, not too surprisingly, that the redundant survivor function for the above case is intermediate between the redundant identical pair and the nonredundant case.

It is all very well to talk knowingly about survivor functions, but what does this all mean? In essentially every real application there is no interest in what happens in a large number of cases; the interest is in what will happen in a given single instance. Will adding redundancy, even ideally (neglecting all of the added apparatus required and its effect), always improve reliability to the first failure if the redundancy provides an element of parallelism? It is quite customary to conclude that this is the case after seeing the comparative

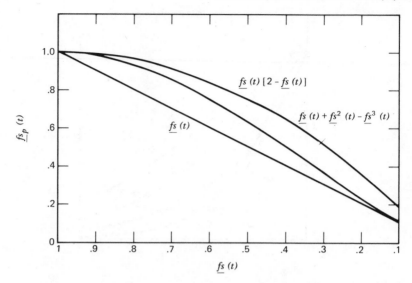

Figure 9.4 The survivor functions for certain redundancies.

survivor functions. *But it is easily demonstrated that this is not the case.*

Consider a single device, be it a component or a system; it has an inherent failure-free operating life that is unknown. Now parallel it with another "identical" device; this device has some other unknown failure-free operating life. Let us call these A and B. There are three possibilities: the life of B is greater than, equal to, or less than the life of A. In the latter two cases the addition of B in parallel with A does not improve the reliability that would have been achieved with A alone. This proves the assertion above. Now, what is the proportion of times that the addition of an element in parallel does improve reliability?

A Monte Carlo experiment was set up to investigate this question. Three sets of 100 random numbers each were generated: one set was labeled A, one B, and the other C. These were placed side by side and it was determined how often A was greater than B, B greater than C, and C greater than A. The results were 44, 49, and 51, with an average of 48. The application of logic to the problem indicates that improvement should occur in one-half the cases if an infinite number of random pairs are compared. This must be the conclusion, since if it were any other proportion, one could not reverse the roles of A and B and get the same result: A and B must be reversible, because both have the same characteristics.

A similar experiment indicates that in triple parallel redundancy the return for the price of three times the equipment in the ideal case (more in real life), that is, adding two additional elements, improves performance over a single element two-thirds of the time. In the case of a two-out-of-three situation improvement over the nonredundant case occurs only one-third of the time. Finally, *two elements in series will be worse than a single element only one-half the time, not all of the time.*

If the above seems to be a very harsh indictment of the payoff for redundancy, it must be noted that parallel operating redundancy does tend to reduce the number of systems prone to short lifetimes, although there is no guarantee that very short lifetimes cannot occur. This reduction is the true meaning conveyed by the survivor functions. Figure 9.2, for example, shows that in an interval that reduces the survivor function of a single element to .9, that is, 10% of the systems will fail in that interval, only 1% of the operating parallel redundancy systems will fail in that same interval. Thus, while early failures are not eliminated, the probability of fielding a system with an early failure is reduced.

Before leaving the subject of ideal redundant systems another important topic must be discussed. The theory given and Figures 9.2 through 9.4 assume *identical new systems.* This is seldom the case, even in one-use systems such as spacecraft and guided missiles, because of the endless testing and repair that goes on before use; it is certainly not the case for equipments that undergo repeated cycles of failure and repair over long periods of time. If it is assumed that the failure law is that of chance, the survivor functions of systems in large aggregates continue to show the attributes of new systems; if the failure law is not chance, the survivor functions will not resemble those shown in this and other texts. Regardless of the assumption, however, the individual system obeys no law other than its own, that it has an inherent operational life that is reduced as testing goes on. Returning to large aggregates, what are the implications of the survivor function crossover exhibited by the two-out-of-three system versus the single system?

The first interpretation not only assumes the conditions underlying the survivor functions of Figure 9.2 but assumes first use of new systems. If the mission time of the system is short compared to the crossover time, the chance of fielding a system that will fail in the mission time is smaller for the two-out-of-three system than for the single nonredundant system; a mission time equal to the crossover time implies equal chances of fielding a system that will survive to the crossover time; a mission time longer than the crossover time predicts the single nonredundant system to be superior in the aggregate! Again, none of this guarantees anything with respect to the behavior of an individual system.

Two-out-of-three systems are universal in aircraft autolanding systems: these are not one-use systems but are expected to perform many times and are subject to maintenance, test, failure, and repair. The interpretation given above is not possible in this case; in fact, no general interpretation is possible. Despite this problem, and the possibility that the more than tripling of equipment may have no real payoff, an autoland system must be subject to monitoring by the pilot: pilots demand the option of aborting a landing or performing it manually if system failure is evident. The penalties of two-out-of-three majority voting are deliberately assumed in order to give the pilot the capacity to determine whether the system is operating properly. This leads to a discussion on the recognition of failure, a system event that is so easily assumed in theory.

9.3   RECOGNIZING FAILURE

9.3.1   Majority Voting Systems: The Inflation of Equipment

One approach to determining whether a digital computation is correct is to compare it with an independent computation made by another digital system; the assumption made is that agreement indicates correct computation. Naturally, this assumes that there is no common mode failure, that is, two failed computers cannot give identical outputs. If this approach to determining nonfailure is adopted, it requires two computers to perform the basic system functions. Since both must operate correctly (survive) for system survival, if both units are identical, the system is a series redundant system; its survivor function is the square of the individual survivor function. This is a grossly inferior survivor function to that of a single unit. To correct this deficiency another computer is added and the system operated on the premise that correct operation is present when any two of the three computers agree. The two-out-of-three survivor function shown in Figures 9.2 and 9.3 corresponds to this voting system. The total system not only includes the three computers, but must also include interconnections and the voting system. If confidence in the latter calls for redundancy as well, these too must be put into majority voting form; but this still leaves a nonredundant tag. Ultimately, a single element system part must be trusted or the inflationary spiral has no end. It is questionable, therefore, whether this elaboration really pays off in enhanced reliability.

9.3.2   Another Failure Detection Method in Standby Systems

It is possible, using sampling schemes at sufficiently high rates, to time share some system operations with system testing. Injecting a test signal and comparing the response to the test signal with the expected response will determine the system state. The Bell System uses this scheme in their Electronic Switching System (ESS): the test signals are injected and the output compared a great many times per second without interfering with the telephone signals. A similar scheme may be used with digital computers: in this case the computer throughput is reduced depending on the fraction of time required for the testing operation. Again, this scheme also requires additional apparatus.

The Bell System ESS equipment uses standby operation: the detection of a failure not only switches in the standby unit, but notifies a maintenance operator that service is needed and indicates the location of the fault down to rather simple modules. The defective unit may then be repaired while the standby unit is in operation. As long as the standby unit operates correctly until the fault is repaired, overall system integrity is maintained. The system has proved quite successful.

A large scale digital computer using the same general approach is on the market. It is finding popular acceptance in reservation systems and other applications requiring a very high percentage of on time. The organization of this computer is such that each unit queries the next unit in the signal path to determine whether the signal will be properly processed. A fault is automatically removed from operation, the signal rerouted, and a maintenance signal generated. Units may be replaced without shutting down the computer.

9.4 CONCLUSIONS

Redundancy is not a panacea. On the most general level there is serious question as to whether the penalties due to extra equipment do not, in fact, destroy the advantages expected. Extreme care in design and construction can produce very high levels of reliability without redundancy; redundancy is not a substitute for poor design or workmanship. In fact, it must be a solution of last resort, to be used where no other way of satisfying a requirement exists.

One area where it must be seriously considered is one-use application (no possibility of repair or an unacceptable economic penalty in repair): spacecraft, earth orbit (without the space shuttle), solar system probes, undersea telephone cables, and some highly complex weapon systems, for example. Manned spacecrafts add the element of personnel safety to the economic pressures for reliability. Safety is an overwhelming factor in the civil aircraft system, both aircraft and air traffic control. Finally, there are long term services where interruption must be minimal and equipment used for long periods of time and go through repeated cycles of failure and repair.

Standby redundancy seems to be the method of choice in this last application; there is no way in which service interruption can be minimized except by redundancy; standby redundancy is the most economic approach. Standby redundancy is also possible in one-use equipment with which communication is possible. Some communication satellites have provided standby redundancy for selected elements of the satellite; these can be switched by command as long as the command link operates. This would also be possible in undersea telephone cables.

Civil air transports represent an interesting mixture: communication gear, navigation, flight instrumentation, primary flight controllers, engines, and other equipment employ parallel operating redundancy, at the least. Present autoland equipment depends on majority voting. For obvious reasons the aircraft aerodynamic surfaces are not redundant although emergency flight is possible in some aircraft even when some part of these structures are damaged or destroyed. The air traffic control system uses standby redundancy at selected installations.

As a closing illustration of performance, Figure 9.5 presents the results of a Monte Carlo simulation. Three 100-random-number groups from the uni-

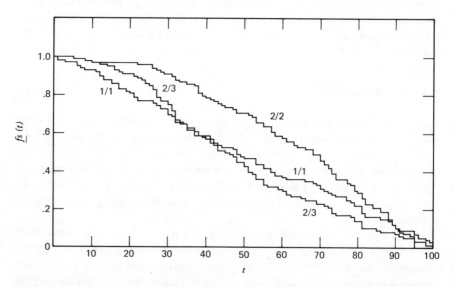

Figure 9.5 Monte Carlo simulation of 300 systems of 100 components each, from a discrete, uniform distribution. Actual survival function for 100 systems in a nonredundant configuration, actual survival function for 200 systems combined into 100 operating redundancy systems, and actual survival function for 300 systems combined into 100 two-of-three voting configurations.

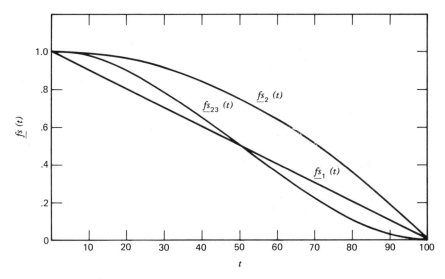

Figure 9.6 Continuous theoretical survivor functions corresponding to those of Figure 9.5.

form distribution (0, 99) were generated. The survivor functions for a nonredundant parallel operating redundancy and the two-out-of-three systems are displayed. The analogous continuous survivor functions are

$$\underline{fs}_1(t) = 1 - t/100$$

$$\underline{fs}_2(t) = 1 - t^2/10^4$$

$$\underline{fs}_{23}(t) = (1 - t/100)^2 (1 + 2t/100)$$

These are shown in Figure 9.6. The survivor functions of Figure 9.5 generally behave like those in Figure 9.6. Once again, the futility of precise calculations of survivor functions is shown, even in the case of a sample of 100.

REFERENCES

Miller, L.E. *Reliability of Semiconductor Devices for Submarine-Cable Systems, Proceedings of the IEEE*, Vol. 62, No. 2, 1974.

CHAPTER TEN

Introduction to Renewal Theory and Mean Time Between Failures

10.1 THE DIFFERENCE BETWEEN MTTFF AND MTBF

The MTBF (mean time between failures) is the cornerstone of current practice in reliability theory; it is often confused with the MTTF (mean time to failure). In its treatment of new systems this text has carefully defined the MTTF and has offered a new term, the MTTFF, the mean time to first failure. Emphasis has been placed on the fact that the MTTFF cannot be determined for a single system by the study of a single system; it is an average over a large number of identical systems.

The MTBF is associated with repeated cycles of failure and repair in a single system; it can be defined and determined for a single system by studying a single system. As developed under renewal theory, the MTBF cannot be measured in a short interval of a system's life; when determined in the manner defined in renewal theory, it should be the same for identical systems. This does not mean that it is an average over a large number of identical systems, but that it is an individual attribute that is the same in identical systems.

Current practice, however, is to make short term measurements of the MTBF. Figure 1.1 is typical of the result of this practice, even when a relatively large number of "identical" systems are available. It is not unusual to take an average of this spread of results and advertise the outcome as the "true MTBF." The following theory does not support the prediction of short term MTBFs.

10.2 THE ORDINARY RENEWAL PROCESS

The literature attacks the problem of the MTBF with the examination of a fundamental process, "the ordinary renewal process." This, the simplest renewal process possible, the behavior of a system composed of only one component, is applied by superposition to illuminate the behavior of complex multiple component systems. The ordinary renewal process assumes the existence of a single kind of component that can be randomly drawn from an infinite population of a known time-to-failure distribution. The process starts with putting one such component into operation. When it fails it is replaced with a new component drawn from the parent population. When that component fails it is replaced by another new component. This process continues without limit. Any objection to the notion of instant replacement may be disposed of by considering the sequence of operating intervals only. Successive operating intervals (failure times) are recorded.

Now consider placing a large number of these same components in operation at the same instant and recording the failure times. It is known that the average failure time approaches a limit, the MTTF, as the number of components under test increases without limit. Considering the ordinary renewal process again, it is clear that as it proceeds without limit the ensemble of operating intervals (failure times) have to be identical to those experienced in the experiment above. Hence the average time between failures in the renewal process will reach a limit as the sequence continues without limit. This limit, the MTBF, must numerically equal the MTTF for the component. Thus the MTBF of an ordinary renewal process based on a time-to-failure distribution $f(t)$, now a time-between-failures distribution, is

$$\int_0^\infty t\, f(t)\, dt$$

for the continuous distribution. An analogous relationship occurs for the discrete distribution

$$\sum_{n=1}^{L} t_n f(t_n)$$

Inasmuch as the MTBF of the ordinary renewal process occurs time and again in subsequent discussion, it is convenient to adopt a special symbol for it, ρ. Again, although numerically equal to the MTTF of a component with distribution $f(t)$, ρ denotes the MTBF of the ordinary renewal process, a process involving the failure and replacement of a single component.

10.3 DEFINITION OF THE MODIFIED RENEWAL PROCESS

Suppose the renewal process has started with a used component and then utilized new components, or with a finite renewal process based on one distribution and then shifted to another distribution. These are considered to be modified renewal processes. These may be treated in either of two ways: the exceptions at the start may be deleted, in which case the ordinary renewal process remains, or the process may be allowed to go on indefinitely without excluding the exceptions. In the latter case the final ordinary renewal process will swamp the effects of the exceptions and still give the same MTBF in the limit.

10.4 PROPERTIES OF THE ORDINARY RENEWAL PROCESS

Cox (1962) gives two definitions of "recurrence time" associated with the ordinary renewal process: "backward" and "forward" recurrence time. The backward recurrence time is the age of a component at a time t during the renewal process; it is the interval between the time of the last renewal (failure) and t. The forward recurrence time is the interval remaining between t and the next renewal; it is the life remaining in the component at time t.

The number of renewals in the interval $(0, t)$, not counting the starting component as a renewal, is denoted as $N(t)$. Thus the number of renewals in an interval (t_1, t_2) is

$$N(t_2) - N(t_1)$$

The renewal function $H(t)$ is the mean value of $N(t)$ in the interval $(0, t)$. The meaning of "the mean value of $N(t)$" is the average of the values for $N(t)$ obtained when the ordinary renewal process is truncated at time t and repeated over and over without limit. It follows, therefore, that the mean value of the number of renewals in the interval (t_1, t_2) is

$$H(t_2) - H(t_1)$$

The renewal density $h(t)$ may now be defined

$$h(t) = \frac{d}{dt} H(t) \tag{10.1}$$

In terms of meaning, $h(t)\, dt$ is the mean number of renewals to be expected in an interval dt about t.

10.5 $H(t)$ AS A FUNCTION OF $f(t)$

The probability that $N(t)$ is greater than or equal to n is by definition $F_n(t)$. It is the case that

$$F_1(t) = F(t) = \int_0^t f(x)\, dx \qquad (10.2)$$

that is, the probability that at least one failure has occurred in the interval $(0, t)$ is the cumulative probability of $f(t)$ in that interval. Now $F_2(t)$ is the probability that at least two failures have occurred in the interval $(0, t)$. This must be the probability that at least one failure has occurred followed by at least another failure. Mathematically,

$$F_2(t) = \int_0^t F_1(x) f(t - x)\, dx = \int_0^t F_1(t - x) f(x)\, dx$$

This may be repeated to give

$$F_n(t) = \int_0^t F_{n-1}(t - x) f(x)\, dx \qquad (10.3)$$

Note that $F_2(t)$ is the cumulative probability that the standby unit in a standby redundancy system has been switched in and failed, hence the survivor function shown in equation (9.4). This correspondence is not accidental, since $F_2(t)$ is the probability that the second unit in the ordinary renewal process has failed. By the same interpretation, the survivor function for an r-wise standby system would be

$$fs_r(t) = 1 - F_r(t)$$

It is now possible to define the probability of exactly n failures in the interval $(0, t)$. Since $F_n(t)$ is the probability that $N(t)$ is equal to or greater than n, the probability that $N(t)$ is less than n must be

$$1 - F_n(t)$$

The probability that exactly n failures have occurred, that is, $N(t)$ is equal to n, must be the probability that $N(t)$ is less than $n + 1$ minus the probability that $N(t)$ is less than n. Thus the probability of exactly n failures is

$$P_n(t) = 1 - F_{n+1}(t) - [1 - F_n(t)]$$
$$= F_n(t) - F_{n+1}(t) \qquad (10.4)$$

Then

$$P_0(t) = F_0(t) - F_1(t)$$

but

$$F_0(t) = 1$$

because $F_0(t)$ is the probability that $N(t)$ is greater than or equal to zero. Therefore

$$P_0(t) = 1 - F_1(t)$$

$$P_0(t) + P_1(t) = 1 - F_1(t) + F_1(t) - F_2(t)$$

$$= 1 - F_2(t)$$

Continuing,

$$F_n(t) = 1 - \sum_{j=0}^{n-1} P_j(t) \tag{10.5}$$

This could have been written directly, since $F_n(t)$ is the probability of n or more failures in the interval $(0, t)$ and $P_j(t)$ is the probability of exactly j failures. It is now possible to derive $H(t)$ in terms of $F_n(t)$. Since $H(t)$ is the average number of failures in the interval $(0, t)$,

$$H(t) = \sum_{n=1}^{\infty} nP_n(t) = \sum_{n=1}^{\infty} n[F_n(t) - F_{n+1}(t)]$$

$$= \sum_{n=1}^{\infty} nF_n(t) - \sum_{n=2}^{\infty} (n - 1)F_n(t)$$

$$= \sum_{n=1}^{\infty} F_n(t) \tag{10.6}$$

Applying equation (10.1),

$$h(t) = \sum_{n=1}^{\infty} f_n(t) \tag{10.7}$$

where

$$f_n(t) = \int_0^t f_{n-1}(t - x) f(x) \, dx$$

An integral equation definition of $H(t)$ is possible. Applying equation (10.3) to equation (10.6) yields

$$H(t) = \sum_{n=1}^{\infty} \int_0^t F_{n-1}(t - x) f(x) \, dx$$

$$= \int_0^t F_0(t - x) f(x) \, dx - \int_0^t \left[\sum_{n=1}^{\infty} F_n(t - x) \right] f(x) \, dx$$

$$H(t) = F(t) + \int_0^t H(t - x) f(x) \, dx \tag{10.8}$$

By differentiation,

$$h(t) = f(t) + \int_0^t h(t - x) f(x) \, dx \tag{10.9}$$

10.6 THE DISTRIBUTION OF RECURRENCE TIMES

Figure 10.1 is the basis of a thought experiment that will be used to develop the distribution of recurrence times. It symbolically shows an infinite number of ordinary renewal processes (those not shown go off the page), all based on the same time-to-failure distribution and having progressed through the interval $(0, t)$. These are arranged one above the other as shown; a given time epoch is a vertical line through the array; renewals are denoted by crosses.

The backward recurrence time, the age of an operating component at time t, is the interval between t and the last renewal preceding t. The distribution of the backward recurrence time at t is found by recording all of the backward recurrence times at t, constructing a histogram, and developing the distribution just as was done in the case of the empirical time-to-failure distribution. Similarly, the distribution may be determined for any time epoch prior to t.

The forward recurrence time distribution presents a philosophical problem. The forward recurrence time is the remaining life in an operating component. In a real sense this cannot be determined at time t, since future failures are undetermined except to a seer or the mind of a mathematician. It is possible to determine remaining life times at some epoch prior to t provided that the distribution $f(t)$ has a finite life. By backing off at least one lifetime from t it is possible to determine all forward recurrence times. This cannot be done if the life of the distribution is infinite, as is the case with most distributions used in statistics.

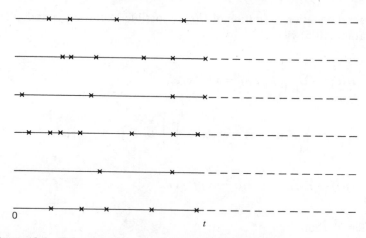

Figure 10.1   Schematic for visualizing recurrence times in a renewal process.

The backward recurrence time distribution, $U(t)$, can be developed as follows. In the case where no renewal has taken place in the interval $(0, t)$ the distribution must be the survivor function for the first component:

$$U(t) = \underline{fs}(t) = 1 - \int_0^t f(x)\,dx$$

If one or more renewals have taken place, the above distribution does not govern; instead, the distribution must be one of times prior to t, for example, $t - x$, where $t - x$ is the time of a renewal and x is the backward recurrence time. The probability that there is a renewal in the interval $(t - x - dx, t - x)$ and that the component renewed fails after x is the product of two probabilities. (Both conditions are necessary by virtue of the definition of backward recurrence time.) The first probability in the product is

$$h(t - x)\,dx$$

The second is

$$\underline{fs}(x)$$

Thus the backward recurrence time distribution $U(t, x)$ is

$$U(t, x) = h(t - x)\,\underline{fs}(x) \qquad (10.10)$$

The forward recurrence time distribution $V(t, u)$ is developed as follows. For $V(t, u)$ to lie in the interval $(u, u + du)$, that is, for the next renewal to lie in the interval $(t + u, t + u + du)$, there are two possibilities: one, the first component in the ordinary renewal process has a failure in the interval

$(t + u, t + u + du)$; two, a renewal occurs in the interval $(t - x, t - x + dx)$ and has a failure time in the interval $(x + u, x + u + du)$, that is, the component fails in the interval $(t + u, t + u + du)$. The first probability is $f(t + u)\, du$; the second is

$$\left[\int_0^t h(t - x) f(x + u)\, dx \right] du$$

Accordingly, the forward recurrence distribution is

$$V(t, u) = f(t + u) + \int_0^t h(t - x) f(x + u)\, dx \qquad (10.11)$$

10.7 THE ORDINARY RENEWAL PROCESS AND EQUILIBRIUM STATES

It will now be demonstrated that the various characteristics of the ordinary renewal process such as $H(t)$, $h(t)$, $U(t, u)$ and $V(t, u)$ approach limiting or equilibrium states as t increases without limit. Starting with the integral equation for $h(t)$,

$$h(t) = f(t) + \int_0^t h(t - x) f(x)\, dx$$

Taking the Laplace transform of both sides,

$$h^*(s) = f^*(s) + h^*(s) f^*(s)$$

where $*(s)$ denotes the Laplace transform. One obtains

$$h^*(s) = \frac{f^*(s)}{1 - f^*(s)} \qquad (10.12)$$

The behavior of $h(t)$ as t increases without limit may be determined using the following property of the transform:

$$\lim_{t \to \infty} h(t) = \lim_{s \to 0} s h^*(s)$$

$$= \lim_{s \to 0} \frac{s f^*(s)}{[1 - f^*(s)]}$$

but this is an indeterminate quantity, that is, $0/0$, since $f^*(0)$ is equal to one. (The Laplace transform of any density function is unity.) This problem may be resolved by applying L'Hospital's rule; this rule requires the independent differentiation of the numerator and denominator with respect to s and again attempting the limit. Thus

$$\lim_{t \to \infty} h(t) = \lim_{s \to 0} \left[-s - \frac{f^*(s)}{d/ds\, f^*(s)} \right]$$

$$= \frac{1}{\displaystyle\int_0^\infty t\, f(t)\, dt}$$

$$= \frac{1}{\rho} \tag{10.13}$$

The behavior of $H(t)$ may be similarly determined for time increasing without limit. Here

$$sH^*(s) = \frac{f^*(s)}{[1 - f^*(s)]}$$

In the limit, as s approaches zero, $sH^*(s)$ becomes large without limit; as a consequence $H(t)$ becomes large without limit as t increases without limit. It is interesting to note that all of this mathematics proves the obvious.

The equilibrium state of the backward recurrence time distribution is easily established, given the result for $h(t)$:

$$\lim_{t \to \infty} U(t, x) = \frac{fs(x)}{\rho} \tag{10.14}$$

In the case of $V(t, u)$

$$\lim_{t \to \infty} V(t, u) = \lim_{t \to \infty} f(t + u) + \lim_{t \to \infty} \int_0^t h(t - x) f(x + u)\, dx$$

$$= 0 + \frac{1}{\rho} \int_0^t f(x + u)\, dx$$

$$= \frac{1}{\rho} \int_u^\infty f(z)\, dz$$

$$= \frac{fs(u)}{\rho} \tag{10.15}$$

which is identical to equation (10.14). Thus in the equilibrium state it is unnecessary to distinguish between backward and forward recurrence time distributions.

It is possible to derive the equilibrium distribution of recurrence time without recourse to the mathematics above. Every renewal has a lifetime; the relative occurrence of the various possible lifetimes is described by the time-to-failure distribution $f(t)$. As t increases without limit every one of these possibilities occurs with the relative frequency described by $f(t)$. Now consider a group of renewals represented by $f(u)\,du$, where u is the lifetime of the component at the time of renewal. As time proceeds u is erased in a linear fashion, thus producing a uniform distribution of forward recurrence time. This is true of every packet of renewals. Thus the sum of all these uniform distributions includes all possible distributions of the equilibrium forward recurrence time. This sum, except for a constant, must be the equilibrium forward recurrence time distribution $V(\infty, u)$:

$$V(\infty, u) = A \int_u^\infty f(z)\,dz = A\,\underline{fs}(u)$$

But $V(\infty, u)$ must be a p.d.f., therefore

$$\int_0^\infty V(\infty, u)\,du = 1 = A \int_0^\infty \underline{fs}(u)\,du = A(\text{MTBF}) = A\rho$$

therefore A is equal to $1/\rho$ and

$$V(\infty, u) = \frac{\underline{fs}(u)}{\rho} \tag{10.16}$$

The equilibrium recurrence time distribution for an ordinary renewal process based on a discrete time-to-failure distribution may now be derived using the same argument:

$$V(\infty, u_j) = \frac{t}{\rho} \sum_{k=j}^L f(u_k) \qquad \underline{t} = u_{j+1} - u_j$$

$$= \frac{t}{\rho}\left[1 - \sum_{k=1}^{i-1} f(u_k)\right]$$

$$= \underline{fs}(u_{j-1}) \frac{t}{\rho} \tag{10.17}$$

Particular notice should be taken of equation (10.17), since by analogy the expected result would have contained $\underline{fs}(u_j)$. The result in equation (10.17), however, is consistent with the conventions established earlier for discrete distributions. $V(\infty, u_0)$ is undefined, $V(\infty, u_1)$ is defined and equal to $1/\rho$, $V(\infty, L)$ is $f(L)/\rho$. $\underline{fs}(u_j)$, on the other hand, would give results inconsistent with these conventions. Incidentally, derivation of the distribution by the analytical methods used in the case of continuous distributions would have been extremely cumbersome.

10.8   EXAMPLES

Inasmuch as the equilibrium distributions of recurrence times for an ordinary renewal process are the product of a constant and the survivor function of the underlying distribution, the material of Chapter Eight provides the means for computing the shape of a number of recurrence time distributions. Figure 10.2 depicts the survivor functions corresponding to a one-part system with underlying distributions ae^{at}, a, ae^{-at}, $a(at)$, and $a(at)^{49}$. (These are plotted in units of at.) Figure 10.3 plots the survivor functions for single components corresponding to modified normal distributions. The graphs correspond to a common peak value for the underlying distributions; μ/σ is

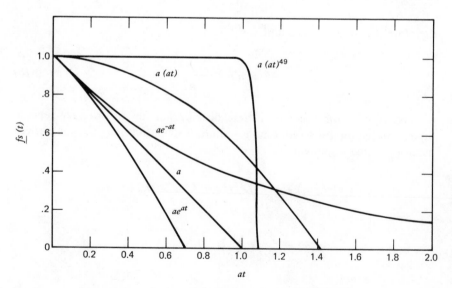

Figure 10.2   Survivor functions of one component systems.

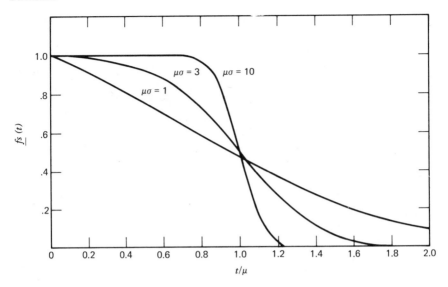

Figure 10.3 Survivor functions of one component systems in a modified normal distribution.

1, 3, and 10. An incidental item of interest is that the equilibrium recurrence time for the exponential distribution $\lambda e^{-\lambda t}$ is also $\lambda e^{-\lambda t}$.

10.9 DISCUSSION

The entire concept of the ordinary renewal process and its mathematical treatment is found in the literature, except for the alternate method of deriving the equilibrium recurrence time distribution. While the treatment ostensibly applies to the properties of the ordinary renewal process, $H(t)$, $h(t)$, and so on are not properties of the single ordinary renewal process but of an infinite array of such processes operating simultaneously.

Despite the impression conveyed by distributions and equilibrium arguments, the single process stubbornly continues to behave in accordance with its underlying distribution $f(t)$, no matter how long the process continues. In fact, each renewal can be considered to be the start of an ordinary renewal process. Although there is definitely an equilibrium process in that as the process continues without limit, the ratio of total time to failures does approach a limit, the MTBF, there is no change in the pattern of renewals. Thus an estimate of the MTBF made in a finite time interval of a renewal process is not affected by the length of time the process has existed prior to the interval in which the estimate is made.

The literature does not address the problem of how long an ordinary renewal process must continue before the ratio of total time to total failures approaches the MTBF to within some requisite tolerance. The solution of this problem is fundamentally related to the problem of determining the number of components that must be put under test to discover an underlying time-to-failure distribution to within some tolerance. This problem has been explored in previous chapters, but no attempt was made to relate the error in an MTTF calculated from a distribution resulting from a test with a finite number of components to the error in the distribution elements. Given such a relationship, the problem would be solved. Perhaps the averaging process inherent in calculating the MTTF reduces the tyranny of large numbers to some extent. Nevertheless, a large number of renewals must be involved if a close tolerance is to be achieved; further, the total time will be a function of both the necessary number of renewals and the life of the underlying distribution.

REFERENCES

Cox, D. R., *Renewal Theory.* Methuen and Co., Ltd., London, 1962.

CHAPTER ELEVEN

Renewal, and MTBF, in Multiple Component Systems

11.1 SUPERPOSITION OF ORDINARY RENEWAL PROCESSES

The basic approach to the treatment of systems composed of a number of identical components, or of many diverse groups consisting of numbers of identical components, is simplicity itself. A system composed of M identical components may be represented as M distinct ordinary renewal processes, all starting at the same time. Renewals (repairs) for M ordinary processes are made by random selection from the same population (spare parts inventory) with underlying distribution $f(t)$. In the case of numbers of components of different kinds corresponding to underlying distributions $f_j(t)$ and numbering M_j components per system, the system is represented by $\sum_{j=1}^{k} M_j$ ordinary renewal processes, where k is the number of different kinds of components in the system. Renewals (repairs) are made, of course, from the appropriate spare parts inventory. A system of M components of the same kind or of different kinds can be represented by a graph such as shown in Figure 10.1.

11.2 THE MTBF OF MULTIPLE COMPONENT SYSTEMS

Using the definition of MTBF developed for the ordinary renewal process, that is, the limiting value of time divided by the number of failures in that time as time increases without limit, it is very simple to derive an analogous MTBF for multiple component systems. This MTBF is not related to customary usage that defines an MTBF over a limited interval in the operating life of a system; a theoretical model for predicting such a finite interval MTBF does not exist in the general case.

Given ρ_j, the MTBF for an ordinary renewal process based on the distribution $f_j(t)$, the number of failures in the interval $(0, t)$, as t increases without limit, is

$$F_j = \frac{t}{\rho_j}$$

If there are M_j of this kind of component in the system, the M_j renewal processes representing this portion of the system will experience M_jF_j failures in that interval. If there are k different kinds of components in the system, the total number of system failures in the interval becomes

$$F = \sum_{j=1}^{k} M_jF_j$$

The system mean time between failures is

$$\text{MTBF}_s = \frac{t}{F} = \frac{1}{\displaystyle\sum_{j=1}^{k} \frac{M_j}{\rho_j}} \tag{11.1}$$

It is clear from equation (11.1) that the MTBF for a system tends to zero as the number of components increases without limit. This is hardly surprising; it would seem obvious. Nevertheless, this result runs into trouble in connection with discrete distributions. The problem arises in the meaning; are we talking about the "time per failure" or the "time between failures"? In the case of the discrete distribution time is not infinitely divisible, the time cells are finite. As a result the time between failures can never be less than the duration of the first time cell t_1. If q failures have taken place in that time cell, the time per failure is t_1/q, but the time between failures is still t_1.

If a distribution of time between failures is defined, $f(tbf)$, the MTBF is defined in the continuous case as

$$\text{MTBF} = \int_0^\infty tbf\, f\,(tbf)\, d\,(tbf) \tag{11.2}$$

in the discrete case as

$$\text{MTBF} = \sum_{n=1}^{L} tbf_n\, f(\text{tbf}_n) \tag{11.3}$$

In the case of $f(tbf_n)$, as the number of parts increases without limit, $f(\underline{tbf_1})$ approaches unity, and the other terms approach zero; accordingly, the MTBF is $\underline{tbf_1}$. This result will be confirmed in later chapters in both theory and Monte Carlo simulation. This enlarges our universe of distributions; in addition to the time-to-failure distribution, its MTTF, and its survivor function, the time-between-failures distribution, its MTBF, and an analogous survivor function are added now and will be explained later.

The result of (11.1) would seem to satisfy anyone content with being able to calculate the MTBF for any system. Actually, it is not satisfying at all. The quantity derived is theoretically achieved only after infinite time; even if a reasonable approximation may be achieved in finite time, that time is likely to be very long compared to the service life of an equipment. Experience indicates that failure behavior changes markedly during service life; an ultimate equilibrium state is questionable even by the time the system is scrapped. Clearly, more analytical tools are needed. Taking a clue from the earlier realization that $H(t)$, $h(t)$, and recurrence time distributions really deal with infinite ensembles of ordinary recurrence processes, the author decided to analyze a system composed of a countless number of components of one kind as an alternative to the study of the ordinary renewal process.

11.3 RENEWAL IN A SYSTEM COMPOSED OF A VERY LARGE NUMBER OF COMPONENTS OF ONE KIND

Figure 11.1 illustrates the general approach to visualizing a renewal process. The upper part of the figure symbolizes a system of many components as a combination of a like number of ordinary renewal processes. The lower portion of the figure covers the same time span and depicts two time epochs, 0 and t. The particular underlying distribution chosen was uniform, with life L, and is displayed as the dotted line on the lower left-hand side. At time zero the forward recurrence time distribution is the underlying distribution itself, that is,

$$h(0, u) = f(u) \qquad (11.4)$$

where $f(t)$ is the component time-to-failure distribution. The time scale for u, the recurrence time variable, is the same as that for t, the system age.

Another forward recurrence time distribution is shown in a solid line on the lower right-hand side as representing the distribution at time t. This happens to be the equilibrium state corresponding to the beginning distribution and would not occur until t became large without limit. Practically, as will be shown later, the equilibrium state for the uniform distribution is reached in about 2.5 lifetimes of the original uniform distribution. Although the for-

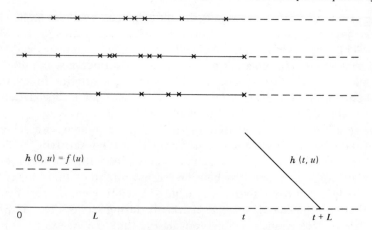

$h\,(0, u) = f\,(u)$ $h\,(t, u)$

0   L t $t + L$

Figure 11.1 Schematic for visualizing a renewal process.

ward recurrence time distribution is normally a probability function, it may be regarded as the actual distribution in this development inasmuch as the component count is large without limit.

The condition expressed in equation (11.4) presumes a new system. It is also possible to start with a system that has aged, where the repair distribution is the same as that for the new system, or where the repair distribution is a new one, representing a change in design. In this case, the representation is

$$h\,(0, u) = W\,(u) \tag{11.5}$$

where $W\,(u)$ is the system state $h\,(t, u)$ when the change is made.

By implication, the discussion has thus far assumed continuous distributions: this is not a necessary condition, it applies equally to discrete distributions. In that case the expressions used are

$$f\,(t_n)\quad f\,(u_j)\quad h\,(t_n, u_j)\quad \text{and}\quad W\,(u_j)$$

As a matter of fact, the development will begin with discrete distributions, since this avoids some philosophical difficulties that occur in the continuous case.

Let us start at some time t_n for which the forward recurrence time distribution is $h\,(t_n, u_j)$. Figure 11.2 displays a hypothetical distribution of this kind; for simplicity it has only four elements. In common with the conventions for discrete distributions, $h\,(t_n, u_0)$ is not defined. The distribution of

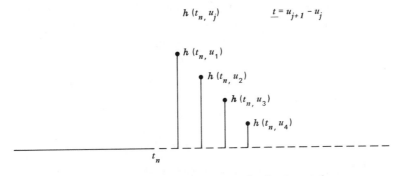

Figure 11.2   Forward recurrence time distribution at time t_n.

Figure 11.2 is based on uniform time cells of duration $\underline{t}$; this will be true of all discrete distributions from this point on. Thus

$$(t_{n+1} - t_n) = (u_{j+1} - u_j) = \underline{t}$$

defining $\underline{t}$. Now assume that the number of system components, M, is finite but very large. It is now possible to state, to a close approximation, that the fraction of system components in each of the j recurrence time states is

$$M h (t_n, u_j) \tag{11.6}$$

The system is now aged for an interval $\underline{t}$. The time epoch is now t_{n+1} and the recurrence time distribution is that shown in Figure 11.3. To a very close approximation $M h (t_n, u_1)$ components have failed; this accounts for the disappearance of $h (t_n, u_1)$ in Figure 11.3. The sum

$$M [h (t_n, u_2) + h (t_n, u_3) + h (t_n, u_4)]$$

is the number of components surviving at t_{n+1}. The numbers of component parts in the surviving state may be expressed as

$$M h (t_n, u_j + \underline{t}) = M h (t_n, u_{j+1}) \tag{11.7}$$

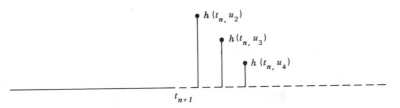

Figure 11.3   Forward recurrence time distribution at time t_{n+1}, after failure but before repair.

for each j. To renew (repair) the system, $Mh(t_n, u_1)$ components are drawn from stock to replace the failed components. Then, to a very close approximation, the system state, in actual numbers of components for each j, is

$$Mh(t_{n+1}, u_j) = Mh(t_n, u_{j+1}) + Mh(t_n, u_1)f(u_j)$$

Dividing by M, the system forward recurrence time distribution at t_{n+1} for each j is

$$h(t_{n+1}, u_j) = h(t_n, u_{j+1}) + h(t_n, u_1)f(u_j) \tag{11.8}$$

The above recursion formula applied again and again will trace the complete history of the system. It applies equally whether the starting distribution is arbitrary, $W(u_j)$, or is $f(u_j)$. The degree of approximation ultimately depends on the number of components but is influenced by the size of $\underline{t}$ and the nature of the underlying distribution.

11.4 PROPERTIES OF $h(t_n, u_j)$

$h(t_n, u_j)$ is a density function. For proof,

$$\sum_{j=1}^{L} h(t_n, u_j) = \sum_{j=1}^{L} [h(t_{n-1}, u_{j+1}) + h(t_{n-1}, u_l)f(u_j)]$$

$$= \sum_{j=2}^{L} h(t_{n-1}, u_j) + h(t_{n-1}, u_1)$$

$$= \sum_{j=1}^{L} h(t_{n-1}, u_j) \tag{11.9}$$

but

$$\sum_{j=1}^{L} h(0, u_j) = \sum_{j=1}^{L} f(u_j) = 1 \tag{11.10}$$

Therefore all of the $h(t_n, u_j)$ are density functions.

The function $h(t_n, u_j)$ reaches an equilibrium state as t_n increases without limit. To establish both the form and fact of equilibrium for this function the behavior of $h(t_n, u_1)$ is considered first. The number of failures in n renewals is, for a very large component count,

$$M \sum_{k=1}^{n} h(t_k, u_1)$$

The time required for n renewals is $n\underline{t}$. Then

$$\text{MTBF}_s = \frac{\rho}{M} = \lim_{n \to \infty} \frac{n\underline{t}}{M \sum_{k=1}^{n} h(t_k, u_1)} \qquad (11.11)$$

Then

$$\lim_{n \to \infty} \left[n - \frac{\rho}{\underline{t}} \sum_{k=1}^{n} h(t_k, u_1) \right] = 0$$

Consequently

$$\lim_{n \to \infty} \left[n + 1 - \frac{\rho}{\underline{t}} \sum_{k=1}^{n+1} h(t_k, u_1) \right] = 0$$

Combining the two equations above yields

$$\lim_{n \to \infty} \left[1 - \frac{\rho}{\underline{t}} h(t_{n+1}, u_1) \right] = 0$$

and

$$h(\infty, u_1) = \frac{\underline{t}}{\rho} \qquad \text{where} \quad \rho = \sum_{j=1}^{L} j\underline{t}f(u_j) \qquad (11.12)$$

Given equation (11.12), the equilibrium state of $h(t_n, u_j)$ as t_n increases may now be derived. From equation (11.8), one has

$$\lim_{n \to \infty} h(t_n, u_{j+1}) = \lim_{n \to \infty} [h(t_{n+1}, u_j) - h(t_n, u_1)f(u_j)]$$

Therefore

$$h(\infty, u_{j+1}) = h(\infty, u_j) - \frac{\underline{t}}{\rho} f(u_j)$$

Applying the above equation

$$h(\infty, u_2) = h(\infty, u_1) - \frac{\underline{t}}{\rho} f(u_1)$$

$$= \frac{\underline{t}}{\rho} [1 - f(u_1)]$$

$$h(\infty, u_3) = h(\infty, u_2) - \frac{t}{\rho} f(u_2)$$

$$= \frac{t}{\rho} [1 - f(u_1) - f(u_2)]$$

Ultimately

$$h(\infty, u_j) = \frac{t}{\rho} \left[1 - \sum_{k=1}^{j-1} f(u_k) \right]$$

$$= \frac{t}{\rho} \underline{fs}(u_{j-1}) \tag{11.13}$$

This is identical to the heuristically derived result in equation (10.17) for the equilibrium forward recurrence time, given a discrete underlying distribution.

Equation (11.12) demonstrates that as the number of components increases without limit in a system with components described by a discrete p.d.f., failures will occur in each interval of length $\underline{t}$ and the number of failures in each such interval will approach $M\underline{t}/\rho$; consequently, the number of failures per unit time will approach M/ρ and the time per failure will approach ρ/M. Mention was made in the above discussion relative to starting the renewal process with some arbitrary distribution $W(u_j)$. In such case, $W(u_j)$ must be defined over the same time cell duration as is $f(u_j)$; the life of $W(u_j)$ need not correspond to that of $f(u_j)$. It can be shown, however, that the ultimate equilibrium state depends only on the repair distribution, $f(u_j)$ and is independent of $W(u_j)$.

11.5 THE VERY LARGE SYSTEM: SINGLE COMPONENT TYPE WITH CONTINUOUS UNDERLYING DISTRIBUTION

If one iterates the recursion formula of equation (11.8) starting at time zero, leaving moot the question of whether the starting distribution $h(0, u_j)$ is $f(u_j)$ or $W(u_j)$ and using time cells of duration $\underline{t}$, one obtains

$$h(\underline{t}, u_j) = h(0, u_{j+1}) + h(0, u_1)f(u_j) \tag{11.14}$$

Now

$$h(2\underline{t}, u_j) = h(\underline{t}, u_{j+1}) + h(\underline{t}, u_1)f(u_j)$$

Combining the above equation with equation (11.14), one has

$$h(2\underline{t}, u_j) = h(0, u_{j+2}) + h(0, u_1)f(u_{j+1})$$

$$+ h(\underline{t}, u_1)f(u_j) \tag{11.15}$$

Similarly

$$h(3\underline{t}, u_j) = h(0, u_{j+3}) + h(0, u_1)f(u_{j+2})$$
$$+ h(\underline{t}, u_1)f(u_{j+1}) + h(2\underline{t}, u_1)f(u_j) \qquad (11.16)$$

The pattern is now obvious, so

$$h(n\underline{t}, u_j) = h(0, u_{j+n}) + \sum_{x=1}^{n} h[(x-1)\underline{t}, u_1]f(u_{j+n-x})$$

or   (11.17)

$$h(n\underline{t}, u_j) = h(0, u_{j+n}) + \sum_{x=0}^{n-1} h[(n-1-x)\underline{t}, u_1]f(u_{j+x})$$

The above expression may be transformed by noting that

$$u_{j+n} = u_j + n\underline{t} \qquad u_{j+n-x} = u_j + (n-x)\underline{t}$$

Accordingly

$$h(n\underline{t}, u_j) = h(0, u_j + n\underline{t}) + \sum_{x=0}^{n-1} h[(n-1)\underline{t} - x\underline{t}, u_1]f(u_j + x\underline{t})$$

$$h(n\underline{t}, u_j) = h(0, u_j + n\underline{t}) + \sum_{x=0}^{(n-1)t} h[(n-1)\underline{t} - x, u_1]f(u_j + x) \qquad (11.18)$$

Note that the summation in x in equation (11.18) is x equal to 0, $\underline{t}$, $2\underline{t}$, and so on.

Equation (11.18) may now be transformed into an integral equation by letting $\underline{t}$ approach zero. This limiting process requires the observance of some mathematical niceties. The recursion formula from which equation (11.18) was derived assumed that $Mh(n\underline{t}, u_1)$ failures occurred for each value of n; this requires that $Mh(n\underline{t}, u_1)$ exceed unity for all values of n. This condition cannot be met if M is finite and constant as t approaches zero. The solution is a step by step process; $\underline{t}$ is decreased in steps and M is increased simultaneously to preserve the base assumption. Now if $\underline{t}$ is allowed to approach zero in this fashion while $n\underline{t}$ is held constant with the value, t, in the limit, equation (11.18) becomes

$$h(t, u) = h(0, u + t) + \int_0^{t} h(t - x, 0)f(u + x)dx \qquad (11.19)$$

It should be noted that as t becomes zero, both $(n - 1)t$ and nt become t and u_1 becomes zero. Equation (11.19) may also be written

$$h(t, u) = h(0, u + t) + \int_0^t h(x, 0)f(u + t - x)dx \qquad (11.20)$$

In the case of a new system, $h(0, u + t)$ is $f(u + t)$; when starting with an arbitrary distribution, $h(0, u + t)$ is $W(u + t)$. Inasmuch as $h(0, u + t)$ approaches zero as t increases without limit, it is seen that the equilibrium state of $h(t, u)$ is independent of the starting distribution.

Some additional correlations with previously derived results are now possible. Replacing $h(0, u + t)$ with $f(u + t)$ in equation (11.20) and setting u equal to zero provides

$$h(t, 0) = f(t) + \int_0^t h(t - x, 0)f(x)dx \qquad (11.21)$$

The integral equation above is identical to that defining $h(t)$ in equation (10.9). Unless the solution to this integral equation is not unique, it follows that

$$h(t, 0) \equiv h(t) \qquad (11.22)$$

The result above should not come as a surprise. $h(t, 0)$ is the fraction of components that fail per unit time about t in a system composed of an infinite number of components of a single type; $h(t)$ is the fraction of renewals that occur per unit time about t in an infinite number of ordinary renewal processes based on a given distribution. Inasmuch as the system and the ensemble of renewal processes are equivalent, the above identity must hold. The derivation, however, is different.

Still another identity is proved. From equation (10.11)

$$V(t, u) = f(t + u) + \int_0^t h(t - x)f(x + u)dx$$

If $h(0, u + t)$ is replaced by $f(u + t)$ in equation (11.19), it is seen that

$$V(t, u) \equiv h(t, u)$$

REFERENCES

Cox, D. R., *Renewal Theory*, Methuen and Co., Ltd., London, 1962.

CHAPTER TWELVE

Solution Methods and Solutions for h(t, u) and h(t_n, u_j)

12.1 EQUILIBRIUM AND TIME TO EQUILIBRIUM

Generally, the attainment of the equilibrium state of $h(t, u)$, $h(t_n, u_j)$, $h(t, 0)$, or $h(t_n, u_1)$ requires time; theoretically, an infinite time, practically, a finite time very much dependent upon the nature of the repair distribution and the degree of approximation desired. ("Repair distribution" is a term that will be used to identify the distribution of the repair population.) There are two situations where theory indicates that the equilibrium is "instant"; however, one is the case where the starting and repair distributions are exponential, $\lambda e^{-\lambda t}$, the other where $W(u)$ is the equilibrium state corresponding to the repair distribution. There is no need to prove the latter assertion mathematically; it is an obvious corollary of the existence of an equilibrium state. For the exponential distribution proof is obtained by substitution in the expression for the equilibrium state:

$$h(\infty, u) = (1/\rho) \, \underline{fs}\,(u)$$

When $f(u)$ is $\lambda e^{-\lambda u}$, $1/\rho$ is λ and $\underline{fs}\,(u)$ is $e^{-\lambda u}$. Thus

$$h(\infty, u) = \lambda e^{-\lambda u} \tag{12.1}$$

Focusing one's attention on the behavior of the forward recurrence time distribution may be very misleading. Ordinary renewal processes, as we have seen, have an instant steady state of their own, that is, the pattern of their renewal behavior is fixed from the instant the process starts, regardless of the behavior of the forward recurrence time distribution. This does not really conflict with what has been found about the forward recurrence time distribution; after all, the discussion has amply explained that $h(t, u)$ is a snapshot of an infinite number of ordinary renewal processes. In the case of the exponential distribution, for example, $h(t, u)$ has instant equilibrium; yet the determination that a single ordinary renewal process is based on an exponential takes the time (number of renewals) necessary to make the discovery of an empirical distribution. It is obvious, therefore, that the relationship between the time to equilibrium of the forward recurrence time distribution and the equilibrium of renewal processes ranges from a complete disconnect in the case of the single ordinary renewal process to a complete connect in the case of the system with countless components. What happens between these limits?

12.2 SOLUTIONS FOR $h(t, u)$: CONTINUOUS DISTRIBUTIONS

Given

$$h(t, u) = f(t + u) + \int_0^t h(t - x, 0) f(u + x) \, dx$$

the general solution may be simplified by separating it into two steps. A simpler integral equation is derived from the above by setting u equal to zero. Having accomplished the solution for $h(t, 0)$, computing $h(t, u)$ no longer requires solution of an integral equation; in principal, it is only an integration. Thus attention is focused on the solution for the density function

$$h(t, 0) = f(t) + \int_0^t n(t - x, 0) f(u + x) \, dx \tag{12.2}$$

The solution for this equation has been determined and is given in equation (10.7):

$$h(t, 0) = \sum_{n=1}^{\infty} f_n(t)$$

$$f_n(t) = \int_0^t f_{n-1}(t - x) f(x) \, dx$$

and

$$f_1(t) = f(t)$$

the underlying distribution for the components.

The same solution can be obtained by application of the Laplace transform:

$$h^*(s, 0) = f^*(s)[1 - f^*(s)]^{-1}$$

$$= f^*(s) \sum_{n=0}^{\infty} f^{*n}(s)$$

$$= f^*(s) + f^{*2}(s) + f^{*3}(s) + \cdots$$

The inverse transforms of the above are

$$f(t) = f_1(t)$$

$$f_2(t) = \int_0^t f(t - x) f(x) \, dx = \int_0^t f_1(t - x) f(x) \, dx$$

$$f_3(t) = \int_0^t f_2(t - x) f(x) \, dx$$

$$\vdots \qquad\qquad \vdots$$

giving the same result.

In the case where the starting distribution is $W(u)$, the equation to be solved is

$$h(t, 0) = W(t) + \int_0^t h(t - x, 0) f(x) \, dx$$

The Laplace transform of both sides of this equation is

$$h^*(s, 0) = W^*(s) + h^*(s, 0) f^*(s)$$

Therefore,

$$h^*(s, 0) = W^*(s)[1 - f^*(s)]^{-1}$$

$$= W^*(s)[1 + f^*(s) + f^{*2}(s) + f^{*3}(s) + \cdots]$$

The inverse transforms of these equations are

$$W(t) = W_1(t)$$

$$W_2(t) = \int_0^t W_1(t - x) f(x) \, dx$$

$$W_3(t) = \int_0^t W_2(t - x) f(x) \, dx$$

$$\vdots \qquad\qquad \vdots$$

Then

$$h(t, 0) = \sum_{n=1}^{\infty} W_n(t) \qquad (12.3)$$

The equilibrium value of $h(t, 0)$ in the above case is also $1/\rho$; thus the starting distribution has no effect on the equilibrium state. The proof of the equilibrium state is identical to that for the case where the starting distribution is $f(t)$.

One can do an interesting little exercise with the solution for $f_n(t)$, assuming the starting and repair distributions to be $\lambda e^{-\lambda t}$. It may be easily shown, using the Laplace transform, that

$$f_n(t) = \frac{\lambda e^{-\lambda t}(\lambda t)^{n-1}}{(n-1)!}$$

This particular expression is known in the literature as the special Erlangian distribution with n stages. An ordinary renewal process of this type, with an exponential underlying distribution and an Erlangian operating time density, is called a **Poisson process**.

Now

$$h(t, 0) = \sum_{n=1}^{\infty} f_n(t) = \lambda = \frac{1}{\rho} \qquad (12.4)$$

This result closes a circle. It has been previously noted that given the distribution $\lambda e^{-\lambda t}$, $h(t, 0)$ achieves instant equilibrium; the above result confirms this.

For further understanding of the nature of both $h(t, 0)$ and solution methods for it consider the case where $f(t)$ is a uniform distribution of magnitude $1/L$ over the interval $(0, L)$. It happens that the general method of solution just covered in this chapter, that of developing $h(t, 0)$ as an infinite sum of convolution integrals, is not the best way to develop the desired solution. It is possible to develop a solution in closed form that does not require an infinite summation. As before,

$$h*(s, 0) = f*(s)[1 - f*(s)]^{-1} \qquad (12.5)$$

$$f*(s) = \frac{1}{L} \int_0^L \frac{e^{-st}}{dt}$$

$$= \frac{1 - e^{-sL}}{sL} \qquad (12.6)$$

Substituting and rearranging,

$$h^*(s, 0) = \frac{1 - e^{-sL}}{L(s - 1/L)}\left[1 + \frac{e^{-sL}}{L(s - 1/L)}\right]^{-1}$$

$$= (1 - e^{-sL}) \sum_{n=0}^{\infty} \frac{(-1)^n e^{-nsL}}{L^{n+1}(s - 1/L)^{n+1}}$$

$$= \sum_{n=0}^{\infty} \left(\frac{(-1)^n e^{-nsL}}{L^{n+1}(s - 1/L)^{n+1}} - \frac{(-1)^n e^{-(n+1)sL}}{L^{n+1}(s - 1/L)^{n+1}}\right) \qquad (12.7)$$

Then

$$h(t, 0) = \sum_{n=0}^{\infty} \left(\frac{(-1)^n e^{t/L - n}(t/L - n)^n}{n!L}\right.$$
$$\left. - \frac{(-1)^n e^{t/L - n - 1}(t/L - n - 1)^n}{n!L}\right) \qquad (12.8)$$

where t/L must be equal to or greater than n in the first term in equation (12.8) and t/L must be equal to or greater than $n + 1$ in the second term. It is now possible to write expressions for $h(t, 0)$. For

$$(0, L) \qquad h(t, 0) = \frac{e^{t/L}}{L}$$

$$(L, 2L) \qquad h(t, 0) = \frac{e^{t/L}}{L}\left(1 - \frac{t/L}{e}\right)$$

$$(2L, 3L) \qquad h(t, 0) = \frac{e^{t/L}}{L}\left[1 - \frac{t/L}{e} + \frac{(t/L)(t/L - 2)}{2!e^2}\right]$$

$$(3L, 4L) \qquad h(t, 0) = \frac{e^{t/L}}{L}\left[1 - \frac{t/L}{e} + \frac{(t/L)(t/L - 2)}{2!e^2} - \frac{(t/L)(t/L - 3)^2}{3!e^3}\right]$$

(12.9)

and so on. This is obviously a herculean task in itself; to develop $h(t, u)$ by integration is an even more strenuous task. It is no wonder, therefore, that the renewal literature terms the "renewal equation" as "intractable." Fortunately, at least for graphical purposes, the interval $(0, 4L)$ is sufficient to depict the behavior; this is because within realistic tolerances $h(t, 0)$ for the uniform distribution has reached equilibrium well within this interval.

Figure 12.1 is the result. Note that the scales used are appropriate to the expressions: time is parametric in t/L and $h(t, 0)$ is plotted in terms of $1/L$, the magnitude of the uniform distribution itself. It is seen that equilibrium is closely approximated in about $2.5L$, and is $2/L$ as expected.

The formal solution for $h(t, 0)$ for one other distribution follows. In this instance the convolution integral series is the method of choice; no attempt is made to reach equilibrium. The distribution is

$$f(t) = \frac{1}{1 - a} \qquad a \leq t \leq 1 \quad \text{and zero elsewhere} \qquad (12.10)$$

This time-to-failure distribution is shown in Figure 12.2. The resulting $h(t, 0)$ for the interval $(0, 3)$ is given below:

$$(0, a) \qquad h(t, 0) = 0$$

$$(a, 1) \qquad h(t, 0) = \frac{1}{1 - a}$$

$$(1, 2a) \qquad h(t, 0) = 0$$

$$(2a, 1 + a) \qquad h(t, 0) = \frac{t - 2a}{(1 - a)^2}$$

$$(1 + a, 2) \qquad h(t, 0) = \frac{-(t - 2)}{(1 - a)^2} \qquad\qquad (12.11)$$

$$(2, 3a) \qquad h(t, 0) = 0$$

$$(3a, 1 + 2a) \qquad h(t, 0) = \frac{(t - 3a)^2}{2(1 - a)^3}$$

$$(1 + 2a, 2 + a) \qquad h(t, 0) = \frac{1}{1 - a} - \frac{(t - 1 - 2a)^2 + (t - 2 - a)^2}{2(1 - a)^3}$$

$$(2 + a, 3) \qquad h(t, 0) = \frac{(t - 3)^2}{2(1 - a)^3}$$

This function is shown in Figure 12.3 for $a = 0.8$. As time increases, the succeeding pulses are smeared more and more, until they join; further increase

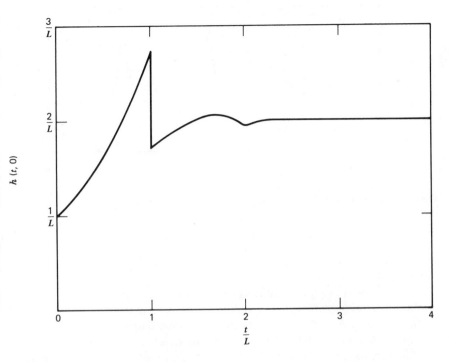

Figure 12.1 The renewal density function $h(t, 0)$ for a uniform distribution.

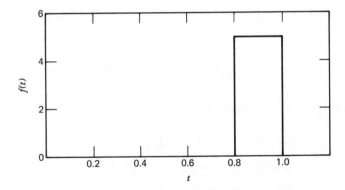

Figure 12.2 A hypothetical narrow dispersion distribution.

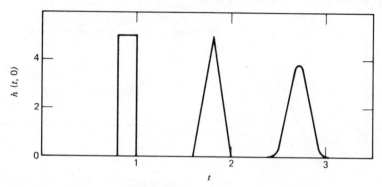

Figure 12.3 Renewal density function $h(t, 0)$ for a continuous narrow dispersion distribution.

in time shows an oscillating behavior that decreases in amplitude as it approaches the equilibrium value.

The time to a practical equilibrium is a function of the dispersion of the original distribution, that is, the degree to which a approaches unity. In the limit, as a becomes unity, the distribution becomes a delta function at $t = 1$, a "one hoss shay" distribution in which all failures occur only at $t = 1$. Equilibrium is never achieved in this instance; $h(t, 0)$ is an endlessly repeating delta function at t equal to 1, 2, and so on. Nevertheless, equilibrium theory predicts a steady state for $h(\infty, 0)$ that is unity, namely, $1/\rho$, and an equilibrium recurrence time distribution, $h(\infty, u)$ that is a uniform distribution over the interval in u, $(0, 1)$. This apparent contradiction is explained by solving the integral equation for $h(t, 0)$ for the "one hoss shay" distribution.

First consider the case where the initial distribution and the repair distribution are both $f(x)$. The appropriate integral equation is

$$h(t, 0) = f(t) + \int_0^t h(t - x, 0)\, f(x)\, dx$$

Given that $f(x)$ is a delta function at $x = 1$, $\delta(1)$, one has

$$h(t, 0) = 0 \qquad 0 \leq t < 1$$
$$h(1, 0) = \delta(1) + h(0,0) = \delta(1) \qquad\qquad (12.12)$$
$$h(t, 0) = 0 + h(t - 1, 0) \qquad 1 < t \leq \infty$$

Accordingly, $h(t, 0)$ is $\delta(1)$ at t equal to 1, 2, and so on and zero everywhere else. Now consider the case where the initial distribution is $W(u)$, a uniform distribution in the interval (0, 1). The appropriate integral equation is

$$h(t, 0) = W(t) + \int_0^t h(t - x, 0) f(x) \, dx$$

Given that $f(x)$ is a delta function at $x = 1$, one has

$$h(t, 0) = 1 \qquad 0 = t < 1$$

$$h(1, 0) = 0 + h(0, 0) = 1$$

$$h(t, 0) = 0 + h(t - 1, 0) \qquad 1 < t \leq \infty$$

Thus, $h(t, 0)$ is unity for all values of t, and, if one starts with the theoretical equilibrium recurrence distribution, one obtains the theoretical equilibrium value for $h(t, 0)$, unity.

The behavior of $h(t, 0)$ for the distribution of equation (12.10) is typical of any distribution of similar characteristics, namely, a limited dispersion about some non zero value of t. A decreasing dispersion lengthens the time to "practical" equilibrium; equilibrium is never reached if the dispersion is zero.

The solution examples for $h(t, 0)$ for underlying uniform and narrow dispersion distributions should suffice to demonstrate the intractability of equations (11.19) and (12.2) to classical methods of solution. While there are some tricks available that ease the situation in certain specific cases, there is no point in further pursuit of classical methods when a powerful and simple approach is available that solves both for $h(t, u)$ and $h(t, 0)$ for any underlying distribution.

12.3 DISCRETE DISTRIBUTIONS, COMPUTER SOLUTIONS FOR $h(t_n, u_j)$

The starting point is equation (11.8),

$$h(t_{n+1}, u_j) = h(t_n, u_{j+1}) + h(t_n, u_1) f(u_j)$$

This is easily transformed into a computer algorithm. First, the time cell duration $\underline{t}$ is made unity; this fits computer operation very nicely and does not constrain the solution in any way. Since t_n is $n\underline{t}$ and u_j is $j\underline{t}$, the recursion formula may be written

$$h(n + 1, j) = h(n, j + 1) + h(n, 1) f(j) \tag{12.13}$$

with the understanding that n refers to t and j to u. To effect a computer solution to equation (12.13) two registers are required, each having the same number of memory locations, the number of locations corresponding to the maximum number of time cells desired for the distributions $f(j)$ and $h(n, j)$. One of these registers serves as the lookup table for $f(j)$; the other is used as a shift register, that is, it may have its contents shifted to adjacent locations. The lookup register is loaded with $f(j)$, the other register, which is the location for $h(n, j)$ in the solution, is loaded with the starting distribution of $h(n, j)$, namely, $h(0, j)$. This starting distribution may be $f(j)$ or the arbitrary $W(j)$.

Computation starts by shifting the $h(n, j)$ register in a downward j sense by one location. This causes $h(0, 1)$ to exit the register; it is stored. To effect repair the contents of the $f(j)$ register are serially read, multiplied by $h(0, 1)$, and the product summed to the contents of the corresponding $h(n, j)$ location. The next shifting of the $h(n, j)$ register produces $h(1, 1)$. Repair is accomplished as described, except that $h(1, 1)$ is now the multiplier. This process is continued for as long as the user desires. The result is the time history not only of $h(n, 1)$, the density function for the discrete case, but of $h(n, j)$ as well, which may be read from the $h(n, j)$ register whenever desired. This process has been programmed for the Texas Instruments TI-59 calculator for a maximum of 20 time cells. The program is provided in the Appendix.

Figure 12.4 illustrates the continuous solution for $h(t, 0)$ for a uniform underlying distribution (recall Figure 12.1), together with the corresponding 20 time cell and five time cell versions of $h(n, 1)$; all underlying distributions have the same life L. The equilibrium values are different, as they should be. For the continous case, $h(\infty, 0)$ is $2/L$, for the discrete case it is $(2g/L)/(g + 1)$, where g is the number of time cells in the distribution. Thus it is $1.905/L$ for the 20 cell case and $1.667/L$ for the five cell case. The correspondence to $h(t, 0)$ is best for the 20 cell case, as one might expect. Remarkably, at least for the uniform distribution, the time to practical equilibrium is about the same for all these distributions. It will be shown later that this does not hold true for distributions generally, particularly those that approach the "one hoss shay" (small dispersion) distribution.

Figure 12.5 displays $h(14, j)$ for the 20 time cell discrete uniform distribution and Figure 12.6 displays $h(19, j)$ for the same sequence. Figure 12.7 is $h(60, j)$; this closely approximates the equilibrium distribution; the solid line is the equilibrium state of $h(t, 0)$ for the continuous uniform distribution with the same life. Figure 12.8 is $h(15, j)$ for the five time cell discrete uniform distribution; it too is a very good approximation to the equilibrium state.

This computer routine is based on discrete distributions and cannot be applied to the law of chance failure, because that distribution, $\lambda e^{-\lambda t}$, has an

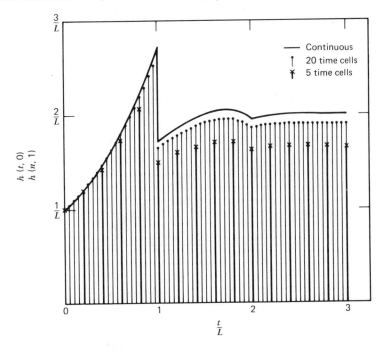

Figure 12.4   Renewal density function $h(t, 0)$ for a continuous uniform distribution (—); renewal density function $h(n, 1)$ for a discrete uniform distribution with 5 time cells (*) and 20 time cells ($\cdot$).

infinite life and cannot be modeled as a finite discrete distribution. It is possible, however, to model $h(n, j)$ for distributions of the type $ae^{\delta at}$, as long as δ is not -1. Figure 12.9 illustrates $h(n, 1)$ for the distribution $ae^{-0.99at}$; Figure 12.10 displays $h(n, 1)$ for the distribution $ae^{-0.5at}$, a distribution falling between the law of chance failure and the uniform distribution.

Figures 12.2 and 12.3 displayed a narrow dispersion distribution and $h(t, 0)$ for the interval $(0, 3)$; these were for a continuous underlying distribution. Figure 12.11 shows $h(n, 1)$ for the first 60 steps for the corresponding discrete underlying distribution. Figure 12.12 is the forward recurrence time distribution for the discrete case at the 60th step, $h(60, j)$. Figures 12.3 and 12.11 may be compared directly.

The next series of figures shows the behavior of $h(n, j)$ and $h(n, 1)$ for a set of modified normal distributions with various dispersions. Figure 12.13 shows a starting distribution $h(0, j)$ with a mean value of 0 and a standard deviation of 7; the lower part of the figure is the equilibrium distribution $h(\infty, j)$. Figure 12.14 displays the behavior of $h(n, 1)$ for this distribution for

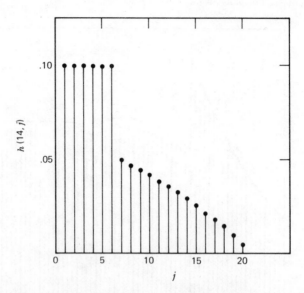

Figure 12.5 Theoretical forward recurrence time distribution $h(14, j)$ for a discrete uniform distribution with 20 time cells.

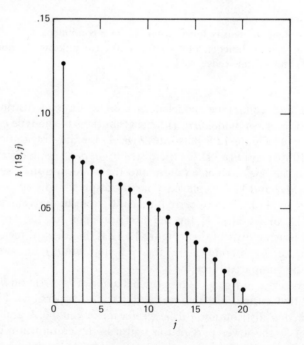

Figure 12.6 Theoretical forward recurrence time distribution $h(19, j)$ for a discrete uniform distribution with 20 time cells.

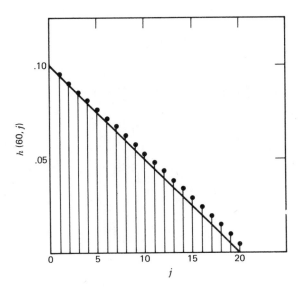

Figure 12.7 Theoretical forward recurrence time distribution $h(n, j)$ at age 60 for a discrete, uniform distribution with 20 time cells (approximate equilibrium). Analogous continuous function shown as solid line.

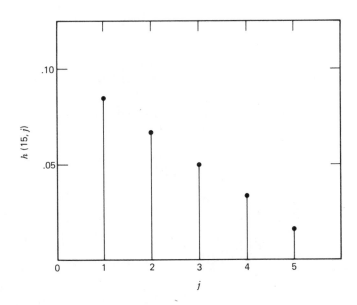

Figure 12.8 Theoretical forward recurrence time distribution $h(n, j)$ at age 15 for a discrete, uniform distribution with five time cells (approximate equilibrium).

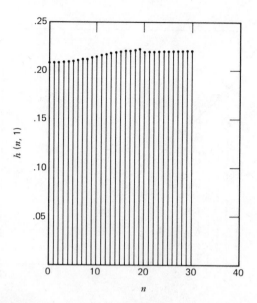

Figure 12.9 Theoretical renewal density function $h(n, 1)$ for the discrete 20 time cell version of $a\,e^{-0.99a\,t}$.

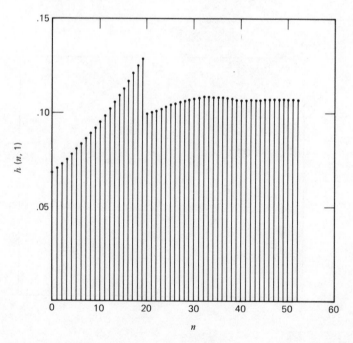

Figure 12.10 Theoretical renewal density function $h(n, 1)$ for the discrete 20 time cell version of $ae^{-0.5at}$.

158

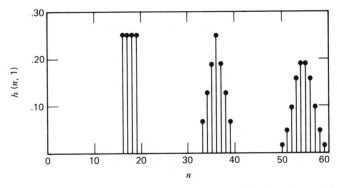

Figure 12.11   Theoretical discrete 20 time cell version of the function of Figure 12.3.

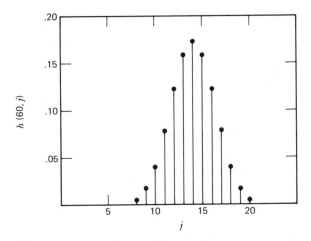

Figure 12.12   Theoretical forward recurrence time distribution $h(60, j)$ for the distribution whose renewal density function is shown in Figure 12.11.

the interval $(0, 60)$ in n. Figures 12.15 and 12.16 display corresponding behavior for a mean of 10.5 and a standard deviation of 10.5/3. Similarly, Figures 12.17 and 12.18 cover the behavior for a mean of 15.5 and a standard deviation of 1.55. Note that while $h(n, 1)$ of the distribution with the greatest dispersion essentially reaches equilibrium in 1.5 distribution lifetimes, $h(n, 1)$ of the distribution with a value of 10 for the ratio of the mean to the standard deviation has not reached that state of equilibrium in 10 lifetimes; in fact it takes about 25 lifetimes to come within 1% of equilibrium.

Finally, to show the effects of infant mortality and the bathtub curve, another set of figures is provided. Figure 12.19a displays a uniform distribution to which has been added an infant mortality characteristic. The hazard

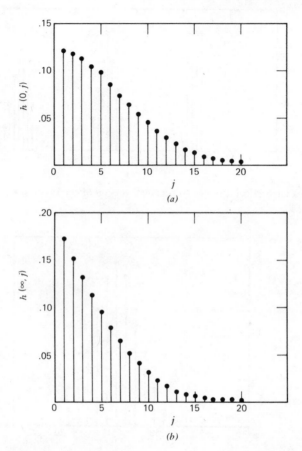

Figure 12.13 Discrete normal distribution with mean 0 and standard deviation, 7: (*a*) starting and repair time-to-failure distribution; (*b*) theoretical equilibrium forward recurrence time distribution.

function $\lambda(j)$ is shown in Figure 12.19*b*. Figure 12.20 is the resulting density function $h(n, 1)$; the first dip in $h(n, 1)$ corresponds to the dip in $\lambda(j)$ and is relatively constant at the bottom. The later dips and ultimate constant behavior of $h(n, 1)$ are primarily due to the uniform portion of the underlying distribution. Figure 12.21 is yet another distribution exhibiting a bathtub curve. This distribution was deliberately contrived to provide an infant mortality period, a basic wearout behavior, and a very wide "bathtub bottom." The distribution is displayed in Figure 12.21*a* and the hazard function in Figure 12.21*b*. Figure 12.22 displays the behavior of the density function $h(n, 1)$. The effect of the bathtub bottom is quite pronounced in a time equal to the lifetime of the underlying distribution and is still quite evident during a

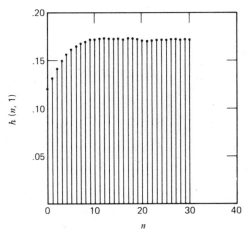

Figure 12.14 Discrete normal distribution with mean 0 and standard deviation, 7: theoretical renewal density function $h(n, 1)$.

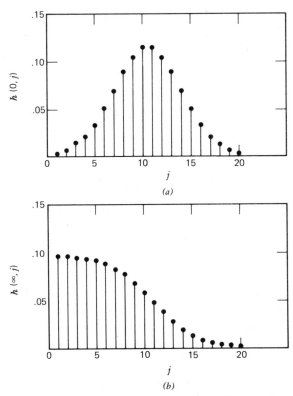

Figure 12.15 Discrete normal distribution with mean 10.5 and standard deviation 10.5/3: (a) starting and repair time-to-failure distribution; (b) theoretical equilibrium forward recurrence time distribution.

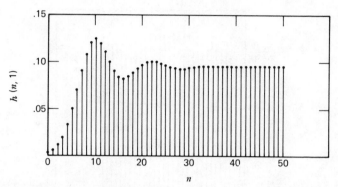

Figure 12.16 Discrete normal distribution with mean 10.5 and standard deviation 10.5/3: theoretical renewal density function $h(n, 1)$.

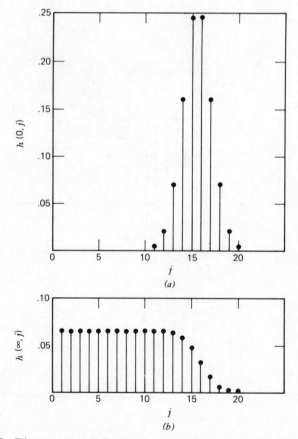

Figure 12.17 Discrete normal distribution with mean 15.5 and standard deviation 1.55: (*a*) starting time-to-failure distribution; (*b*) theoretical equilibrium forward recurrence time distribution.

162

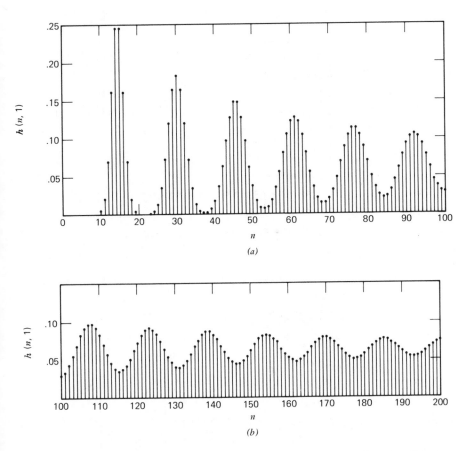

Figure 12.18 Theoretical renewal density function $h(n, 1)$ corresponding to a discrete, normal distribution with mean 15.5 and standard deviation 1.55: (a) n from 0 to 100; (b) n from 100 to 200.

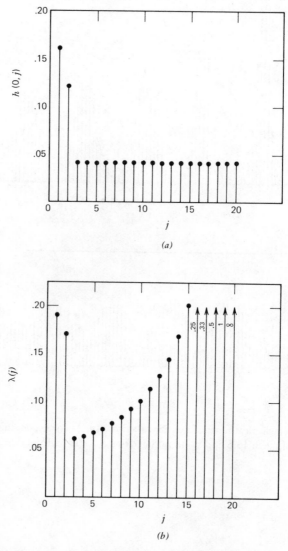

Figure 12.19 (*a*) Hypothetical distribution and (*b*) its hazard function.

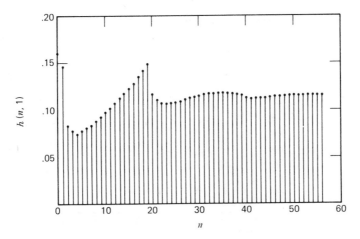

Figure 12.20 Theoretical renewal density function, $h(n, 1)$, for the distribution in Figure 12.19.

second interval of the same length. Ultimately, the oscillatory behavior due to the narrow dispersion portion of the distribution becomes dominant as the function proceeds to equilibrium.

The power of computer solutions should be evident from the foregoing examples. Classical methods of solution would be unbelievably laborious, if not impossible, especially with respect to arbitrary distributions. The computer solutions so easily obtained provide not only the density function but the total distribution of $h(n, j)$; should greater detail (more time cells per distribution) be required, a computer with a greater memory capability than the TI-59 is necessary. As memory and detail are increased, throughput will decrease unless a greater speed capability is also provided. Despite our ability to solve the renewal equation, we are far from a complete understanding of the renewal process; more theory is required, as is simulation of actual renewal processes.

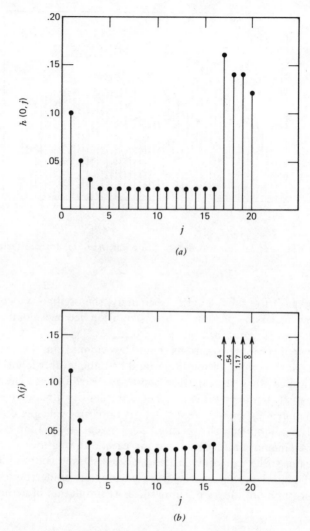

Figure 12.21 (*a*) Hypothetical distribution and (*b*) its hazard function.

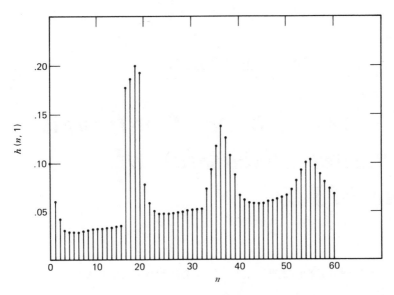

Figure 12.22 Theoretical renewal density function $h(n, 1)$, for the distribution in Figure 12.21.

CHAPTER THIRTEEN

Renewal Theory Continued: Further Discussion of the MTBF

13.1 TIME-BETWEEN-FAILURES DISTRIBUTIONS

Before continuing with further theoretical developments, it is appropriate that we summarize what has been accomplished to this point, what was provided by way of explanation of system behavior, and what yet remains to be explained about system behavior. Consideration of the ordinary renewal process, the behavior of a single component system as it goes through endless cycles of failure and repair, leads to the determination of the MTBF for that process. Further, it was found that the renewal behavior of any system could be represented as a combination of ordinary renewal processes of the same number as the components of the system, no matter how many kinds and numbers of components were contained in the system. This notion provided the means to compute the MTBF for such complex systems.

The concepts of renewal function, renewal density, and recurrence time distributions were developed with respect to the ordinary renewal process. It was shown that the forward recurrence time distribution could be reinterpreted as the actual, not probable, distribution for a single system comprised of an infinite number of identical components and a discrete underlying distribution. Further, a recursion formula was developed which provided the basis for a computer solution for the entire life span of the forward recurrence time distribution; this filled the "intractable" gap between time zero and the equilibrium state. This computer solution provided an easy means for studying the time behavior of the forward recurrence time distributions corresponding to various underlying distributions. But another gap was unfilled, the gap between systems consisting of one component only and those consisting of countless components.

The literature partially attacks this gap by investigating equilibrium time-between-failures distributions for systems with finite numbers of identical components. The notion of time-between-failures distributions was mentioned in Section 11.2, but little was said and a rather awkward symbolism was employed. A serious treatment requires a convenient symbolism; from this point forward, the time-between-failures distribution will be symbolized as

$$b(v) \tag{13.1}$$

The MTBF must then be

$$\text{MTBF} = \int_0^\infty v b(v) \, dv \tag{13.2}$$

The analog of the survivor function is

$$\underline{fe}(v) = 1 - \int_0^v b(z) \, dz \tag{13.3}$$

Mathematically, it follows that

$$\text{MTBF} = \int_0^\infty \underline{fe}(v) \, dv \tag{13.4}$$

Reasoning by analogy, there may exist a time-between-failures distribution $b(v)$ such that the survivor analog for M identical renewal processes operating in combination is

$$\underline{fe}_s(v) = \left[1 - \int_0^v b(z) \, dz \right]^M \tag{13.5}$$

$$= \underline{fe}(v)^M$$

The above terminology applies to continuous time-between-failures distributions. The discrete distribution versions are obtained by following the same mathematical rules given earlier for time-to-failure distributions.

It is easy to look at the mathematical formulation and accept it without pondering the real meaning of a time-between-failures distribution. A simple interpretation is possible in the case of the single ordinary renewal process, here

$$b(v) = f(v) \tag{13.6}$$

where $f(t)$ is the continuous underlying time-to-failure distribution. The interpretation is that $b(v)$ is a distribution that may be discovered by examining the intervals between renewals in the infinite sequence of any ordinary renewal process.

As soon as the system consists of two or more components, the interpretation requires modification. To discover $b(v)$ now requires that the system be in equilibrium; then $b(v)$ may be discovered by examining an infinite sequence of the equilibrium state for the combination of ordinary renewal processes that constitute the system. There is no interpretation possible except in the equilibrium state; therefore investigation of time-between-failures distributions cannot cover the period prior to equilibrium.

The expression for MTBF should be clear; it is the calculation of the mean value of time between failures. The analog of the survivor function expresses the fraction of times between failures that exceed v, hence the particular symbolism. The mathematics that provides the calculation of the MTTF from the survivor function of the time-to-failure distribution equally provides the MTBF from the analog survivor function of the time-between-failures distribution.

13.2 EQUILIBRIUM STATE; CONTINUOUS TIME-BETWEEN-FAILURES DISTRIBUTIONS

Cox develops a time-between-failures analog survivor function and its associated time-between-failures distribution for the equilibrium state of M simultaneous, identical ordinary renewal processes with continuous underlying distributions. Denoting $U(v)$ as the system equilibrium backward recurrence time, the probability that $U(v)$ is greater than v is the analog survivor function of $U(v)$. Thus

$$1 - \int_0^v U(u) \, du = \int_v^\infty U(u) \, du = \left[\frac{1}{\rho} \int_v^\infty fs(u) \, du \right]^M \qquad (13.7)$$

where $(1/\rho) \int_v^\infty fs(u) \, du$ is the analog survivor function corresponding to the equilibrium recurrence time distribution. This survivor function is interpretable, for equation (13.7), as the probability that the individual equilibrium process recurrence time exceeds v. It then follows that the negative derivative with respect to v of the probability that $U(v)$ is greater than v is

$$U(v) = \frac{M}{\rho} fs(v) \left[\frac{1}{\rho} \int_v^\infty fs(u) \, du \right]^{M-1} \qquad (13.8)$$

$U(v)$ is a p.d.f., that is,

$$\int_0^\infty U(v)\,dv = 1$$

Cox then states that since the MTBF for the system is ρ/M, the system analog survivor function $\underline{fe}_s(v)$, that is, the probability that the times between failures exceed v, is

$$\underline{fe}_s(v) = \frac{\rho}{M}\,U(v) = \underline{fs}(v)\left[\frac{1}{\rho}\int_v^\infty \underline{fs}(u)\,du\right]^{M-1} \tag{13.9}$$

It then follows that the system time-between-failures distribution is

$$b_s(v) = \frac{-d}{dv}\,\underline{fe}_s(v)$$

$$= f(v)\left[\frac{1}{\rho}\int_v^\infty \underline{fs}(u)\,du\right]^{M-1} + \frac{1}{\rho}(M-1)\underline{fs}^2(v)\left[\frac{1}{\rho}\int_v^\infty \underline{fs}(u)\,du\right]^{M-2}$$

$$\tag{13.10}$$

Setting M equal to one in equation (13.10) yields

$$b_s(v) = f(v)$$

This is a necessary result if the development is correct; further, regardless of the value of M, the MTBF is

$$\text{MTBF} = \int_0^\infty \underline{fe}_s(v)\,dv = \frac{\rho}{M}$$

This follows from equation (13.9) and the fact that $U(v)$ is a p.d.f. This too is a necessary result.

13.3 EQUILIBRIUM STATE; DISCRETE TIME-BETWEEN-FAILURES DISTRIBUTIONS

Cox (1962) does not develop these equilibrium relationships for the case of the discrete underlying distribution. While it would seem reasonable that the discrete case would develop in an identical fashion, this does not quite occur.

Our development starts with the discrete equilibrium recurrence time distribution given in equation (11.13):

$$h(\infty, u_j) = \frac{t}{\rho} \; \underline{fs}(u_{j-1}) = \frac{t}{\rho} \left[1 - \sum_{k=1}^{j-1} f(u_k) \right]$$

Writing the analog survivor function for the system recurrence time distribution,

$$1 - \sum_{k=1}^{j} U(v_k) = \left[1 - \frac{t}{\rho} \sum_{k=1}^{j} \underline{fs}(v_{k-1}) \right]^{M} \tag{13.11}$$

then

$$U(v_j) = \left[1 - \sum_{k=1}^{j-1} U(v_k) \right] - \left[1 - \sum_{k=1}^{j} U(v_k) \right]$$

$$= \left[1 - \frac{t}{\rho} \sum_{k=1}^{j-1} \underline{fs}(v_{k-1}) \right]^{M} - \left[1 - \frac{t}{\rho} \sum_{k=1}^{j} \underline{fs}(v_{k-1}) \right]^{M} \tag{13.12}$$

It can be seen that $U(v_j)$ is nonzero only for values of j one through L. Further, it can be shown that it is a p.d.f., that is

$$\sum_{j=1}^{L} U(v_j) = 1$$

This follows from the fact that $(t/\rho)\, fs(v_{j-1})$ is a p.d.f. It is at this point that Cox multiplies $U(v)$ by ρ/M and indicates that the time-between-failures distribution is obtained by taking the negative time derivative of this product. That multiplier is not appropriate to the discrete case; some method is necessary to discover it. To develop a distribution from $U(v_j)$ the analog of the negative time differentiation must be employed. Thus

$$b(v_j) = -[U(v_j) - U(v_{j-1})]$$

$$= U(v_{j-1}) - U(v_j) \tag{13.13}$$

Equation (13.13) must be interpreted with care. For example, straight substitution yields

$$b(v_1) = U(v_0) - U(v_1)$$
$$= -U(v_1)$$

Inasmuch as $U(v_1)$ is positive, and $b(v_1)$ must be positive, the above result is nonsense. Actually, the least value of v for which $b(v)$ is defined is v_2. Thus

$$b(v_2) = U(v_1) - U(v_2)$$

The greatest value of v for which $b(v)$ may be defined is

$$b(v_{L+1}) = U(v_L)$$

It is evident, therefore, that $b(v_j)$ has L defined terms despite the above situation. This behavior stems from the attempt to use $U(v_j)$, a p.d.f., as a survivor function. A survivor function must be unity when its argument is zero; $U(v_0)$ is zero, however. This problem did not occur in connection with the development for the continuous distribution; according to equation (13.8), $U(0)$ is M/ρ.

The dilemma may be resolved by redefining $U(v_j)$ as follows:

$$\underline{U}(v_j) = \left[1 - \frac{t}{\rho} \sum_{k=1}^{j} \underline{fs}(v_{k-1}) \right]^M - \left[1 - \frac{t}{\rho} \sum_{k=1}^{j+1} \underline{fs}(v_{k-1}) \right]^M \quad (13.14)$$

Then

$$\underline{U}(v_0) = \underline{U}(0) = 1 - \left(1 - \frac{t}{\rho} \right)^M \quad (13.15)$$

Following the procedure used in the continuous case, the system time-between-failures analog survivor function is defined as

$$\underline{fe}_s(v_j) = \frac{\underline{U}(v_j)}{\underline{U}(v_0)} \quad (13.16)$$

Now

$$\underline{fe}_s(v_0) = 1 \quad (13.17)$$

Further,

$$b_s(v_j) = \underline{f}e_s(v_{j-1}) - \underline{f}e_s(v_j) \qquad 1 \le j \le L \tag{13.18}$$

$$b_s(v_j) = f(v_j) \qquad M = 1 \tag{13.19}$$

giving the desired result. It may be shown by substitution that

$$\sum_{j=1}^{L} b_s(v_j) = 1 \tag{13.20}$$

Another interesting property of this distribution is

$$\lim_{M \to \infty} b_s(v_1) = 1 \tag{13.21}$$

Properties (13.20) and (13.21) combine to prove that all but $b_s(v_1)$ are zero when M approaches infinity. This demonstrates one of the two predictions made in Section 11.2. Now

$$\text{MTBF}_s = \underline{t} \sum_{j=0}^{L-1} \underline{f}e_s(v_j) = \frac{\underline{t}}{\underline{U(v_0)}} \sum_{j=0}^{L-1} \underline{U(v_j)}$$

$$= \frac{t}{1 - \left(1 - \dfrac{t}{\rho}\right)^M} \tag{13.22}$$

Therefore

$$\lim_{M \to \infty} \text{MTBF}_s = \underline{t} \tag{13.23}$$

$$\lim_{\underline{t} \to 0} \text{MTBF}_s = \frac{\rho}{M} \tag{13.24}$$

Equation (13.23) demonstrates the other prediction of Section 11.2.

Equation (13.24) ties the discrete and continuous developments together, since the limit of equation (13.24) is the reduction to the continuous case. It is also a means for determining the conditions under which a system with components described by a discrete distribution will adequately model the equilibrium state of a system whose components are described by the corresponding continuous distribution.

The difference between equation (13.22) and ρ/M is due to the fact that simultaneous multiple component failures are possible in the discrete case and not possible in the continuous case. A condition that makes equation (13.22) reasonably approach ρ/M should therefore indicate that the discrete distribution reasonably approximates the continuous distribution as far as modeling system renewal behavior in the equilibrium state. Such a condition is

$$\frac{Mt}{\rho} \le 0.1$$

Given a distribution of finite life L and the number of time cells in the distribution w, the above relation may be restated as

$$\frac{ML}{w\rho} \le 0.1$$

or

$$w \ge \frac{10ML}{\rho} \qquad (13.25)$$

Now L/ρ ranges from a minimum value of unity to infinity for a distribution with infinite life, such as the exponential distribution. Nevertheless, for reasonable approximations L/ρ will be generally less than four, thus

$$w \ge 40M \qquad (13.26)$$

will insure a very good modeling of a continuous case. Possibly, this condition is too rigorous by at least a factor of two.

The result of equation (13.23) is not unique to discrete distributions; there is at least one continuous distribution that exhibits analogous behavior, the "one hoss shay" distribution. A distribution of this type is the limit case of distributions described in Sections 8.3 and 8.4, for example. The "one hoss shay" distribution is one whose value is zero everywhere except at $t = L$, where it is a delta function; the only time to failure is L. The MTTF of this distribution is L, the MTTFF of an M component system of such components is L. An ordinary renewal process based on this distribution has an MTBF of L. Although an equilibrium distribution is defined for it, $\underline{fs}(t)/L$, this equilibrium is never reached, since $h(t, u)$ is periodic in L forever. The MTBF of a system with M such components must obviously be L, since the system fails totally (M components at once) as t becomes L, $2L$, $3L$, and so on. Since M components fail at each of these instants, the ratio of the total time to the total failures is L/M. Thus the MTBF remains L and the time per failure approaches zero as M becomes large without limit.

13.4 NONEQUILIBRIUM STATES

In principle, the renewal state of any kind of system is provided by the proper combination of ordinary renewal processes. A much more useful result is a statement of that principle in closed mathematical form. While no hope is provided for a closed form for the most general case, a system with a finite number of many different kinds of components, some closed form results have been provided for systems composed of identical components. A complete, statistically satisfying theory has been provided for the ordinary renewal process, but this result is not very useful to the practicing reliability engineer. Presumptively, a closed theory has been provided for the equilibrium state of a system composed of a finite number of identical components; additionally, the author has provided a lifetime description of the behavior of a system composed of an infinite number of identical components. In this latter case we still do not know how well this approximates a system with a large but finite number of components.

We are still left to somehow provide a closed form description of the behavior of systems in the nonequilibrium state. What is an appropriate way to describe that state? The discussion on renewal processes and the MTBF clearly show that this state cannot be characterized by an MTBF that changes with system age; the MTBF requires equilibrium to have meaning. Another possibility assumes the viability of adapting the MTTFF to the renewal process. This requires that the state of a system at any time t can be considered to be a random sampling of a hypothetical component time-to-failure distribution that represents the renewal history of all identical systems. If that hypothetical component time-to-failure distribution is represented as $\overline{rn}(t, u)$, the survivor function for such systems in the aggregate should be

$$\underline{fs}(t, u) = \left[\int_u^\infty \underline{rn}(t, x)\, dx \right]^M \tag{13.27}$$

In the above context the system is assumed to have M identical components and the survivor function is interpreted as that fraction of the aggregate of such systems surviving the interval $(t, t + u)$. The mean time to the next failure (MTTTNF) is therefore

$$\text{MTTTNF} = \int_0^\infty \left[\int_u^\infty \underline{rn}(t, x)\, dx \right]^M du \tag{13.28}$$

In the equilibrium state the MTTTNF must be the same as the MTBF, since the MTTTNF must be the same after each renewal (definition of equilibrium). This provides a connection between $rn(\infty, u)$, the time-to-failure distribution for the system in the equilibrium state defined after each renewal, and the time-between-failures distribution. Thus

$$\int_0^\infty \left[\int_u^\infty \underline{rn}(\infty, x)\, dx\right]^M du = \int_0^\infty \underline{fe}_s(v)\, dv$$

$$= \int_0^\infty \underline{fs}(v)\left[\frac{1}{\rho}\int_v^\infty \underline{fs}(u)\, du\right]^{M-1} dv$$

(13.29)

One solution of the above is

$$\left[\int_v^\infty \underline{rn}(\infty, x)\, dx\right]^M = \underline{fs}(v)\left[\frac{1}{\rho}\int_v^\infty \underline{fs}(x)\, dx\right]^{M-1}$$

(13.30)

Then

$$\underline{rn}(v) = \frac{-d}{dv}\left\{\underline{fs}(v)^{1/M}\left[\frac{1}{\rho}\int_v^\infty \underline{fs}(x)\, dx\right]^{1-1/M}\right\}$$

(13.31)

Returning to the entire time domain of renewal, the previous work provides two possibilities for consideration:

$$\left[\int_u^\infty \underline{rn}(t, x)\, dx\right]^M = \left[\int_u^\infty h(t, x)\, dx\right]^M$$

(13.32)

or

$$\left[\int_u^\infty \underline{rn}(t, x)\, dx\right]^M = \frac{h(t, u)}{h(t, 0)}\left[\int_u^\infty h(t, x)\, dx\right]^{M-1}$$

(13.33)

The right-hand side of equation (13.33), in the limit as t approaches infinity, becomes

$$\frac{h(\infty, u)}{h(\infty, 0)}\left[\int_u^\infty h(\infty, x)\, dx\right]^{M-1}$$

another way of writing equation (13.30).

The proposal of equation (13.32) gives proper results for t equal to zero, where $h(0, u)$ is $f(u)$, but becomes increasingly flawed, generally, as the system ages. The proposal of equation (13.33) agrees with the theory developed for the equilibrium state, but is flawed for the nonequilibrium state. As we shall see, there are conditions where one or both of these proposals are satisfactory, or at least not too far from such a happy state.

The exponential distribution again proves its remarkable mathematical convenience in that it trivializes the problem above; both equations (13.32) and (13.33) yield identical results in this case and $\underline{rn}(t, u)$ is $\lambda e^{-\lambda u}$. If the underlying distribution is a "one hoss shay" (narrow dispersion) type, the use of $h(t, u)$ for $\underline{rn}(t, u)$ works with complete satisfaction.

In the case of the uniform distribution the assumption of $h(t, u)$ for $\underline{rn}(t, u)$ provides the following survivor function at equilibrium:

$$\underline{fs}(\infty, u) = \left(1 - \frac{u}{L}\right)^{2M} \tag{13.34}$$

On the other hand, assuming equation (13.31), which gives the correct result for the equilibrium state, gives

$$\underline{fs}(\infty, u) = \left(1 - \frac{u}{L}\right)^{2M-1} \tag{13.35}$$

Thus, if M is sufficiently large, the assumption of $h(t, u)$ for $\underline{rn}(t, u)$ will be quite satisfactory in the case of the uniform distribution. These examples clearly show that the nature of the underlying distribution plays a major role in determining the suitability of the two proposals above.

Lacking a suitable situation, there is still a fallback, $h(t, 0)$. Recalling that the average number of failures per unit time is $Mh(t, 0)$ in an M component system, $h(t, 0)$ may be used as a measure of the density of renewals (failures) throughout system life. It gives the correct result in all cases of the equilibrium state, M/ρ failures per unit time, but is flawed at time zero except in the case of the exponential distribution. For example, $Mh(0, 0)$ for the uniform distribution is M/L; the reciprocal of the MTTFF is $(M + 1)/L$. The difference is negligible for large values of M, but substantial when M is equal to unity. These flaws, however, are minor in the context of understanding the behavior of systems. Although the discussion has so far only considered continuous distributions, it also holds good for discrete distributions; the trend measure is $h(t_n, u_1)$ in this instance. This is a most useful result, since computer solutions for $h(t_n, u_1)$ are conveniently available.

Figure 13.1 illustrates the use of the density function $h(t, 0)$ for forecasting the general behavior of systems with more than one kind of compo-

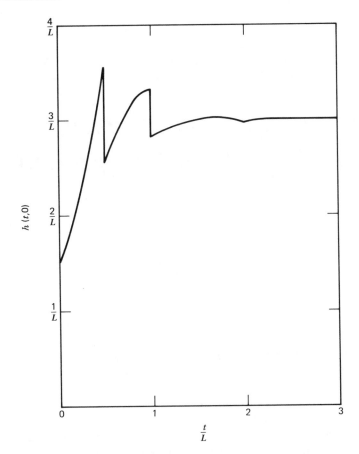

Figure 13.1 Theoretical renewal density function $h(t, 0)$ for a system composed of equal number of components of two kinds from continuous, uniform distributions with unequal lifetimes.

nent. The graph represents the equivalent density function for a system of equal numbers of components from two distinct uniform distributions, one having twice the life of the other. For convenience the illustration is plotted in terms of the life of the longer lived components.

CHAPTER FOURTEEN

Monte Carlo Simulation Systems of One Component Kind

14.1 NUMBER OF FAILURES AND TIME-BETWEEN-FAILURES ONLY

This basic system simulation is one that manufactures a new system, ages it to failure, repairs it, ages it to failure again, repairs it, and so on, while keeping track of the system age, the total number of failures, and the ratio of the total time to the total failures at each renewal cycle. Implementation requires a means of generating random numbers, uniform, normal, exponential, or other, as required. The system is itself implemented as a shift register in a computer, a register with the same number of memory positions as time cells in the underlying distribution. The time cell duration t is taken as unity; this is natural to computer simulation, simple, and does not restrict the results in any manner.

The manufacture of a new system of M parts is the process by which M random numbers of the desired sort are generated and stored in the appropriate positions of the shift register. This is most easily explained by example. Let us consider a 20 time cell distribution and the random numbers from 1 through 20. Delineate the sequence of positions in the shift register correspondingly, 1 through 20. Assume the first number generated is 16; sum 1 into position 16 of the shift register. Given that the next number is 8; sum 1 into position 8. Suppose the next number is 16; sum 1 into position 16. At this point in the proceedings position 8 contains a 1, position 16 a 2, and all the others, 0. The process is continued until M random numbers have been generated and stored by the process given above. Manufacture is now complete and the sum of the contents of the shift register positions is M.

To age the new system by a unit interval the shift register is shifted once in the decreasing sense of the position index, that is, the contents of all positions are simultaneously moved such that the contents of 20 go to 19, 19 to 18, and so on. This dumps the contents of position 1. The contents are examined: if zero, no failure has occurred after one time unit of system life; if nonzero, component failures have occurred equal in number to the number dumped. In either case, 1 is summed into a memory location which is the repository of system age, the number of failures is summed into another memory location which holds the total number of component failures. If failure has occurred, the system age, the total number of component failures, and the ratio of the age to the total number of component failures are reported to be followed by system repair. Repair is accomplished by generating a random number for each failed component and summing 1's into the shift register in the appropriate manner; the sum of the shift register contents will be M again after repair. If no failure has occurred, there is no reporting and no repair. The system is now aged another single time unit, the dump examined, and the appropriate actions repeated.

The time between system failures is the number of agings between successive system failures, regardless of the number of component failures involved in each system failure. This may be determined by inspection of records or calculated and reported by the computer. Thus the basic mechanization gives the time between system failures, the number of component failures at each system failure, the system age, the total component failures, and the ratio of the system time to the total number of component failures; it does not provide information on the time-to-failure distribution at various stages in system life or the time-between-failures distribution. Additional mechanization must be provided for the acquisition of such information.

14.2 IMPLEMENTING ADDITIONAL FEATURES

Monte Carlo simulation enables us to explore the behavior of real systems. It will allow the determination of the time-to-failure distribution of the system components following equilibrium, the same distribution at a given system age prior to equilibrium, or the distribution corresponding to the renewal just following a specific system age. When the system component count is sufficiently large such that the contents of the system shift register (basic mechanization) fairly represent the underlying distribution, these distributions may be determined by reading the shift register contents in the basic scheme of Section 14.1.

To determine these and other distributions when the component count is small one must sum samples of the distribution of interest. This requires that the elements in the summation are indeed samples of the same distribution. By definition, successive renewal states of a single system in equilibrium must be samples of the equilibrium distribution whether it be the time-to-failure or the time-between-failures distribution. Prior to equilibrium, however, this scheme of summing successive states of a single system will not do, since the distribution is in constant change. Instead, one must sum the distributions of a large number of identical systems of the same age or, perhaps, the renewal state immediately following a given age. The simulated identical systems for this purpose cannot be based on an identical sequence of random numbers but must be based on different samples of the random number distribution.

A computer mechanization that allows the summation of successive postequilibrium samples requires the addition of two registers to the basic system. Neither is a shift register: one is used to contain the sum of the samplings of the system shift register; the other, the samplings of the time-between-failures distribution. The system for investigating pre-equilibrium behavior requires only one additional register over the basic system: a register to contain the sum of the samples of the time-to-failure distribution. In this case systems are manufactured and aged, the contents of the system shift register summed into the storage register, and the systems discarded. The output is the summation of all of the distribution samples. Programs for the basic postequilibrium and pre-equilibrium simulations are provided in the Appendix.

14.3   1000 COMPONENT SYSTEM FROM A UNIFORM DISTRIBUTION WITH 20 TIME CELLS

A thousand components, with an average of 50 per time cell, should provide uniformity to within 50 ± 14; Figure 14.1, the system time-to-failure distribution just after manufacture, shows extremes of 66 and 39, rather good agreement. This is an excellent example of the tyranny of large numbers; to improve this by a factor of five, to get 50 ± 3, would require 25,000 components!

Figure 14.2 graphs the density function $h(n, 1)$; its completion required the total generation of about 6500 random numbers, including manufacture. This graph should be compared with the corresponding plot in Figure 12.4, the theoretical $h(n, 1)$ for a uniform distribution of 20 time cells. The comparison of ordinates can be made by recognizing that L of Figure 12.4 is 20.

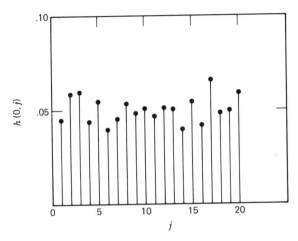

Figure 14.1 As manufactured distribution of 1000 components from a uniform discrete distribution with 20 time cells.

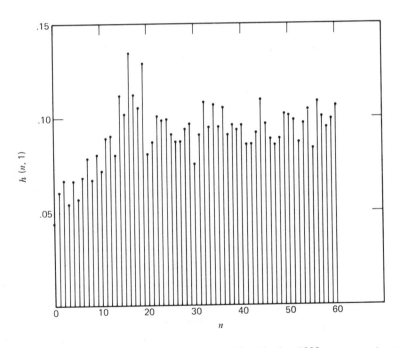

Figure 14.2 Actual renewal density function $h(n, 1)$ of a 1000 component system from a uniform discrete distribution with 20 time cells.

183

The similarity is striking, dispite the variability due to the tyranny of large numbers.

Figures 14.3, 14.4, and 14.5 are graphs of the system time-to-failure distributions $h(14, j)$, $h(19, j)$, and an essential equilibrium distribution $h(60, j)$, respectively. Direct comparison with Figures 12.5, 12.6, and 12.7, the corresponding theoretical distributions, shows the similarity.

Some vital statistics are notable. The theoretical MTTF of a uniform time-to-failure distribution of 20 time cells is 10.5; with 1000 components the theoretical ratio of the total time to the total number of failures is 0.0105 in the equilibrium state. The actual result during the last 20 time units of the simulation was 0.01053! The total of all findings and comparisons certainly indicate that for the uniform distribution, at least, and a minimum of about 50 components per time cell, an adequate description of system behavior is given by Mh (t_n, u_j).

14.4 EQUILIBRIUM BEHAVIOR OF A TWO COMPONENT SYSTEM FROM A UNIFORM DISTRIBUTION WITH 20 TIME CELLS

The previous arguments and the simulation of Section 14.3 indicate that a reasonable theory is available for systems containing a large number of com-

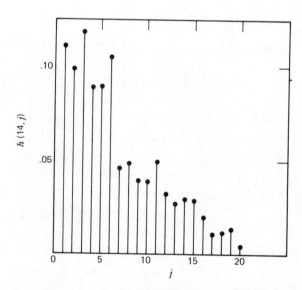

Figure 14.3 Actual forward recurrence time distribution $h(14, j)$ of a 1000 component system from a uniform discrete distribution with 20 time cells.

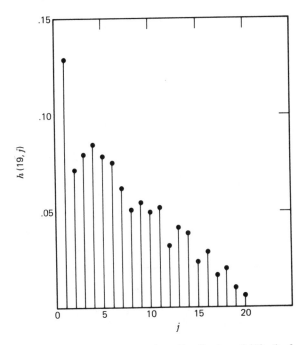

Figure 14.4   Actual forward recurrence time distribution, $h(19, j)$ of a 1000 component system from a uniform discrete distribution with 20 time cells.

ponents. It appears that the greatest theoretical difficulties occur between the ordinary renewal process, a one component system, and systems of a few components. The test of theory with greatest rigor, therefore, should be the simulation of a two component system. This simulation has been run for the equilibrium state, given a discrete uniform distribution with 20 time cells. The computer mechanization used provided for summing both the system time-to failure and the time-between-failures distributions. The experiment was run by first aging the system for a time that essentially guarantees a steady state for the uniform distribution, erasing all summations and calculations of the MTBF and so on for that period, and starting again with the retention of only the system time-to-failure distribution at that age. The system was then run in the equilibrium state for enough successive renewals to provide 1000 failures and the summations taken.

The resulting experimental data agreed remarkably with the theory developed for discrete distributions. First, with respect to sheer numerical results the ratio of the total time to the total number of failures was 5.31, versus a theoretical 5.25. The MTBF was 5.65, versus a theoretical 5.51 [see equation (13.22)]. If the ratio of the total time to the total number of failures,

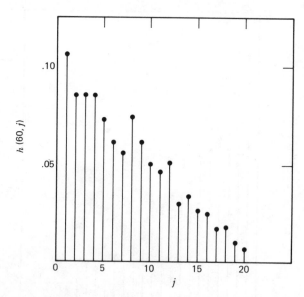

Figure 14.5 Actual forward recurrence time distribution $h(60, j)$ age 60 (equilibrium), of a 1000 component system from a uniform discrete distribution with 20 time cells.

5.31, is used as indicative of the real MTTF of the distribution, then the MTBF is theoretically 5.57, versus the actual 5.65.

The most remarkable results have to do with the distributions recorded. Figure 14.6 is the time-between-failures distribution derived from summation; Figure 14.7 is the system time-to-failure distribution recorded. Figure 14.8 is the analog survivor function constructed from the data shown in Figure 14.6. It is determined from

$$\underline{f}e_s(v_j) = 1 - \sum_{K=1}^{j} b(v_k) \qquad j = 0, 1, \ldots, L \qquad (14.1)$$

As expected, the sum of the terms, the MTBF, is 5.65. Figure 14.9 is the system survivor function constructed from the data in Figure 14.7, the actual summed component system time-to-failure distribution. It was determined from

$$\underline{f}s_s(u_j) = \left[1 - \sum_{K=1}^{j} rn(\infty, u_k) \right]^2 \qquad j = 0, 1, \ldots, L \qquad (14.2)$$

The sum of the terms is 5.68! This is a remarkable demonstration of equation (13.27). The correspondence of Figures 14.8 and 14.9 demonstrates the ap-

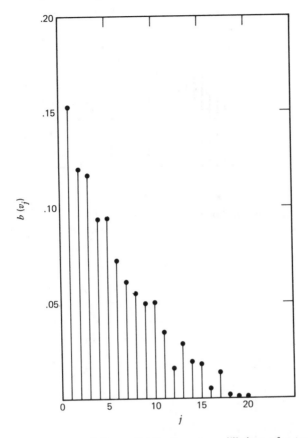

Figure 14.6 Time-between-failures distribution at equilibrium of a two component system from a uniform discrete distribution with 20 time cells.

plicability of equation (13.29). The identity of the survivor functions can only come about if equation (13.29) is a correct solution. Figure 14.10, the theoretical plot of fe_s (v_j) based on equation (13.16), completes the trio of survivor function graphs. The remarkable correspondence of the data in Figures 14.8, 14.9, and 14.10 is almost embarrassing.

14.5 EQUILIBRIUM BEHAVIOR OF A TWO COMPONENT SYSTEM FROM A UNIFORM DISTRIBUTION WITH TWO TIME CELLS

The best test of equation (13.22), the equilibrium MTBF for the discrete case, is a simulation that enhances the difference between the MTBF and

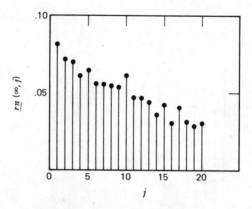

Figure 14.7 Summed component time-to-failure distribution at equilibrium of a two component system from a uniform discrete distribution with 20 time cells.

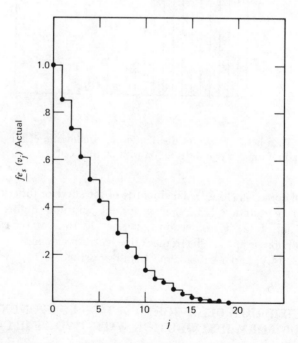

Figure 14.8 Analog survivor function corresponding to Figure 14.6.

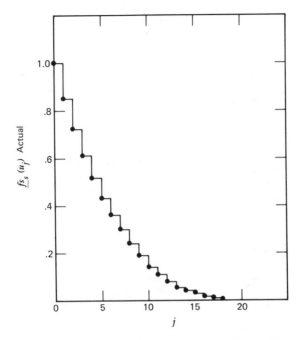

Figure 14.9   System survivor function corresponding to Figure 14.7.

ρ/M, the ratio of the total time to the total number of failures. That simulation is a two component system based on a two cell distribution. For this case and the uniform distribution the theoretical value for the MTBF is 1.125, and for $\rho/2$, 0.75. The results of a simulation involving 600 consecutive renewals were 1.15 and 0.75, respectively. This should be satisfactory affirmation of the difference between the MTBF and ρ/M for discrete distributions.

14.6 NONEQUILIBRIUM BEHAVIOR OF A TWO COMPONENT SYSTEM FROM A UNIFORM DISTRIBUTION WITH 20 TIME CELLS

The simulation employed in this investigation provided for the summation of the system time-to-failure distributions of independent renewal processes of the same kind and of the same age. As an additional feature, the simulation also provided the means for summing such distributions following the first renewal subsequent to the chosen system age.

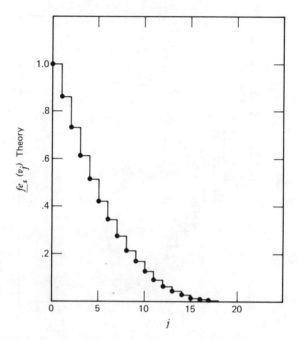

Figure 14.10   Theoretical analog survivor function at equilibrium for a two component system from a uniform discrete distribution with 20 time cells.

Figure 14.11 is the outcome of of a simulation of independent system renewals to a given age. The underlying distribution was discrete uniform, with 20 time cells; systems consisted of two components. The data represents a summation over 500 independent system renewal sequences, 14 time units in age. Figure 14-11 should be compared with Figure 12.5, the theoretical $h(14,j)$, and Figure 14.3, the time-to-failure distribution for the 1000 component system at age 14. As far as one may determine, the distribution of Figure 14.11 corresponds to $h(14, j)$ and is so labeled.

Figure 14.12 is a record of the same sequence of renewals as that for Figure 14.11 except that the distribution was summed not at age 14 but immediately after the renewal just following age 14. The data indicates that the average time of renewal was 14.8; as a result one might expect that the summed distribution might correspond to $h(15, j)$. Figure 14.12 indicates that this may be the case; it looks like the distribution of Figure 14.11 aged by one time unit. This simulation was performed to see the effect of summing distributions at the first renewal following a specific age, compared to summing at a given age. The effect was not great in this experiment and it

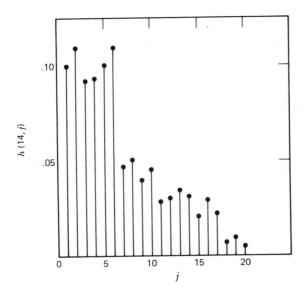

Figure 14.11 Summation of the forward recurrence time distribution $h(14, j)$ over 500 independent two component systems based on a component uniformly discrete distribution with 20 time cells.

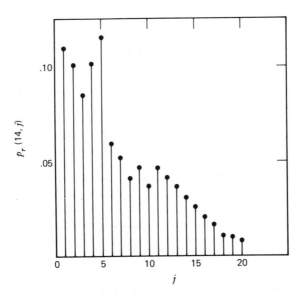

Figure 14.12 Summation of the forward recurrence time distribution at the first renewal following age 14 over 500 independent two component systems; the underlying component distribution for all systems is uniformly discrete with 20 time cells.

becomes increasingly smaller as the number of system components is increased.

14.7 SIMULATING THE BEHAVIOR OF EXPONENTIAL SYSTEMS

Theory indicates that systems composed of many kinds of components described by exponential distributions behave like a single component drawn

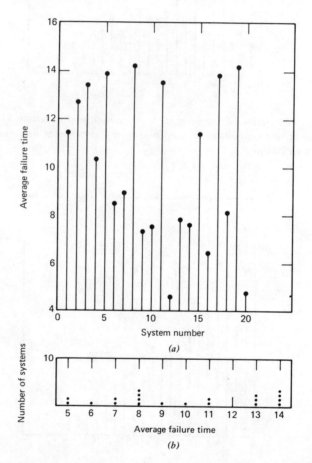

(a)

(b)

Figure 14.13 Behavior of systems constructed with components obeying the exponential distribution: (*a*) average time per failure plotted against system number; (*b*) histogram of average failure times.

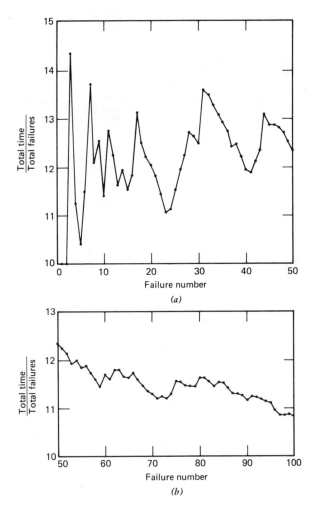

Figure 14.14 Behavior of a single system constructed with components obeying the exponential distribution: (a) ratio of total time to total failures at failure numbers 1 to 50; (b) ratio of total time to total failures for failure numbers 50 to 100; (c) ratio of total time to total failures for failure numbers 100 to 150; (d) ratio of total time to total failures for failure numbers 150 to 200.

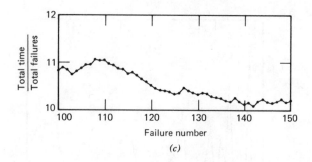

(c)

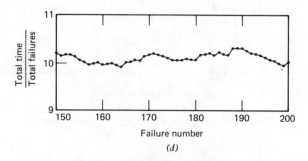

Failure number

(d)

Figure 14.14   Continued

from an exponential distribution. That single component distribution is of the form

$$\lambda e^{-\lambda t}$$

where

$$\lambda = \sum_{K=1}^{j} \lambda_k M_k$$

for a system of M_k exponential components of each kinds. Accordingly, the renewal behavior of any kind of system composed of exponential components is equivalent to the behavior of an ordinary renewal process based on the exponential distribution.

Figures 14.13, 14.14a, and 14.14b summarize the results. There were generated 200 consecutive random exponential numbers for λ equal to 0.1. These were treated as 20 independent systems, sequentially aged for 10 renewals and as a single system aged for 200 renewals. Figure 14.13a shows the point estimates of the system MTBFs (total time to total failures ratio) as they occurred in sequence. Figure 14.13*b* is a histogram of this same data aggregated into unit intervals centered on integral values of time units. These estimates vary by about 3 to 1 and are not clustered at the theoretical MTBF, 10. This is indicative of the futility of estimating or demonstrating MTBFs in exponentially based systems on the basis of a few failures.

Figures 14.14*a*, *b*, *c*, and *d* illustrate another fact of life with respect to determining the MTBF. In this particular experiment it took 120 renewals before the MTBF estimate came within 6% of the known theoretical value. Even at 200 renewals, however, the estimate still fluctuates appreciably about the theoretical value. In view of the fact that the support for the exponential description depends on the existence of the bottom of a bathtub curve, is the duration of that bottom sufficient to determine the MTBF of such a system?

CHAPTER FIFTEEN

Monte Carlo Investigation of Systems Based on Normal Distributions

15.1 INTRODUCTION

Narrow dispersion distributions such as normal distributions are considered to be characteristic of components that fail owing to wearout; in particular, it is thought that mechanical components behave in this fashion. Systems of components that behave according to such distributions are largely ignored in the literature; even mechanical parts of electronic systems are treated as though their descriptive distributions were exponential. The conventional approach to mechanical reliability has been in terms of factors of safety; this is not probabilistic nor does it in any way provide a time history of the failure process. Relatively recent probabilistic approaches to mechanical reliability are also deficient in providing a time history but do define a probability of failure.

There is no basic theoretical reason why mechanical components must be treated uniquely with respect to a theory of reliability; basic theory applies given appropriate distributions describing the components. Although it is possible to argue about the nature of the distributions that properly models wearout, one may safely say that precise data to settle the argument does not exist; furthermore, precise details will have practically no effect on the gross behavior of systems and gross behavior is all that one should expect from theory.

Accordingly, this text will assume the modified normal distribution to be an adequate model, modified in the sense that probabilities for negative time are not permitted, and in the Monte Carlo case the distribution will be discrete and have a finite number of time cells. This latter constraint eliminates the infinite positive tails of the distribution. Care must be taken in the discrete case, of course, to pick the model so that there is little probability of occurrence beyond the last time cell. This requires that the mean be located relative to the field of the discrete distribution such that the sum of the mean and two standard deviations does not fall beyond the last time cell. As far as system behavior is concerned, however, only one parameter is critical: the ratio of the mean to the standard deviation. Thus the absolute values of the mean and the standard deviation have only to do with the mechanics of the simulation.

15.2 THE 50 TIME CELL NORMAL DISTRIBUTION WITH MEAN 40 AND STANDARD DEVIATION 4

The above distribution has been simulated using a computer program described in the Appendix. Figure 15.1 is the distribution one obtains from the first 1000 samples of the simulation for a normal distribution with mean 40 and standard deviation 4. Its general shape and magnitudes grossly approximate the underlying distribution; 1000 samples are insufficient to discover a smooth approximation.

Figure 15.2 displays an ordinary renewal process (one component system) based on the distribution of Figure 15.1. The graphic format displays time-between-failures versus the failure (renewal) number. It is actually a display of the first 80 numbers of the normal distribution routine for the parameters of Figure 15.1. The actual mean after 40 failures is 39.7. The figure displays an equilibrium state: the fluctuations about the constant time between failures (TBF) exceeds the two σ limits only once.

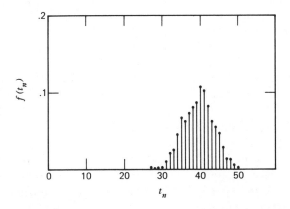

Figure 15.1 Computer generated discrete normal distribution: first 1000 samples; mean, 40; standard deviation, 4.

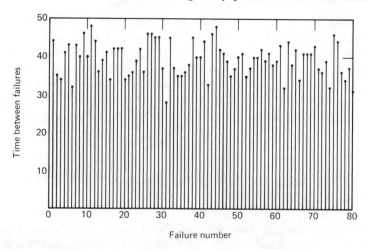

Figure 15.2   Ordinary renewal process based on a discrete normal distribution with mean 40 and standard deviation 4.

15.3   A TWO COMPONENT SYSTEM FROM A NORMAL DISTRIBUTION WITH MEAN 40 AND STANDARD DEVIATION 4

Figures 15.3*a* and *b* display the renewal behavior of this system for the first 180 failures. The infrequent double failures are treated by ascribing the time since the last failure to one of the failures, the other is considered to occur with zero delay. The behavior is startling; the previous development of renewal theory fosters the notion that the renewal process must ultimately produce an equilibrium state, regardless of the distribution and the component count. This view of an equilbrium state is more than the notion that $h(t, o)$ will approach the limiting value ρ/M; it also includes the concept of an approximate regularity in time between failures that persists indefinitely once equilibrium has been reached. Figure 15.3*a* indicates that such an equilibrium state has been reached by about the 40th failure; it does not persist beyond the 60th failure, however. At this point the system behavior returns to the behavior expected, initially, from a new system: the equilibrium state is unstable. This state of affairs is repeated again and again, but the duration of the two phases varies.

As a check on the hypothesis that Figures 15.3*a* and *b* do actually show the system achieving equilibrium and then losing it, an experiment was conducted in which the system was configured in its equilibrium state at the start, rather than manufacturing the system with the first two samples of the random normal numbers. This experiment was based on the fact that instant

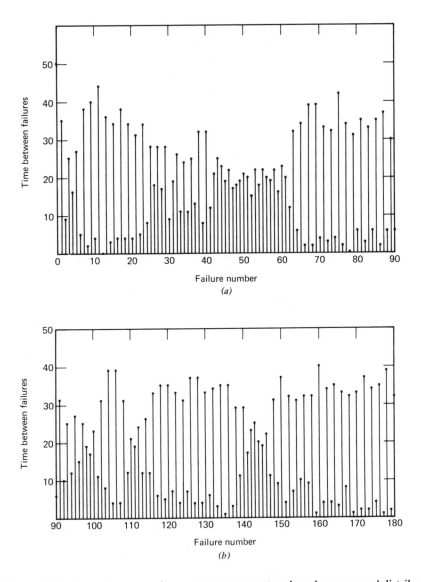

Figure 15.3 Renewal process of a two component system based on a normal distribution with mean 40 and standard deviation 4: (*a*) failure number from 0 to 90; (*b*) failure number from 90 to 180.

equilibrium is achieved for the forward recurrence time distribution if the starting distribution duplicates the equilibrium state.

The initial equilibrium state of the system was achieved by configuring it with one component with life 20 and one component with life 40. The result is shown in Figure 15.4: the equilibrium state is very short lived. Inasmuch as these experiments are conducted with the same sequence of pseudorandom normal numbers each time, behavior may be compared by properly superimposing figures. The superposition of Figure 15.4 upon Figure 15.3*a*, making due allowance for the first two failures due to the equilibrium starting distribution, shows identity to Figure 15.3*a* following failure two in that figure, except for a random fluctuation of two time units in the time between failures. The above result would seem to confirm the hypothesis.

15.4 THEORY AND EXPERIMENT: EQUILIBRIUM STABILITY

The behavior noted is illustrative of the gulf between probability theories that really deal only in large numbers and those that deal with the behavior of systems of small numbers. It is possible, however, to explain the instability noted in Section 15.3. Prior to this explanation the manner of providing a starting equilibrium must be developed. We already know that the MTBF of any system is ρ/M, regardless of the distribution or parts count. Ideally the

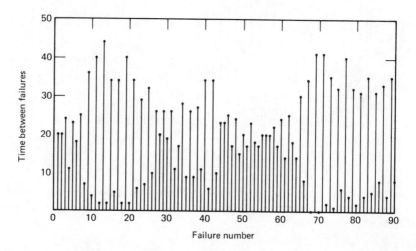

Figure 15.4 Renewal process with equilibrium start, of a two component system from a discrete normal distribution with mean 40 and standard deviation 4.

equilibrium distribution should produce one failure each ρ/M time units. Accordingly, the ideal equilibrium distribution for the simulation under investigation is a component in the 20th time cell and one in the 40th time cell; this provides a spacing of ρ/M, 20.

Aging the system by 20 time units causes one failure and leaves the system with one component in the 20th time cell. Assume that the repair component, randomly drawn, has a life of 48 time units, the mean plus 2σ. The repaired system now has components in the 20th and 48th time cells. After 20 more time units a failure occurs and leaves the system with one component in the 28th time cell. Assume the replacement component has a life of 32 time units, the mean minus 2σ. The system now has components in the 28th and 32nd time cells. After 28 time units another failure occurs, leaving one component in the fourth time cell. Assume the repair component has a life of 48 time units; the system now has components in the 4th and 48th time cells. After the next failure, four time units later, assume that the repair component has a life of 44 units; the system now has two components in the 44th time cell: the next failure, 44 time units later, will be a double failure. Had this repair component occurred with a life of 42, an overlap would have occurred and components would have been located in the 42nd and 44th time cells.

The scenario above is typical of what happens. Intuitively, one would expect that stability must depend on the ratio of ρ/M to σ. An analysis of the behavior of the first two renewals of a system starting in equilibrium yields conditions for avoiding overlap (insuring equilibrium stability) that do depend on this ratio. The only condition that will avoid an overlap at the first renewal is

$$\rho/M > j\sigma$$

where the repair component has a life of $\rho - j\sigma$, with j greater than zero. The value for j,3, virtually guarantees stability; 2 runs some small risk of instability, and 1 virtually guarantees instability.

A condition that avoids overlap at the second and first renewals, given that the life of the first repair component is $\rho + j\sigma$ and the life of the second is $\rho - j\sigma$, is

$$\rho/M > 2j\sigma$$

No other sequence of these lifetimes produces instability. Thus ρ/M greater than 6σ virtually guarantees stability for two renewals (M plus two failures) after an equilibrium start.

The analysis for three and more renewals becomes so complex that one must resort to experimental methods to determine the condition for stability. The experimental approach was a series of two component renewal processes based on a normal distribution with mean 40 and a series of standard deviations. Figure 15.5a displays the behavior of such a two component system with an equilibrium start and a standard deviation of 2. Figure 15.5b is identical, except that the standard deviation is 1. Figures 15.6a and b are the corresponding processes for a nonequilibrium start. It is quite clear that, unlike the situation portrayed by Figures 15.3 and 15.4, the equilibrium state definitely persists over 30 failures when the standard deviation is 1, and it may persist for the case of the standard deviation equal to 2. In fact, a simulation run for a standard deviation of 2½ definitely shows that 2 is very likely the borderline case. This one investigation, therefore, indicates that equilibrium stability, in the sense employed in this chapter, requires ρ/M to exceed 10σ.

Despite the logic of the scenario explaining equilibrium instability, the reader may wonder whether the results of the simulation represent a fortuitous sequence of random normal numbers. Now the region between the 45th and 60th failures in Figure 15.3a suggests a region in the random normal number sequence where the variations from the mean are fortuitously limited. This suggestion is confirmed by Figure 15.2. Accordingly, one might expect that a simulation starting at the 45th random normal number in the

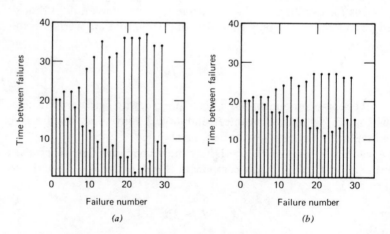

Figure 15.5 Renewal process, with equilibrium start, of a two component system from a discrete normal distribution with mean 40 and standard deviation (a) 2; (b) 1.

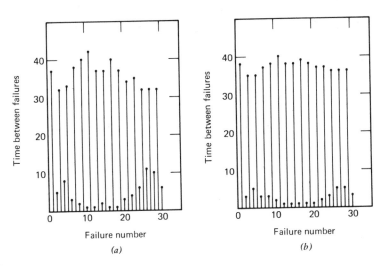

Figure 15.6 Renewal process of a random start of a two component system from a discrete normal distribution with mean 40 and standard deviation (a) 2; (b) 1.

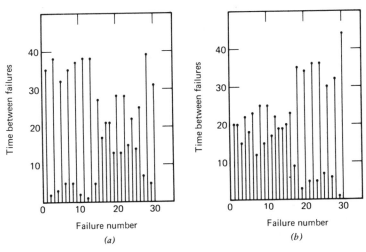

Figure 15.7 Renewal process of a two component system from a discrete normal distribution with mean 40, standard deviation 4, and an altered random number sequence: (a) random start; (b) equilibrium start.

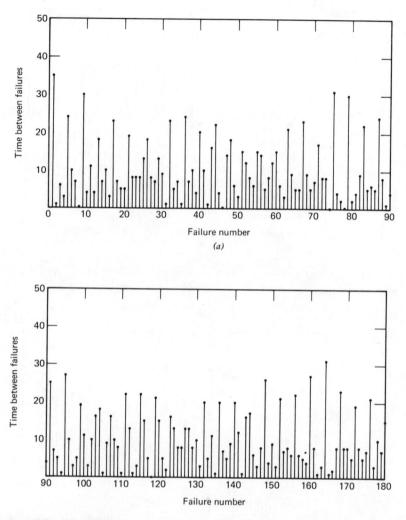

Figure 15.8 Renewal process of a four component system from a discrete normal distribution with mean 40 and standard deviation 4: (*a*) failure number from 0 to 90; (*b*) failure number from 90 to 180.

sequence would behave as though the standard deviation were smaller than it actually was, at least until the 60th random normal number is encountered. the first half of Figure 15.7*b* with Figure 15.5*b* confirms the expectation. The Figure 15.7*a* displays the first 30 failures for the two-part system with non-equilibrium start, and Figure 15.7*b* shows the corresponding equilibrium start. A comparison of the first half of Figure 15.7*a* with Figure 15.6*b* and

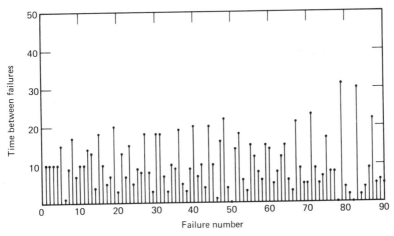

Figure 15.9 Renewal process of a four component system from a discrete normal distribution with mean 40 and standard deviation 4 with equilibrium start.

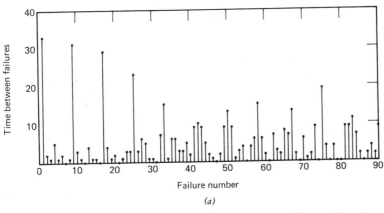

(a)

Figure 15.10 Renewal process of an eight component system from a discrete normal distribution with mean 40 and standard deviation 4: (*a*) failure number from 0 to 90; (*b*) failure number from 90 to 180.

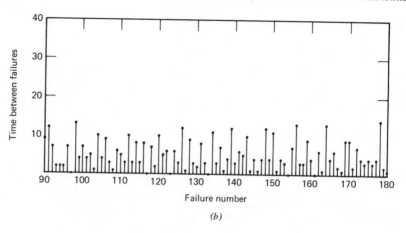

(b)

Figure 15.10   Continued

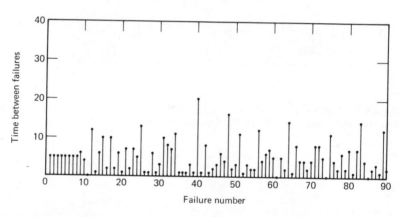

Figure 15.11   Renewal process of an eight component system from a discrete normal distribution with mean 40 and standard deviation 4, with equilibrium start.

emergence from this fortuitously quiet sequence of random normals at about the 15th failure rapidly produces the instability already noted in previous simulations.

15.5   THE EFFECT OF INCREASED COMPONENT COUNT

The next series of figures hold the mean at 40 and the standard deviation at 4, but increase the component count. This increase has the effect of decreasing ρ/M and should further increase instability. Figures 15.8a and b show the nonequilibrium start sequence for four components; Figure 15.9 shows the result of an equilibrium start. Finally, Figures 15.10a,b, and 15.11 display the corresponding simulations for eight components. The clear cut behavior shown by the two component system tends to become blurred as the component count increases; certainly, equilibrium instability is very much in evidence.

These results lead to the troubling conclusion that equilibrium and a large component count are mutually exlcusive, at least in the sense of equilibrium being a sequence of time-between-failures contained between the limits of 0 and 2 ρ/M without overlap. This does not violate the notion that the ratio of the total time to the total number of failures must eventually be ρ/M, however. Resorting to renewal theory based on discrete, finite distributions cannot illuminate the problem; systems based on such distributions always show an equilibrium state if the component count is sufficiently large: the time between failures becomes the duration of the first time cell. This conclusion, if correct, leads to the prediction that equilibrium in systems with a large number of components will show considerable variation of the time-between-failures relative to the MTBF.

CHAPTER SIXTEEN

An Assortment of Interesting Topics

16.1 AIRCRAFT ENGINE MAINTENANCE AND SAFETY STRATEGIES

No sensible discussion of aircraft engine maintenance and safety strategies is possible without valid data on the failure behavior of both new and zero-time overhaul engines. The MTTFF (mean time to first failure) is required in each case, as well as the standard deviation about that mean. Valid data is defined as data that conforms to a high confidence, statistically speaking; this means very large test samples or exceedingly conservative one-sided estimates.

Assuming that such data is available, it is customary to attempt the discovery of the underlying distribution. Since this would require more data than is realistically available, assumptions and fits of typical distributions are the usual approach. On the assumptions that the time-to-failure behavior is that of wearout, assumptions of normal or Weibull distributions would be typical, one would resort to the use of "goodness of fit" criteria and a chosen distribution. If this determination is treated solely as an exercise in statistical arithmetic, it will be replete with chi-square statistics and exquisite precision.

It has been a major premise of this book to temper statistical concepts with reality when dealing with reliability; this is based on the assumption that reliability theory should deal with the real world and not be treated as a purely arithmetic exercise. The previous chapter dealt with Monte Carlo simulations of situations that can have a direct bearing on the subject of aircraft engine replacement strategies; those simulations assumed a normal distribution. Figure 15.1 displays the actual distribution derived from 1000 samples of a typical normal distribution. Despite the symmetry of the underlying distribution and the large sample size, this display is obviously asymmetrical and lumpy. From a purely statistical point of view an analyst might argue that an asymmetric distribution might fit better than a normal one, given the absence of any a priori information.

To examine the consequences of the details of the fit of an assumed distribution another Monte Carlo simulation was performed in which the assumed distribution differed substantially from the normal. The actual distribution determined from 1000 samples of this distribution is shown in Figure 16.1. The distribution is a uniform narrow dispersion with mean 40 and standard deviation 4.33. Although the author wished to duplicate the standard deviation of the normal distribution, the discrete nature of the distribution made it impossible to hold the same mean and standard deviation; the choice was mean 39 and standard deviation 4, or mean 40 and standard deviation 4.33.

Figures 16.2a,b, and 16.3 are to be compared with Figures 15.3a,b, and 15.4. These are all renewal processes for two component systems, differing only in the underlying distributions. Considering the fact that there would be differences even if they all corresponded to identical underlying distributions, there is considerable gross similarity in these renewal processes. Although the uniform narrow dispersion distribution should be less prone to equilibrium instability, it can be seen that both distributions produce instability. The obvious conclusion is that concern over minor details of an underlying distribution is unwarranted insofar as renewal behavior is concerned; the mean and the standard deviation are the important parameters. These should suffice for the discussion of aircraft engine replacement.

The single engine aircraft case is almost trivial. Failure cannot be tolerated in flight, takeoff, or landing. The only reasonable strategy is

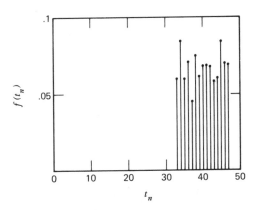

Figure 16.1 Computer generated discrete uniform narrow dispersion distribution, first 1000 samples, with mean 40 and standard deviation 4.33.

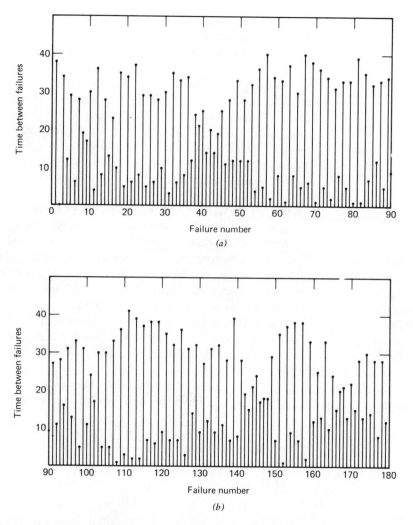

Figure 16.2 Renewal process of a two component system from a discrete uniform narrow dispersion distribution with mean 40 and standard deviation 4.33: (*a*) failure number from 0 to 90; (*b*) failure number from 90 to 180.

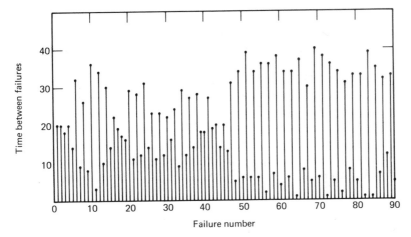

Figure 16.3 Renewal process, with equilibrium start, of a two component system from a discrete uniform narrow dispersion distribution with mean 40 and standard deviation 4.33.

replacement at least 3σ prior to the MTTFF, assuming that these parameters are well known for both new and zero-time overhaul engines.

Multiengine aircraft are another story. Well designed multiengine aircraft are capable of acceptable performance with one engine out on a two and three engine aircraft and perhaps even two engines out on a four engine aircraft. There is no question that safety is well served by following the single engine replacement strategy on multiengine aircraft; it is rather a drastic strategy, however, from an economic standpoint. From a pure workload point of view, ignoring workload leveling in the shop, the most economic approach is engine replacement on failure, that is, a renewal process. But safety is served with this strategy only if the probability of simultaneous or near simultaneous failure is very small. The best guarantee of such a state is an equilibrium state, that is, that the forward recurrence times of the engines are equally spaced.

The experiments of Chapter Fifteen showed that an equilibrium state, once established, will be maintained in a renewal process only if the dispersion of the underlying distribution is very small compared to ρ/M. If this criterion can be validly established, the equilibrium state may be easily established. Given a new twin engine aircraft, one engine is replaced by a new engine or its equivalent when the aircraft has operated for a time $\rho/2$. Thereafter engines are replaced by new engines or their equivalent whenever engine failures occur. The engine removed with half its life still available may be used to outfit some other aircraft, a new one, for instance. A similar but more complex scheme may be used for three and four engine aircraft to establish the equilibrium state. Note that all of the engines, original equipment, and replacement must have the same time-to-failure characteristics for this scheme to work. This is why knowledge of overhauled engines is also required. If these behave like new engines, there is no problem; if they do not, the surprising conclusion is that only overhauls should be used in this scheme.

The more likely situation is a standard deviation that will not maintain equilibrium. Maintaining safety in this situation will require extensive record keeping and frequent reestablishment of the equilibrium state; this implies removal of unfailed engines each time equilibrium is reestablished.

16.2 A MAINTENANCE STRATEGY FOR LIGHT BULB REPLACEMENT

This section addresses itself to the maintenance of general lighting in large buildings. There is seldom a requirement to replace lamps in general lighting fixtures on a failure by failure basis. Accordingly, failures (multiple, usually) may be replaced on a periodic basis, the period being generally less than the mean life of the lamps. The most desirable situation is one in which the number failing per period is roughly constant. This implies the equilibrium state.

The assumption of periodic replacements, recognition of failure only in discrete time cells, is perfectly suited to the behavior of discrete distributions. Preceding portions of this book have demonstrated that the behavior of a system with a very large component count (general lighting is such a system) will closely approximate Mh $(n, 1)$ failures per time cell. Accordingly, the ideal maintenance strategy is the establishment of the equilibrium state, since this implies roughly equal failures per time cell (replacement period). There is general agreement that lamp bulbs behave normally with an essentially narrow dispersion; this in turn implies an unacceptably long time to equilibrium. Thus the attainment of the desirable maintenance state requires the forcing of a rapid establishment of equilibrium.

This is similar to the strategy suggested for aircraft engines, but the large numbers and low unit cost of lamps preclude a deterministic attack on the problem; what is needed is a way to make the system help in the matter. The proposed forcing method for equilibrium is based on the knowledge that the periodic number of failures in the equilibrium state will be roughly Mt/ρ, where $\underline{t}$ is the replacement period. The scheme for forcing equilibrium requires that from the beginning at least Mt/ρ replacements be made each period, even if this requires replacing good lamps as well as failed lamps. The good lamps taken out of service are not discarded but are subsequently used as replacements with an admixture of new lamps from stock as the scheme is continued. It is expected that equilibrium will be established within roughly the lamp lifetime and will be signalled by a marginal requirement to replace good lamps. Thereafter replacement of lamps will be on failure only.

16.3 TIRE WARRANTIES

Automobile tire behavior is a prime candidate for reliability theory application. The numbers involved run into the millions, the failure behavior is clearly one of wearout, and the system numbers are well defined. Today, with the advent of the "spare only" spare, the new car system is four tires, the replacement, four or two tires. The continuous modified normal distribution is an obvious choice as the model of the time-to-failure distribution.

The tool for analysis of manufacturer's risk of a warranty claim is the survivor function $fs_s(t)$. For example, the survivor function for a system of four components (new car or four tire replacement) is the probability of survival of all four tires in time t, now interpreted as the miles driven. Thus a value of .99 for $fs_s(w)$ (w is the warranted mileage), indicates a 1% risk of a warranty claim on one or more tires on the car. The parametric representation developed in Chapter Eight is exceedingly useful in this application; by developing $fs_s(t)$ parametric in t/μ, where μ is the peak of the distribution, a set of universal curves can be provided in which μ need not be specific and risks may be expressed in terms of ranges of t/μ.

This may be more easily understood by referring to Figures 16.4 and 16.5. These have been computed using the programs of Appendix C. The parametric representation above is easily obtained, since β is zero in this case; this value of β is obtained by setting T equal to μ in equation (8.30). Each figure has a series of curves corresponding to a specific value for μ/σ; thus a spectrum of possible normal distributions are made available without having to specify either μ or σ.

As an example, assume the manufacturer knows that a specific tire design conforms by test to a normal distribution with a μ/σ of five. Assume further that the warranty risk the manufacturer is willing to assume on a set of new car tires is 4%. This set of conditions corresponds to a value of 0.534 for t/μ, according to Figure 16.5. As a consequence, if the test results have determined that μ is 50,000 miles, the warranty cannot exceed 27,000 miles. A μ/σ of eight, however, allows a warranty of 36,000 miles. The two tire case would allow warranties of 29,000 and 37,000 miles, respectively.

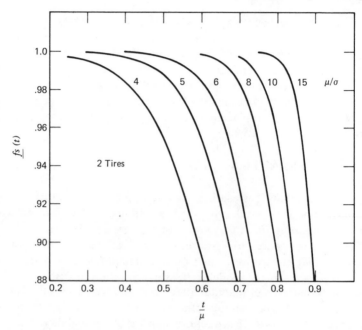

Figure 16.4   Tire warranty risk charts: replacement pairs.

Clearly these charts are useless unless the manufacturer has very specific knowledge of the time-to-failure distribution of his tire design. In the ideal case, where the manufacturer can design to a specific distribution, the charts may be used in reverse. Consider a warranty that is to be 80% of μ and a 4% risk for new car tires: μ/σ must then be 10. A warranty of 40,000 miles would then require a design with a μ of 50,000 miles and a σ of 5000 miles. If the designer is incapable of designing a tire to a μ/σ of 10, or this becomes an economic impossibility, the manufacturer will not be able to achieve a warranty that is 80% of μ. Clearly, a design to a warranty that is a smaller fraction of μ allows for considerably broader variations in manufacturing process control and quality; However, to keep the warranty fixed in the face of the larger variation requires a higher value of μ. Thus these charts permit tradeoff decisions.

16.4   RENEWAL BEHAVIOR: A SYSTEM WITH TWO COMPONENT TYPES

A Monte Carlo simulation was conducted to generate the renewal behavior of a system of two different distributions, containing four components each.

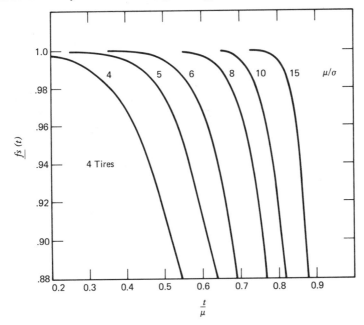

Figure 16.5   Tire warranty risk charts: new car or four wheel replacement.

One distribution is the normal one, with mean 40 and standard deviation four; the other is a uniform distribution with life 40. The renewal behavior for the mixed eight component system was obtained by manually combining the renewal sequences individually generated for each of the four component systems. The sequence for the normally distributed four component system is shown in Figures 15.8*a* and *b*; the sequence for the uniformly distributed four component system is shown in Figure 16.6. The combined eight component system renewal process is shown in Figure 16.7. To put this sequence into perspective it should be compared to the sequence shown in Figures 15.10*a* and *b*. It is evident that the four components that are uniformly distributed have completely masked the effects of the normally distributed components; the combined eight component sequence exhibits more irregularity downstream than does the normally distributed eight component system.

The process required to generate the results of Figure 16.7 is laborious, requiring two complete renewal sequences by computer and a tedious manual operation. Investigation of systems based on multiple component types should be carried out on computers; machines more capable than the TI-59 are required. Some readers may have the inclination and the facilities to carry these investigations further.

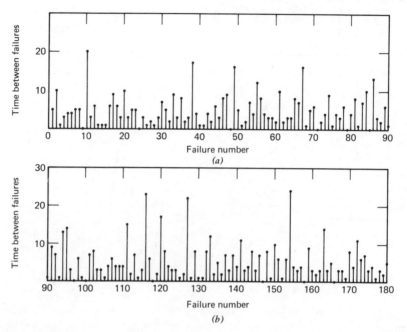

Figure 16.6 Renewal process of a four component system, from a discrete uniform distribution, with life 40: (*a*) failure number from 0 to 90; (*b*) failure number from 90 to 180.

16.5 PARALLEL REDUNDANCY UNDER RENEWAL

Two component system renewal processes are the perfect vehicle for investigating parallel redundancy under renewal. The definition of system failure in a parallel redundant system is simultaneous failure of both elements. Theoretically, given continuous distributions, this cannot happen; practically, failure of a system occurs when both elements fail within a defined interval. In the case of nonrepairable systems the interval is the mission time; in repairable systems the interval is the time required to repair the failed unit.

The analyses that dwell only on the MTTFF of nonrepairable operating parallel redundant systems fail to give the true flavor of their operation. For an exponential distribution the MTTFF is $3/2\lambda$; the silence about the standard deviation about that mean tends to lull many users into thinking that individual systems of this type are failure free in that interval. The fact is that the standard deviation is 82% of the mean and the survival times of individual parallel redundant systems vary widely. Figure 16.8 displays the

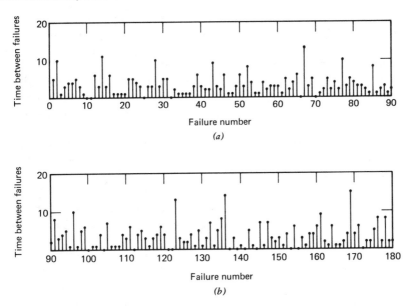

Figure 16.7 Renewal process of an eight component system from combined discrete uniform and normal distributions: (*a*) failure number from 0 to 90; (*b*) failure number from 90 to 180.

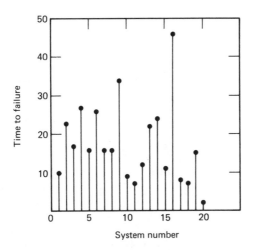

Figure 16.8 Twenty independent operating redundant pair systems consisting of components exponentially distributed with $1/\lambda = 10$; system time-to-failure.

result of a simulation of 20 independent exponentially distributed pairs in parallel; $1/\lambda$ is 10. The mean is 17.5, somewhat higher than the prediction of 15; the failure times range from 2 to 46! Parallel operating redundancy does not guarantee against short system failure times.

The two component system renewal process is the ideal vehicle for investigating the behavior of operating parallel redundancy in repairable systems. Figure 16.9 is the renewal history of a single two component system, exponentially distributed, with $1/\lambda$ equal to 10. There are five instances of the simultaneous failure of both components in the system. Thus, if the maximum repair time is less than one time unit, the system fails every 100 time units, on the average. If the repair time is between one and two time units, a one time unit interval between failures also constitutes a system failure; there are now 14 failures (5 + 9), for an average system failure time of 36. For a repair time between two and three time units there is a total of 29 failures (5 + 9 + 15), for an average time between system failures of 17. A repair time between three and four time units results in a system failure time of 13. Thus, even with the last and most severe definition, the system failure time average is superior to that of a nonredundant system, where it is 10. Unless the repair time is sufficiently short, however, the parallel redundant system may not be sufficiently better to justify the doubling of maintenance costs.

Before leaving the topic of repairable parallel redundant systems, let us look at the same system as above, but normally distributed with mean 40 and standard deviation 4. The nonredundant system behavior is shown in Figure 15.2; the basic data for evaluating the operating repairable parallel redundant system is displayed in Figures 15.3a and b. With a repair time of one standard deviation, the average system life is 100. A repair time of 2σ gives an average life of 67, and 3σ, 53.

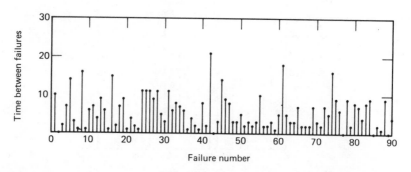

Figure 16.9 Renewal process of a two component system from an exponential distribution with $1/\lambda = 10$.

One should not concentrate on the averages given in the examples to the exclusion of the failure-to-failure behavior of a system. The exponentially distributed system, using a repair time of under two time units, experiences time-between-failure intervals of 10, 26, 17, 33, 34, 7, 100, 7, 32, 72, 103, 47, 2, and 10. The most rigorous definition of system failure, simultaneous failure of both components, yields time-between-failure intervals of 10, 256, 175, 47, and 12. Neither series is a model of regularity. The important finding is that variations from averages have been neglected in both emphasis and use in the application of reliability theory.

CHAPTER SEVENTEEN

Some Parting Observations

17.1 THE NO-DOWNTIME COMPUTER

The September 1980 *IEEE Spectrum* contains an article by Robert Bernhard on the super-reliable computer, which quotes the following from a NASA goal.

> Avionics computers of the 1990s are self-repairing, and they are so reliable that they remain operational despite multiple hardware or software failures. The pilot is excluded from the flight-stabilizing loop since no human intervention could be swift or precise enough to handle the advanced airframes of the 1990s. The airframes are more fuel-efficient than previous models, but they are less stable and require the continuous action of super-reliable computers—and so the computers are as indispensable to flight as wings.

> The computers are designed to break down so rarely—less than once in a human lifetime—that conventional bench and field tests cannot certify their reliability. However, the Federal Aviation Administration has adopted new certification procedures that emphasize mathematical models and simulations of the system over actual tests. The FAA's new procedures indicate that the computers are actually predicted to break down less often than the wings are expected to fall off planes in flight.

> Still, an anxiety lingers among some senior pilots and engineers: The certification procedures, though brilliantly conceived, are nevertheless based largely on theory, not field tests. The calm could therefore be shattered any day by the sudden emergence of undiscovered hardware or software bugs, leading to disturbing system malfunctions.

The author must say that he fully shares the anxiety that is said to linger among some senior pilots and engineers. The argument that computers can be made as reliable as wings is yet to be demonstrated; wings are reliable today as a result of much hard and demonstrable experience. A final rebuttal, in the author's own mind, is that one cannot do without wings and fly, but one can fly without computers.

The article goes on to say that the FAA has no exact reliability requirement for such a computer, but NASA calls for a "mean frequency of 10^{-9} such failures per 10 hour flight." The article further states that this figure, at any rate, is almost impossible to estimate with adequate confidence limits by conventional tests prior to service. The required number of trials would take years to perform, and so another solution must be found. This is the understatement of the year.

The reliability demonstration demanding the minimum number of computers under test is described in Section 4.5. Using that criterion, a test in which 9×10^8 computers operated without failure for 10 hours would demonstrate that the probability of failure in that period did not exceed 10^{-9}, with a confidence of 60%! A requirement for a 99% confidence requires 4.6×10^9 computers operated without failure during that 10 hour period. Increasing the test time to 10,000 hours reduces these numbers by a factor of 1000, but failure free operation is now required for 10,000 hours. Such demonstrations are patently impossible, but is that reliability necessary? The reliability of aircraft wings have not been demonstrated to this degree.

The super-computers that have been proposed are literally cases of redundancy "run amok" and this is not said in a pejorative sense. Both architecture and estimates of reliability are based on a theory that assumes exponential component distributions. Although no mention is made that the computers be considered nonrepairable, it is not clear whether it is intended that failed components be repaired, even though the computer can operate successfully in the face of certain failures. The reliability requirement as stated only refers to "mean performance"; has the variance and the fact that it is the individual computer that must be reliable been considered? Are the proposed designs based on a benign world in which vendors deliver exponentially distributed components to reliablility specifications, perfect factories, harmless transportation, and installation operations and an aircraft environment free of potentially harmful mechanical and electrical disturbances? A lightning stroke may leave a wing still operating; will the electrical energy coupled to the computer leave the crucial microcircuits undamaged?

17.2 SOFTWARE RELIABILITY

The specifications and discussions in Section 17.1 on "no-downtime" computers assume perfect (bug free) software. In recent years the U.S. Defense

Department has included software under the "reliability umbrella." From a management point of view this is completely logical, since a user is concerned about system function, and a system failure is a failure regardless of cause. From an engineering point of view, however, many, including the author, believe that the use of the term "software reliability" implies similar failure mechanisms at work in both hardware and software; there is disagreement that this is the case and therefore disagreement with the use of the term. On the most elementary level software is a set of instructions used to accomplish some specific task; it may be incorrect for its task, but it cannot be unreliable; it will repeat these errors in completely reliable fashion. Unreliable hardware, on the other hand, does not reliably fail in a specific manner each time it is operated, unless it has a design defect that reliably causes the failure. In that respect it is like incorrect software and the solution for both hardware and software is redesign. There are hardware failures that are misinterpreted as software failures; these are due to failures in the hardware where the program resides. These are legitimate hardware reliability problems. They give rise to a failure mode that is cured by reloading the program.

This discussion does not preclude statistical descriptions of the degree to which a given program may be error free. The complexity of the programs in modern embedded computer systems is so great that it is impossible to determine if such programs are error free; hence the probabilistic statement of error. This does not prove identity to hardware reliability, which is also couched in probabilistic terms.

17.3   THE ROLE OF RELIABILITY THEORY IN THE ACQUISITION OF RELIABLE EQUIPMENT

It may be disappointing to reliability theorists to realize that organizations responsible for very high reliability equipment development and manufacture make very little use of reliability theory. Almost exclusively, the effort is placed on design, component requirements, procurement, factory practice, and installation. An excellent example of the relative role is given in the Bell System paper on "Reliability of Semiconductor Devices for Submarine Cable Systems"; the small concession to theory covers one paragraph. Even in U.S. Defense Department weapons procurement the great precision in predicting MTBFs finally gives way to selecting components that come in reliability classes which differ by an order of magnitude. Ultimately, the entire theoretical exercise reduces to making a choice between Class S or Class B microcircuits, between JAN, JANTX, JANTXV, and so on. In the final analysis the theory plays a very minor role in the hardware gestation but a major role in contractual negotiations.

17.4 NONREPAIRABLE AND REPAIRABLE EQUIPMENT

Preceding discussions have emphasized the difference between the time-to-first-failure of an equipment and the behavior of an equipment under renewal; this distinction is lacking in much of current theory and certainly in much of its application. The theoretical justification is the assumption of simultaneous exponentiality for all system components. The result has been the universal description of all devices in terms of the MTBF, reparable or not. Even if nonrepairables are properly assessed in terms of their MTTFF, the notion of describing performances in terms of survivor functions becomes rather ridiculous when applied to systems with very short service lives. Couching the performance of artillery shells or bombs in terms of survivor functions will appear ridiculous to many, but describing ICBMs in such terms is taken very seriously. Yet no manager can give credence to a description that predicts the fraction surviving a flight time short of the target; the manager's interest is in the fraction that complete the mission. Accordingly, the fraction successful is a more appropriate measure of quality than an MTTFF.

17.5 PRECISION, THE MEAN, AND THE INDIVIDUAL

Our current culture is rife with statistics quoted with great precision. Here are some taken from the press.

In 1979, the speed of the average driver on the highway was 55.8 miles per hour.

In 1979, the average TV viewer spent 7 hours and 22 minutes in daily viewing; this was 2 minutes more than last year.

74.5% of manufacturng capacity was utilized in August, this is 0.1% more than the previous month.

The average costs for yearly repair and maintenance for many cars in many cities was given to the nearest cent.

Unemployment changed 0.1% from the previous month.

All of this is very precise and nonsensical. There is no way in which these parameters can be measured to the precision claimed, even if the entire country was taken as a sample. Reliability calculations suffer from the same malaise.

Even if the mean is quoted to some reasonable precision that reflects the reality of the supporting data, what comfort does the mean give to the individual? Suppose it is literally true that the MTBF of some particular computer is 1000 hours and that the underlying component distributions of these computers are truly exponential; then the fraction surviving a 100 hour mission is usually calculated to be .905. As far as the agency that has to provide maintenance on these computers is concerned, this figure is approximately correct in indicating the fraction of 1000 computers in service that will require repair after 1000 have experienced 100 hours of life. For the individual whose life may depend on the computer this number merely means that the chance of an individual computer surviving the mission is approximately 9 out of 10. It is no guarantee that the individual computer will not be one of the casualties. Certainly, exquistite precision in the calculation of $e^{-t/1000}$ has no meaning in the individual case.

REFERENCES

Bernhard, R. "The 'No-Downtime' Computer," *IEEE Spectrum*, **17**, No 9, 33 (1980)

Miller, L. E. "Reliability of Semiconductor Devices for Submarine-Cable Systems," *Proceedings of the IEEE*, **62** No. 2 (1974).

100 Random Numbers in Ascending Order

358	12765	32639	54914	77921
582	14342	33062	56349	81525
725	14577	34914	57392	83473
742	15011	36857	57948	85475
1011	15664	37570	58492	89579
2368	17955	39975	61129	89634
2488	18584	40961	62765	90725
4213	20575	42167	63553	91245
4711	21382	42595	63976	91567
5366	22368	46503	64364	91921
6907	24130	46573	65797	91977
7056	25976	48360	67412	92157
7119	26418	48663	68379	93093
7523	27001	51085	69011	93969
8962	28277	52162	69578	95012
9429	28918	52210	69884	96301
9763	29334	53916	70060	97336
10365	29515	53976	72295	97628
10480	29676	54092	72905	98427
10493	32363	54164	76072	99562

The Texas Instruments Programmable 59

B.1 GENERAL REMARKS

All calculations and simulations appearing in this book have been processed on the Texas Instrument TI-59. The long run time and considerable output involved in many of these computations dictate the use of its companion printer, the PC—100C; manual operation would be utterly impractical. Despite the modest speed and memory capability of the device, it was sufficiently capable for the explorations necessary to the development of the material. Those readers who have access to more powerful computational means and who are so inclined may use the same basic algorithms to conduct computations not subject to the limitations of the TI-59.

B.2 RANDOM NUMBER GENERATION

The TI-59 provides auxiliary Solid State Software Modules that supply specialized programs. Among these are ML-15 of the Master Library and ST-02 of the Applied Statistics Library that provide for the generation of uniform and normal random numbers. The programs described and listed in the Appendix, except in one instance, do not use the programs of ML-15 or ST-02 but provide their own random number routines. The algorithms used are taken from Machol. The generation of random uniform numbers in the field (0, 1) is provided by an algorithm that only requires repeated multiplication. It involves a multiplier,

$$7^7$$

a first random number,

$$r_1 = \text{Fractional part } [(7^7)^2 \times 10^{-6}]$$

and a recursion formula for subsequent random numbers,

$$r_{i+1} = \text{Fractional part } [7^7 r_i]$$

To provide integer random numbers in a field $(0, n - 1)$,

$$ir_i = \text{Integer part } (nr_i)$$

Random exponential integer numbers are generated by

$$eir_i = \text{Integer part } \left[- \left(\frac{1}{\lambda} \right) \ln r_i \right]$$

Random normal integer numbers are generated by

$$nir_i = \text{Integer part } [\sigma(-2 \ln r_{i-1})^{1/2} \cos (2\pi r_i) + m]$$

where m is the mean and σ is the standard deviation. In the case of exponential and normal random numbers means are provided to reject negative numbers and numbers that exceed the number of time cells used.

REFERENCE

Machol, R. T. *System Engineering Handbook.* McGraw-Hill, New York 1965, pp. 40-28 and 40-29.

TI-59 Programs for Chapter Eight

C.1 SURVIVOR FUNCTIONS PROGRAM

C.1.1 Table C.1, Program Listing

Table C.1, Program Listing

000	91	R/S	051	42	STD	101	14	14	151	12	12
001	76	LBL	052	17	17	102	12	B	152	23	LNX
002	11	A	053	55	÷	103	75	-	153	55	÷
003	99	PRT	054	02	2	104	43	RCL	154	43	RCL
004	42	STD	055	95	=	105	10	10	155	08	08
005	00	00	056	42	STD	106	95	=	156	95	=
006	98	ADV	057	06	06	107	55	÷	157	99	PRT
007	81	RST	058	00	0	108	53	(	158	43	RCL
008	76	LBL	059	42	STD	109	43	RCL	159	11	11
009	12	B	060	15	15	110	10	10	160	75	-
010	99	PRT	061	42	STD	111	75	-	161	01	1
011	55	÷	062	16	16	112	01	1	162	95	=
012	43	RCL	063	81	RST	113	54	)	163	55	÷
013	00	00	064	76	LBL	114	85	+	164	43	RCL
014	95	=	065	16	A'	115	01	1	165	08	08
015	42	STD	066	43	RCL	116	95	=	166	95	=
016	14	14	067	06	06	117	45	Y×	167	75	-
017	81	RST	068	99	PRT	118	43	RCL	168	01	1
018	76	LBL	069	43	RCL	119	00	00	169	95	=
019	13	C	070	07	07	120	95	=	170	94	+/-
020	99	PRT	071	75	-	121	68	NOP	171	45	Y×
021	42	STD	072	43	RCL	122	71	SBR	172	43	RCL
022	08	08	073	08	08	123	02	02	173	00	00
023	42	STD	074	95	=	124	22	22	174	95	=
024	09	09	075	42	STD	125	61	GTD	175	68	NOP
025	69	DP	076	13	13	126	00	00	176	71	SBR
026	29	29	077	65	×	127	66	66	177	02	02
027	81	RST	078	43	RCL	128	76	LBL	178	22	22
028	76	LBL	079	06	06	129	17	B'	179	61	GTD
029	10	E'	080	75	-	130	43	RCL	180	01	01
030	42	STD	081	43	RCL	131	06	06	181	30	30
031	06	06	082	07	07	132	99	PRT	182	76	LBL
032	81	RST	083	95	=	133	01	1	183	18	C'
033	76	LBL	084	94	+/-	134	85	+	184	43	RCL
034	14	D	085	36	PGM	135	43	RCL	185	06	06
035	99	PRT	086	14	14	136	08	08	186	99	PRT
036	42	STD	087	11	A	137	65	×	187	45	Y×
037	07	07	088	65	×	138	43	RCL	188	43	RCL
038	36	PGM	089	43	RCL	139	14	14	189	08	08
039	14	14	090	13	13	140	95	=	190	65	×
040	11	A	091	55	÷	141	42	STD	191	43	RCL
041	36	PGM	092	53	(	142	12	12	192	09	09
042	14	14	093	01	1	143	45	Y×	193	65	×
043	12	B	094	75	-	144	43	RCL	194	43	RCL
044	42	STD	095	43	RCL	145	06	06	195	14	14
045	10	10	096	10	10	146	95	=	196	95	=
046	81	RST	097	54	)	147	42	STD	197	99	PRT
047	76	LBL	098	95	=	148	11	11	198	43	RCL
048	15	E	099	99	PRT	149	65	×	199	06	06
049	99	PRT	100	36	PGM	150	43	RCL	200	45	Y×
050	98	ADV									

Table C.1 *(Continued)*

201	43	RCL
202	09	09
203	65	×
204	43	RCL
205	14	14
206	95	=
207	75	-
208	01	1
209	95	=
210	94	+/-
211	45	Y×
212	43	RCL
213	00	00
214	95	=
215	68	NOP
216	71	SBR
217	02	02
218	22	22
219	61	GTO
220	01	01
221	84	84
222	22	INV
223	87	IFF
224	00	00
225	02	02
226	38	38
227	53	(
228	53	(
229	24	CE
230	75	-
231	01	1
232	54	)
233	33	X²
234	75	-
235	01	1
236	54	)
237	94	+/-
238	99	PRT
239	42	STO
240	18	18
241	98	ADV
242	44	SUM
243	15	15
244	53	(
245	24	CE
246	65	×
247	43	RCL
248	06	06
249	54	)
250	44	SUM

251	16	16
252	43	RCL
253	18	18
254	32	X¦T
255	93	.
256	00	0
257	01	1
258	77	GE
259	02	02
260	66	66
261	43	RCL
262	17	17
263	44	SUM
264	06	06
265	92	RTN
266	43	RCL
267	15	15
268	65	×
269	43	RCL
270	17	17
271	95	=
272	99	PRT
273	42	STO
274	15	15
275	43	RCL
276	16	16
277	65	×
278	02	2
279	65	×
280	43	RCL
281	17	17
282	75	-
283	43	RCL
284	15	15
285	33	X²
286	95	=
287	34	ΓX
288	42	STO
289	16	16
290	99	PRT
291	98	ADV
292	43	RCL
293	15	15
294	75	-
295	43	RCL
296	16	16
297	95	=
298	99	PRT
299	43	RCL
300	15	15

301	85	+
302	43	RCL
303	16	16
304	95	=
305	99	PRT
306	98	ADV
307	81	RST
308	76	LBL
309	19	D'
310	03	3
311	06	6
312	03	3
313	07	7
314	02	2
315	01	1
316	02	2
317	07	7
318	00	0
319	01	1
320	69	OP
321	01	01
322	69	OP
323	05	05
324	86	STF
325	00	00
326	91	R/S
---	--	

C.1.2 Partitioning

Normal, banks one and two.

C.1.3 Solid State Software Module Master Library ML-14

C.1.4 Nomenclature

M Number of components.
β Parametric constant, normal function.
ϕ μ/σ for normal function.
γ Parametric constant, exponential and power functions.
δ Coefficient, exponential and power functions.
d Increment in t/T.

C.1.5 Data Entry

These entries may be made in any order and are retained.

Enter M, press A.
Normal function: enter β, press C, enter ϕ, press D.
Exponential or Power function: enter γ, press B, enter δ, press C.

C.1.6 Standard Solution

For a sequence of calculations corresponding to $d/2$, $3d/2$, $5d/2$, ...,
leading finally to the MTTFF, σ_s, and ending when $\underline{fs}(t) \leq .01$:

Enter d, press E; for parallel redundancy, also press D'.
Then press A' for normal function calculations, B' for an exponential
calculation, or C' for a power function calculation. See sequences of t/T, $Tf(t)$,
$\underline{fs}_s(t)$, and at the end, MTTFF, MTTFF $- \sigma_s$, and MTTFF $+ \sigma_s$.

The accuracy with which MTTFF and σ_s are computed depends on the
choice of d. A choice suitable for graphing $\underline{fs}_s(t)$ is usually adequate for the
computation of MTTFF and σ_s.

C.1.7 Solution for a Single Value of t/T

Enter t/T, press E'; for parallel redundancy, also press D'.
Press A', B', or C', depending on the function.
Press R/S as soon as the solution appears.

C.1.8   Solution for a Sequence Starting From a Specific t/T.

Enter d, press E, enter t/T, press E'; for parallel redundancy, also press D'. Press A', B', or C', depending on the function.

The MTTFF, σ_s, and other calculations at the end are incorrect in this instance and are ignored.

C.1.9   To Continue Calculations Beyond $\underline{fs}_s(t) = .01$

The program must be modified to accomplish this: Press GTO 257, press LRN, press 0, press LRN. To remove the modification reload the program or press GTO 257, press LRN, press 1, press LRN.

C.2   SOLUTION FOR β, NORMAL DISTRIBUTION

C.2.1   Table C.2, Program Listing

Table C.2, Program Listing

000	91	R/S		049	42	STO
001	76	LBL		050	12	12
002	11	A		051	55	÷
003	36	PGM		052	53	(
004	14	14		053	24	CE
005	11	A		054	75	-
006	36	PGM		055	53	(
007	14	14		056	43	RCL
008	12	B		057	11	11
009	42	STO		058	85	+
010	20	20		059	43	RCL
011	81	RST		060	99	99
012	76	LBL		061	54	)
013	12	B		062	71	SBR
014	42	STO		063	00	00
015	00	00		064	86	86
016	69	OP		065	54	)
017	30	30		066	65	×
018	75	-		067	43	RCL
019	43	RCL		068	99	99
020	00	00		069	54	)
021	65	×		070	42	STO
022	43	RCL		071	11	11
023	20	20		072	43	RCL
024	95	=		073	98	98
025	42	STO		074	32	X:T
026	13	13		075	43	RCL
027	81	RST		076	12	12
028	76	LBL		077	50	I×I
029	13	C		078	77	GE
030	42	STO		079	00	00
031	99	99		080	42	42
032	81	RST		081	43	RCL
033	76	LBL		082	11	11
034	14	D		083	22	INV
035	42	STO		084	52	EE
036	98	98		085	81	RST
037	81	RST		086	53	(
038	76	LBL		087	36	PGM
039	15	E		088	14	14
040	42	STO		089	11	A
041	11	11		090	36	PGM
042	53	(		091	14	14
043	43	RCL		092	12	B
044	11	11		093	75	-
045	85	+		094	43	RCL
046	71	SBR		095	13	13
047	00	00		096	54	)
048	86	86		097	92	RTN

233

C.2.2   Partitioning

10 OP 17, bank one.

C.2.3   Algorithms

The following equation, equation (8.29),

$$\int_{\beta}^{\infty} E(y)\, dy - \frac{\gamma}{M} - \left(1 - \frac{\gamma}{M}\right)\psi = 0$$

is solved by iteration using Newton's method.

C.2.4   Nomenclature

ϕ μ/σ.
M Number of components.
γ Parametric constant.

C.2.5   Solution

Enter ϕ, press A, enter γ/M, press B, enter *guess*, press E; see β. Time of solution is dependent on the *guess*.

C.2.6   Modifications

Two constants are stored in registers 98 and 99 and are entered into these registers when the program card is read. 10^{-10} is stored in 98; it is the accuracy constant, that is, the iterative solution stops only after the equation above approaches zero to better than 10^{-10}. The constant in 99, 10^{-6}, defines a derivative in the solution. These may be altered, if desired, as follows. To change the contents of 98, enter the new value, press D. To change the contents of 99, enter the new value, press C. To record these on the program cards so that they are automatically entered whenever the program is loaded, rewrite the program card with new entries in the registers.

APPENDIX D

Program for the Discrete Renewal Distribution Function $h(t_n, u_j)$

D.1 INTRODUCTORY COMMENTS

The program, as written, can be substantially shortened by resorting to DSZ and IND routines; this would provide for additional time cells but would invoke a heavy penalty in throughput. The additional time cells do not add to understanding and were considered a poor tradeoff.

Twenty time cells need not be used if less will do; in such cases the throughput may be increased by program modification, in which unnecessary portions of sequences are bypassed by using GTOs.

D.2 TABLE D.1, PROGRAM LISTING

Table D.1, Program Listing

000	91	R/S	051	32	X:T	101	48	EXC	151	43	RCL
001	76	LBL	052	00	0	102	40	40	152	19	19
002	12	B	053	61	GTO	103	42	STO	153	65	×
003	42	STO	054	01	01	104	19	19	154	43	RCL
004	18	18	055	01	01	105	65	×	155	33	33
005	42	STO	056	76	LBL	106	43	RCL	156	95	=
006	00	00	057	13	C	107	39	39	157	44	SUM
007	81	RST	058	00	0	108	95	=	158	53	53
008	76	LBL	059	42	STO	109	42	STO	159	43	RCL
009	14	D	060	16	16	110	59	59	160	19	19
010	42	STO	061	76	LBL	111	43	RCL	161	65	×
011	40	40	062	15	E	112	19	19	162	43	RCL
012	00	0	063	48	EXC	113	65	×	163	32	32
013	42	STO	064	59	59	114	43	RCL	164	95	=
014	00	00	065	48	EXC	115	38	38	165	44	SUM
015	42	STO	066	58	58	116	95	=	166	52	52
016	41	41	067	48	EXC	117	44	SUM	167	43	RCL
017	42	STO	068	57	57	118	58	58	168	19	19
018	42	42	069	48	EXC	119	43	RCL	169	65	×
019	42	STO	070	56	56	120	19	19	170	43	RCL
020	43	43	071	48	EXC	121	65	×	171	31	31
021	42	STO	072	55	55	122	43	RCL	172	95	=
022	44	44	073	48	EXC	123	37	37	173	44	SUM
023	42	STO	074	54	54	124	95	=	174	51	51
024	45	45	075	48	EXC	125	44	SUM	175	43	RCL
025	42	STO	076	53	53	126	57	57	176	19	19
026	46	46	077	48	EXC	127	43	RCL	177	65	×
027	42	STO	078	52	52	128	19	19	178	43	RCL
028	47	47	079	48	EXC	129	65	×	179	30	30
029	42	STO	080	51	51	130	43	RCL	180	95	=
030	48	48	081	48	EXC	131	36	36	181	44	SUM
031	42	STO	082	50	50	132	95	=	182	50	50
032	49	49	083	48	EXC	133	44	SUM	183	43	RCL
033	42	STO	084	49	49	134	56	56	184	19	19
034	50	50	085	48	EXC	135	43	RCL	185	65	×
035	42	STO	086	48	48	136	19	19	186	43	RCL
036	51	51	087	48	EXC	137	65	×	187	29	29
037	42	STO	088	47	47	138	43	RCL	188	95	=
038	52	52	089	48	EXC	139	35	35	189	44	SUM
039	42	STO	090	46	46	140	95	=	190	49	49
040	53	53	091	48	EXC	141	44	SUM	191	43	RCL
041	42	STO	092	45	45	142	55	55	192	19	19
042	54	54	093	48	EXC	143	43	RCL	193	65	×
043	42	STO	094	44	44	144	19	19	194	43	RCL
044	55	55	095	48	EXC	145	65	×	195	28	28
045	42	STO	096	43	43	146	43	RCL	196	95	=
046	56	56	097	48	EXC	147	34	34	197	44	SUM
047	42	STO	098	42	42	148	95	=	198	48	48
048	57	57	099	48	EXC	149	44	SUM	199	43	RCL
049	42	STO	100	41	41	150	54	54	200	19	19
050	58	58									

201	65	×
202	43	RCL
203	27	27
204	95	=
205	44	SUM
206	47	47
207	43	RCL
208	19	19
209	65	×
210	43	RCL
211	26	26
212	95	=
213	44	SUM
214	46	46
215	43	RCL
216	19	19
217	65	×
218	43	RCL
219	25	25
220	95	=
221	44	SUM
222	45	45
223	43	RCL
224	19	19
225	65	×
226	43	RCL
227	24	24
228	95	=
229	44	SUM
230	44	44
231	43	RCL
232	19	19
233	65	×
234	43	RCL
235	23	23
236	95	=
237	44	SUM
238	43	43
239	43	RCL
240	19	19
241	65	×
242	43	RCL
243	22	22
244	95	=
245	44	SUM
246	42	42
247	43	RCL
248	19	19
249	65	×
250	43	RCL
251	21	21
252	95	=
253	44	SUM
254	41	41
255	43	RCL
256	19	19
257	65	×
258	43	RCL
259	20	20
260	95	=
261	44	SUM
262	40	40
263	97	DSZ
264	00	00
265	00	00
266	63	63
267	43	RCL
268	18	18
269	42	STO
270	00	00
271	43	RCL
272	19	19
273	99	PRT
274	01	1
275	44	SUM
276	16	16
277	43	RCL
278	16	16
279	77	GE
280	02	02
281	85	85
282	61	GTO
283	00	00
284	63	63
285	81	RST
286	76	LBL
287	11	A
288	04	4
289	00	0
290	22	INV
291	90	LST
292	81	RST

D.3 PARTITIONING

Normal, banks one and two.

D.4 ALGORITHM

$$h(n + 1, j) = h(n, j + 1) + h(n, 1) f(j)$$

D.5 Nomenclature

k	Multiplier.
$h(0, j)$	Initial distribution.
$f(j)$	Repair distribution.
$h(n, 1)$	Renewal density function.
$h(n, j)$	nth forward recurrence time distribution.

D.6 DATA ENTRY

Load $f(j)$ into registers 20 through 39, register by register, using the STO instruction.

If $h(0, j)$ is to be $f(j)$, enter 1, press D; this will load $f(j)$ into the $h(n, j)$ registers.

If for any reason $kh(n, j)$ is required as the output, enter k, press D; this loads $kf(j)$ into the $h(n, j)$ registers.

If $h(0, j)$ is to be different than $kf(j)$, load it register by register into registers 40 through 59, using the STO instruction.

The load may be inspected by pressing A; the printer will print the contents of registers 40 through 59.

$f(j)$ is always retained during any of the above steps and during any solution. One may start over by entering k and pressing D, or entering $h(0, j)$.

D.8 SOLUTIONS

D.8.1 Single Steps, One at a Time, $n = 0, 1\ 2, \ldots$

Enter zero, press B. Press C repeatedly, see $h(n, 1)$. To see $h(n, j)$ at any time, press A.

D.8.2   Groups of _g_ Steps, One Group at a Time, _n_ = _g_, 2_g_, 3_g_, ...

Enter _g_, press B. Press C repeatedly, see $h(mg, 1)$. To see $h(mg, j)$, press A.

D.8.3   _j_ Groups of _g_ Steps

Enter _g_, press B, unless _g_ has been previously entered. Enter _j_, press $x \rightleftharpoons t$, press C, see sequence of $h(n, 1)$. When the solution is completed, press A to see last $h(n, j)$.

To obtain additional groups after the initial _j_ groups have been completed, press E repeatedly for one group at a time, or enter the new total number of groups desired, press $x \rightleftharpoons t$, press E.

Programs for Monte Carlo Simulations

E.1 INTRODUCTORY REMARKS

This material covers three programs: MC-1, MC-2, and MC-3; these were used to generate the data for the graphical material provided in Chapters Fourteen, Fifteen, and Sixteen. Program MC-1 provided the data for Figures 14.13, 14.14, 15.1 through 15.11, 16.1, and 16.2. MC-2 was used to supply the data for Figures 14.1 through 14.9 and for Section 14.5. MC-3 was used for Figures 14.11 and 14.12.

A common thread runs through all three programs: the random number generation is the same for all (see Appendix B), as is the means for distributing random numbers to appropriate positions in shift registers. MC-1 has the capacity of handling up to 50 time cells, the other programs have a maximum of 20 time cells; the reason for the difference is computer capability. Some of the programs have built in conveniences that are lacking in others; this was simply a matter of sufficient program space.

E.2 PROGRAM MC-1

E.2.1 Introduction

This program was kept as basic as possible to provide the utmost capacity for time cells, 50. Only one shift register was possible: it contains the components of the system as manufactured and during renewal. It is primarily a program for tracing the time between failures in systems with small component counts; with a relatively large number of time cells and properly restricted distributions, the results approximate the behavior of systems with components described by continuous distributions. In its given form the program provides for uniform, exponential, and normal distributions. A slight modification provides for narrow dispersion distributions that are uniform about the mean. Another modification provides for printing lists of the basic random number sequence used in all programs described in this Appendix. This information enables the program user to start a simulation elsewhere than at the beginning of the sequence.

E.2.2 Table E.1, Program Listing

Table E.1, Program Listing

000	91	R/S									
001	76	LBL	051	54	54	101	65	×	151	32	X:T
002	11	A	052	23	LNX	102	89	π	152	00	0
003	47	CMS	053	94	+/-	103	65	×	153	77	GE
004	42	STO	054	65	×	104	43	RCL	154	01	01
005	04	04	055	43	RCL	105	03	03	155	63	63
006	99	PRT	056	04	04	106	54	)	156	05	5
007	07	7	057	95	=	107	39	COS	157	00	0
008	45	Y×	058	71	SBR	108	65	×	158	32	X:T
009	07	7	059	01	01	109	43	RCL	159	22	INV
010	95	=	060	48	48	110	04	04	160	77	GE
011	42	STO	061	87	IFF	111	85	+	161	01	01
012	01	01	062	00	00	112	43	RCL	162	65	65
013	33	X²	063	00	00	113	05	05	163	86	STF
014	55	÷	064	45	45	114	95	=	164	00	00
015	01	1	065	71	SBR	115	71	SBR	165	59	INT
016	52	EE	066	01	01	116	01	01	166	92	RTN
017	06	6	067	67	67	117	48	48	167	85	+
018	95	=	068	97	DSZ	118	87	IFF	168	03	3
019	22	INV	069	00	00	119	00	00	169	00	0
020	52	EE	070	00	00	120	00	00	170	95	=
021	22	INV	071	45	45	121	85	85	171	42	STO
022	59	INT	072	76	LBL	122	71	SBR	172	06	06
023	42	STO	073	18	C'	123	01	01	173	01	1
024	02	02	074	71	SBR	124	67	67	174	74	SM*
025	70	RAD	075	01	01	125	97	DSZ	175	06	06
026	81	RST	076	77	77	126	00	00	176	92	RTN
027	76	LBL	077	61	GTO	127	00	00	177	43	RCL
028	16	A'	078	00	00	128	85	85	178	10	10
029	42	STO	079	45	45	129	76	LBL	179	32	X:T
030	00	00	080	76	LBL	130	10	E'	180	43	RCL
031	99	PRT	081	15	E	131	71	SBR	181	08	08
032	81	RST	082	42	STO	132	01	01	182	22	INV
033	76	LBL	083	05	05	133	77	77	183	77	GE
034	12	B	084	99	PRT	134	61	GTO	184	01	01
035	42	STO	085	43	RCL	135	00	00	185	87	87
036	10	10	086	02	02	136	85	85	186	91	R/S
037	99	PRT	087	42	STO	137	43	RCL	187	01	1
038	91	R/S	088	03	03	138	02	02	188	44	SUM
039	76	LBL	089	71	SBR	139	65	×	189	07	07
040	13	C	090	01	01	140	43	RCL	190	44	SUM
041	86	STF	091	37	37	141	01	01	191	09	09
042	01	01	092	23	LNX	142	95	=	192	00	0
043	76	LBL	093	65	×	143	22	INV	193	48	EXC
044	14	D	094	02	2	144	59	INT	194	79	79
045	71	SBR	095	94	+/-	145	42	STO	195	48	EXC
046	01	01	096	95	=	146	02	02	196	78	78
047	37	37	097	34	ГX	147	92	RTN	197	48	EXC
048	87	IFF	098	65	×	148	22	INV	198	77	77
049	01	01	099	53	(	149	86	STF	199	48	EXC
050	00	00	100	02	2	150	00	00	200	76	76

201	48	EXC	251	48	EXC	301	99	PRT
202	75	75	252	50	50	302	44	SUM
203	48	EXC	253	48	EXC	303	08	08
204	74	74	254	49	49	304	43	RCL
205	48	EXC	255	48	EXC	305	09	09
206	73	73	256	48	48	306	99	PRT
207	48	EXC	257	48	EXC	307	00	0
208	72	72	258	47	47	308	42	STO
209	48	EXC	259	48	EXC	309	09	09
210	71	71	260	46	46	310	43	RCL
211	48	EXC	261	48	EXC	311	07	07
212	70	70	262	45	45	312	99	PRT
213	48	EXC	263	48	EXC	313	55	÷
214	69	69	264	44	44	314	43	RCL
215	48	EXC	265	48	EXC	315	08	08
216	68	68	266	43	43	316	99	PRT
217	48	EXC	267	48	EXC	317	95	=
218	67	67	268	42	42	318	99	PRT
219	48	EXC	269	48	EXC	319	92	RTN
220	66	66	270	41	41			
221	48	EXC	271	48	EXC			
222	65	65	272	40	40			
223	48	EXC	273	48	EXC			
224	64	64	274	39	39			
225	48	EXC	275	48	EXC			
226	63	63	276	38	38			
227	48	EXC	277	48	EXC			
228	62	62	278	37	37			
229	48	EXC	279	48	EXC			
230	61	61	280	36	36			
231	48	EXC	281	48	EXC			
232	60	60	282	35	35			
233	48	EXC	283	48	EXC			
234	59	59	284	34	34			
235	48	EXC	285	48	EXC			
236	58	58	286	33	33			
237	48	EXC	287	48	EXC			
238	57	57	288	32	32			
239	48	EXC	289	48	EXC			
240	56	56	290	31	31			
241	48	EXC	291	48	EXC			
242	55	55	292	30	30			
243	48	EXC	293	32	X:T			
244	54	54	294	00	0			
245	48	EXC	295	67	EQ			
246	53	53	296	01	01			
247	48	EXC	297	87	87			
248	52	52	298	32	X:T			
249	48	EXC	299	42	STO			
250	51	51	300	00	00			

E.2.3 Partitioning

8 OP 17, banks one and two.

E.2.4 Nomenclature

M	Number of components.
R multiplier	The constant multiplier for random number generation.
R_i	The ith random number in the sequence.
UL	The highest integer of the required uniform distribution.
$1/\lambda$	The reciprocal of the exponential failure rate.
σ	The standard deviation of the normal distribution.
μ	The mean of the normal distribution.
Stop number	The number of failures that terminate the computation.

E.2.5 Data Entry

Enter UL $+$ 1, $1/\lambda$, or σ, press A; the first refers to uniform distributions, the second to exponential ones, and the third to normal ones.
Enter M, press A '.
Enter stop number, press B.

E.2.6 Standard Solution

For uniform distribution, press C.
For an exponential distribution, press D.
For a normal distribution, enter $\mu - 1$, press E.
To increase the stop number after an initial stop number has been completed; enter new total stop number, press B. Then press C ', D ', or E ', depending on whether a uniform, exponential, or normal distribution is in process.

E.2.7 To Manufacture Only

Proceed as in standard solution but use stop number of zero.

E.2.8 To Terminate on Time Elapsed

To terminate on time elapsed rather than the number of failures, modify program by press GTO 181, press LRN, press 7, press LRN.

E.2.9 To Start Solution at Arbitrary Point in Random Number Sequence

Enter data in standard way; before initiating standard solution, do the following:

For uniform and exponential distributions, enter the desired random number, press STO 02, proceed with standard solution.

For normal distributions, also enter the preceding random number by keying it into the display, then press STO 03. Proceed with standard solution.

E.2.10 To View the Distribution at any Time

Enter 30, press INV LIST.

E.2.11 Equilibrium Start

Do standard data entry with the exception of entering *M*.

Enter equilibrium distribution by keying 1, STO, into the appropriate registers, 30 through 79.

Start solution by pressing C′ for uniform distribution, D′ for exponential distribution. For normal distribution, enter $\mu - 1$, press STO 05, press E′.

E.2.12 Solution With Uniform Narrow Dispersion Distribution

Modify program by pressing GTO 168, press LRN, press the number

[30 + mean − 1 − ½ (total width of dispersion)] press LRN.

Enter width of dispersion, press A.

Complete data entry and solution in standard form.

E.2.13 To Avoid Printing Some Results

As written, the program prints sequences of number of failures, time since last failure, total elapsed time, total number of failures, and the ratio of the total time to the total number of failures. These instructions are in program steps 301, 306, 312, 316, and 318. Any of these print instructions may be voided by program modification. To void program step, xxx, press GTO xxx, press LRN, press NOP, press LRN.

E.2.14 To Print the Basic Sequence of Random Numbers

Modify program by press GTO 48, press LRN, press PRT, press GTO 45, press RCL, press LRN. To start the process of printing the sequence, press A, press D; to terminate the sequence, press R/S.

Table E.2, First 100 Random Numbers

0.38974209	0.76258100
0.37002210	0.24447760
0.11029770	0.81613500
0.89875032	0.26629920
0.53477740	0.84206370
0.18432440	0.66568320
0.06934790	0.73957290
0.97760921	0.08477950
0.22162410	0.56376790
0.97618470	0.10766570
0.07638520	0.33357434
0.49676306	0.81268420
0.74071810	0.38411490
0.20622310	0.13708800
0.59044180	0.86278300
0.21129320	0.90016290
0.03580610	0.85514830
0.86301204	0.39642090
0.52445160	0.65724590
0.44401510	0.26021900
0.52749610	0.53591510
0.72067860	0.12919550
0.81627470	0.04965550
0.31525630	0.43943615
0.11906860	0.56527630
0.11204896	0.33992690
0.13666449	0.41900430
0.08408710	0.05823190
0.34259471	0.47362129
0.47525510	0.49802710
0.01081590	0.73201180
0.35873362	0.19380220
0.56490730	0.44519320
0.45255990	0.74350440
0.53772250	0.84408390
0.60081370	0.38725170
0.91693480	0.42677030
0.23598990	0.69316990
0.83021400	0.21895080
0.92819610	0.39868280
0.40077580	0.42915760
0.10465650	0.73737370
0.12797876	0.94901390
0.01194570	0.75424100
0.79761502	0.89585770
0.26311610	0.33782480
0.42234040	0.24926400
0.48003420	0.62235020
0.80516720	0.15075420
0.81138390	0.56612950
0.53115200	0.98681450
0.51153220	0.17376650

E.3 PROGRAM MC-2

E.3.1 Introduction

Program MC-2 provides a maximum of 20 time cells in each of three groups of memory registers. Registers 50 through 69 hold the system and are operated as a shift register, 30 through 59 accumulate the distributions found in 50 through 69. Registers 10 through 27 are used to accumulate the time-between-failures distribution; the full 20 time cells are not needed for the time-between failures distribution if the component count is three or more, and requires register 28 only rarely if the component count is two. This economy was dictated by restricted program space.

The particular application of this program is the study of postequilibrium states. Means are provided for manufacturing a system, aging it for a time estimated to be in excess of practical attainment of equilibrium, and clearing the register groups that accumulate system and time-between-failures distributions. On continuation of the renewal process, the postequilibrium system time-to-failure and time-between-failures distributions are accumulated after each successive renewal; this process is terminated after a desired number of renewals (failures).

In addition to providing the particular procedures it was designed for, this program can do everything that MC-1 is capable of, including variations, limited, of course, to a maximum of 20 time cells.

E.3.2 Table E.3, Program Listing

Table E.3, Program Listing

000	91	R/S								
001	76	LBL	051	01	01	101	34	√X	151	92	RTN
002	11	A	052	41	41	102	65	×	152	22	INV
003	47	CMS	053	87	IFF	103	53	(	153	86	STF
004	42	STO	054	01	01	104	02	2	154	00	00
005	04	04	055	00	00	105	65	×	155	32	X:T
006	99	PRT	056	59	59	106	89	π	156	00	0
007	07	7	057	23	LNX	107	65	×	157	77	GE
008	45	Y^x	058	94	+/-	108	43	RCL	158	01	01
009	07	7	059	65	×	109	03	03	159	67	67
010	95	=	060	43	RCL	110	54	)	160	02	2
011	42	STO	061	04	04	111	39	COS	161	00	0
012	01	01	062	95	=	112	65	×	162	32	X:T
013	33	X²	063	71	SBR	113	43	RCL	163	22	INV
014	55	÷	064	01	01	114	04	04	164	77	GE
015	01	1	065	52	52	115	85	+	165	01	01
016	52	EE	066	87	IFF	116	43	RCL	166	69	69
017	06	6	067	00	00	117	05	05	167	86	STF
018	95	=	068	00	00	118	95	=	168	00	00
019	22	INV	069	50	50	119	71	SBR	169	59	INT
020	52	EE	070	71	SBR	120	01	01	170	92	RTN
021	22	INV	071	01	01	121	52	52	171	85	+
022	59	INT	072	71	71	122	87	IFF	172	05	5
023	42	STO	073	97	DSZ	123	00	00	173	00	0
024	02	02	074	00	00	124	00	00	174	95	=
025	70	RAD	075	00	00	125	89	89	175	42	STO
026	81	RST	076	50	50	126	71	SBR	176	06	06
027	76	LBL	077	76	LBL	127	01	01	177	01	1
028	16	A'	078	18	C'	128	71	71	178	74	SM*
029	42	STO	079	71	SBR	129	97	DSZ	179	06	06
030	00	00	080	01	01	130	00	00	180	92	RTN
031	99	PRT	081	81	81	131	00	00	181	43	RCL
032	81	RST	082	61	GTO	132	89	89	182	29	29
033	76	LBL	083	00	00	133	76	LBL	183	32	X:T
034	12	B	084	50	50	134	10	E'	184	43	RCL
035	42	STO	085	76	LBL	135	71	SBR	185	08	08
036	29	29	086	15	E	136	01	01	186	22	INV
037	99	PRT	087	42	STO	137	81	81	187	77	GE
038	91	R/S	088	05	05	138	61	GTO	188	02	02
039	76	LBL	089	43	RCL	139	00	00	189	08	08
040	17	B'	090	02	02	140	89	89	190	43	RCL
041	22	INV	091	42	STO	141	43	RCL	191	07	07
042	90	LST	092	03	03	142	02	02	192	99	PRT
043	91	R/S	093	71	SBR	143	65	×	193	55	÷
044	76	LBL	094	01	01	144	43	RCL	194	43	RCL
045	13	C	095	41	41	145	01	01	195	08	08
046	86	STF	096	23	LNX	146	95	=	196	99	PRT
047	01	01	097	65	×	147	22	INV	197	95	=
048	76	LBL	098	02	2	148	59	INT	198	99	PRT
049	14	D	099	94	+/-	149	42	STO	199	43	RCL
050	71	SBR	100	95	=	150	02	02	200	09	09

Table E.3 (Continued)

201	99	PRT	251	60	60	301	85	+			
202	55	÷	252	44	SUM	302	09	9	351	48	EXC
203	43	RCL	253	40	40	303	95	=	352	59	59
204	08	08	254	48	EXC	304	42	STD	353	48	EXC
205	95	=	255	59	59	305	06	06	354	58	58
206	99	PRT	256	44	SUM	306	32	X!T	355	48	EXC
207	91	R/S	257	39	39	307	42	STD	356	57	57
208	01	1	258	48	EXC	308	00	00	357	48	EXC
209	44	SUM	259	58	58	309	44	SUM	358	56	56
210	07	07	260	44	SUM	310	08	08	359	48	EXC
211	44	SUM	261	38	38	311	65	×	360	55	55
212	28	28	262	48	EXC	312	43	RCL	361	48	EXC
213	00	0	263	57	57	313	28	28	362	54	54
214	48	EXC	264	44	SUM	314	95	=	363	48	EXC
215	69	69	265	37	37	315	44	SUM	364	53	53
216	44	SUM	266	48	EXC	316	09	09	365	48	EXC
217	49	49	267	56	56	317	43	RCL	366	52	52
218	48	EXC	268	44	SUM	318	00	00	367	48	EXC
219	68	68	269	36	36	319	74	SM*	368	51	51
220	44	SUM	270	48	EXC	320	06	06	369	48	EXC
221	48	48	271	55	55	321	00	0	370	50	50
222	48	EXC	272	44	SUM	322	42	STD	371	32	X!T
223	67	67	273	35	35	323	28	28	372	00	0
224	44	SUM	274	48	EXC	324	92	RTN	373	67	EQ
225	47	47	275	54	54	325	01	1	374	03	03
226	48	EXC	276	44	SUM	326	44	SUM	375	25	25
227	66	66	277	34	34	327	07	07	376	61	GTO
228	44	SUM	278	48	EXC	328	44	SUM	377	02	02
229	46	46	279	53	53	329	28	28	378	99	99
230	48	EXC	280	44	SUM	330	00	0	379	76	LBL
231	65	65	281	33	33	331	48	EXC	380	19	D'
232	44	SUM	282	48	EXC	332	69	69	381	04	4
233	45	45	283	52	52	333	48	EXC	382	04	4
234	48	EXC	284	44	SUM	334	68	68	383	42	STD
235	64	64	285	32	32	335	48	EXC	384	00	00
236	44	SUM	286	48	EXC	336	67	67	385	43	RCL
237	44	44	287	51	51	337	48	EXC	386	00	00
238	48	EXC	288	44	SUM	338	66	66	387	85	+
239	63	63	289	31	31	339	48	EXC	388	05	5
240	44	SUM	290	48	EXC	340	65	65	389	95	=
241	43	43	291	50	50	341	48	EXC	390	42	STD
242	48	EXC	292	44	SUM	342	64	64	391	06	06
243	62	62	293	30	30	343	48	EXC	392	00	0
244	44	SUM	294	32	X!T	344	63	63	393	72	ST*
245	42	42	295	00	0	345	48	EXC	394	06	06
246	48	EXC	296	67	EQ	346	62	62	395	97	DSZ
247	61	61	297	03	03	347	48	EXC	396	00	00
248	44	SUM	298	25	25	348	61	61	397	03	03
249	41	41	299	43	RCL	349	48	EXC	398	85	85
250	48	EXC	300	28	28	350	60	60	399	91	R/S

E.3.3 Partitioning

7 OP 17, banks one and two.

E.3.4 Nomenclature

See E.2.4.

E.3.5 Data Entry

See E.2.5.

E.3.6 Standard Solution

Uniform distribution, press C.

Exponential distribution, press D.

Normal distribution, enter $\mu - 1$, press E.

The stop number entered under data entry is that for reaching equilibrium; when the initial process has stopped, press D ', this clears registers 6 through 49.

Enter postequilibrium stop number, press B; this is independent of the number used in the first part of the solution. Now press C ' for the uniform and exponential distributions, E ' for the normal one. To record the accumulated distributions, enter the beginning register number, press B '.

E.4 PROGRAM MC-3

E.4.1 Introduction

Program MC-2 provided means for accumulating time-to-failure and time-between-failures distributions from each renewal of a single system. Program MC-3 only accumulates the time-to-failure distribution, but accumulates this data from any number of independent single systems of a given age. Like MC-2, the maximum number of time cells is 20; the system is contained in registers 20 through 39, the summation in 40 through 59. In addition to the accumulation of data from single systems of a given age, it can also accumulate the same data from single systems at the first renewal following a given age. This latter capability requires a program modification. The modification is the following: press GTO 195, press LRN, press RCL 19, press LRN.

The program manufactures and ages a single system at a time, repairing it at each successive failure, and continuing the renewal process until the specified age has been reached. At this time the time-to-failure distribution of the system is summed into the accumulation register group, the system register group and other registers containing specific system data are cleared (18–39), the next system is manufactured, aged, and read, and so on.

E.4.2   Table E.4, Program Listing

Table E.4, Program Listing

000	91	R/S								
001	76	LBL	051	76	LBL	101	95	=	151	22	INV
002	11	A	052	14	D	102	34	ГX	152	86	STF
003	47	CMS	053	71	SBR	103	65	×	153	00	00
004	42	STD	054	01	01	104	53	(	154	32	X:T
005	04	04	055	40	40	105	02	2	155	00	0
006	99	PRT	056	87	IFF	106	65	×	156	77	GE
007	07	7	057	01	01	107	89	π	157	01	01
008	45	Y^X	058	00	00	108	65	×	158	66	66
009	07	7	059	62	62	109	43	RCL	159	02	2
010	95	=	060	23	LNX	110	03	03	160	00	0
011	42	STD	061	94	+/-	111	54	)	161	32	X:T
012	01	01	062	65	×	112	39	CDS	162	22	INV
013	33	X²	063	43	RCL	113	65	×	163	77	GE
014	55	÷	064	04	04	114	43	RCL	164	01	01
015	01	1	065	95	=	115	04	04	165	68	68
016	52	EE	066	71	SBR	116	85	+	166	86	STF
017	06	6	067	01	01	117	43	RCL	167	00	00
018	95	=	068	51	51	118	05	05	168	59	INT
019	22	INV	069	87	IFF	119	95	=	169	92	RTN
020	52	EE	070	00	00	120	71	SBR	170	85	+
021	22	INV	071	00	00	121	01	01	171	02	2
022	59	INT	072	53	53	122	51	51	172	00	0
023	42	STD	073	71	SBR	123	87	IFF	173	95	=
024	02	02	074	01	01	124	00	00	174	42	STD
025	70	RAD	075	70	70	125	00	00	175	06	06
026	81	RST	076	97	DSZ	126	90	90	176	01	1
027	76	LBL	077	00	00	127	71	SBR	177	74	SM*
028	16	A'	078	00	00	128	01	01	178	06	06
029	42	STD	079	53	53	129	70	70	179	92	RTN
030	00	00	080	71	SBR	130	97	DSZ	180	87	IFF
031	42	STD	081	01	01	131	00	00	181	02	02
032	10	10	082	80	80	132	00	00	182	02	02
033	99	PRT	083	61	GTD	133	90	90	183	69	69
034	81	RST	084	00	00	134	71	SBR	184	43	RCL
035	76	LBL	085	53	53	135	01	01	185	07	07
036	12	B	086	76	LBL	136	80	80	186	32	X:T
037	42	STD	087	15	E	137	61	GTD	187	43	RCL
038	07	07	088	42	STD	138	00	00	188	18	18
039	99	PRT	089	05	05	139	90	90	189	22	INV
040	91	R/S	090	43	RCL	140	43	RCL	190	77	GE
041	76	LBL	091	02	02	141	02	02	191	02	02
042	17	B'	092	42	STD	142	65	×	192	02	02
043	42	STD	093	03	03	143	43	RCL	193	00	0
044	08	08	094	71	SBR	144	01	01	194	32	X:T
045	99	PRT	095	01	01	145	95	=	195	68	NDP
046	91	R/S	096	40	40	146	22	INV	196	00	0
047	76	LBL	097	23	LNX	147	59	INT	197	67	EQ
048	13	C	098	65	×	148	42	STD	198	02	02
049	86	STF	099	02	2	149	02	02	199	69	69
050	01	01	100	94	+/-	150	92	RTN	200	86	STF

201	02	02	251	00	0	301	32	32	351	40	40
202	01	1	252	67	EQ	302	44	SUM	352	43	RCL
203	44	SUM	253	01	01	303	52	52	353	18	18
204	18	18	254	80	80	304	43	RCL	354	99	PRT
205	44	SUM	255	32	X:T	305	31	31	355	55	÷
206	11	11	256	42	STD	306	44	SUM	356	43	RCL
207	44	SUM	257	00	00	307	51	51	357	17	17
208	19	19	258	44	SUM	308	43	RCL	358	99	PRT
209	00	0	259	12	12	309	30	30	359	95	=
210	48	EXC	260	44	SUM	310	44	SUM	360	99	PRT
211	39	39	261	17	17	311	50	50	361	02	2
212	48	EXC	262	00	0	312	43	RCL	362	04	4
213	38	38	263	42	STD	313	29	29	363	42	STD
214	48	EXC	264	19	19	314	44	SUM	364	00	00
215	37	37	265	01	1	315	49	49	365	43	RCL
216	48	EXC	266	44	SUM	316	43	RCL	366	00	00
217	36	36	267	16	16	317	28	28	367	85	+
218	48	EXC	268	92	RTN	318	44	SUM	368	01	1
219	35	35	269	01	1	319	48	48	369	05	5
220	48	EXC	270	44	SUM	320	43	RCL	370	95	=
221	34	34	271	09	09	321	27	27	371	42	STD
222	48	EXC	272	43	RCL	322	44	SUM	372	06	06
223	33	33	273	39	39	323	47	47	373	00	0
224	48	EXC	274	44	SUM	324	43	RCL	374	72	ST*
225	32	32	275	59	59	325	26	26	375	06	06
226	48	EXC	276	43	RCL	326	44	SUM	376	97	DSZ
227	31	31	277	38	38	327	46	46	377	00	00
228	48	EXC	278	44	SUM	328	43	RCL	378	03	03
229	30	30	279	58	58	329	25	25	379	65	65
230	48	EXC	280	43	RCL	330	44	SUM	380	43	RCL
231	29	29	281	37	37	331	45	45	381	10	10
232	48	EXC	282	44	SUM	332	43	RCL	382	42	STD
233	28	28	283	57	57	333	24	24	383	00	00
234	48	EXC	284	43	RCL	334	44	SUM	384	22	INV
235	27	27	285	36	36	335	44	44	385	86	STF
236	48	EXC	286	44	SUM	336	43	RCL	386	02	02
237	26	26	287	56	56	337	23	23	387	43	RCL
238	48	EXC	288	43	RCL	338	44	SUM	388	08	08
239	25	25	289	35	35	339	43	43	389	32	X:T
240	48	EXC	290	44	SUM	340	43	RCL	390	43	RCL
241	24	24	291	55	55	341	22	22	391	09	09
242	48	EXC	292	43	RCL	342	44	SUM	392	22	INV
243	23	23	293	34	34	343	42	42	393	77	GE
244	48	EXC	294	44	SUM	344	43	RCL	394	03	03
245	22	22	295	54	54	345	21	21	395	98	98
246	48	EXC	296	43	RCL	346	44	SUM	396	43	RCL
247	21	21	297	33	33	347	41	41	397	11	11
248	48	EXC	298	44	SUM	348	43	RCL	398	99	PRT
249	20	20	299	53	53	349	20	20	399	55	÷
250	32	X:T	300	43	RCL	350	44	SUM	400	43	RCL
									401	12	12
									402	99	PRT
									403	95	=
									404	99	PRT
									405	04	4
									406	00	0
									407	22	INV
									408	90	LST
									409	81	RST
									410	92	RTN

E.4.3 Partitioning

6 OP 17, banks one and two.

E.4.4 Nomenclature

See E.2.4.

Stop number one, system age.
Stop number two, number of independent systems.

E.4.5 Data Entry

Enter UL + 1, $1/\lambda$, or σ, press A.
Enter M, press A .
Enter stop number one, press B.
Enter stop number two, press B '.

E.4.6 Standard Solution

Uniform distribution, press C.
Exponential distribution, press D.
Normal distribution, enter $\mu - 1$, press E.
To record the accumulated distribution, press D '.

Program for Least Member of a Set of Random Numbers

F.1 INTRODUCTORY REMARKS

This program was used to compute the data underlying Figures 8.2 and 8.3. It will generate M sets of N random numbers, printing the least member, only, of each set of N numbers. It generates uniform and normal random numbers. It uses the TI-59 Master Library program, ML-15, to generate uniform and normal random numbers but discards negative normal random numbers when generated.

F.2 TABLE F.1, PROGRAM LISTING

Table F.1, Program Listing

000	91	R/S							
001	76	LBL	041	76	LBL				
002	11	A	042	15	E				
003	99	PRT	043	22	INV				
004	42	STO	044	86	STF				
005	10	10	045	00	00				
006	01	1	046	43	RCL				
007	42	STO	047	18	18				
008	16	16	048	42	STO	081	00	00	
009	81	RST	049	00	00	082	91	91	
010	76	LBL	050	01	1	083	32	X:T	
011	12	B	051	52	EE	084	42	STO	
012	99	PRT	052	09	9	085	19	19	
013	42	STO	053	22	INV	086	61	GTO	
014	11	11	054	52	EE	087	00	00	
015	81	RST	055	42	STO	088	91	91	
016	76	LBL	056	19	19	089	69	OP	
017	13	C	057	87	IFF	090	20	20	
018	99	PRT	058	00	00	091	97	DSZ	
019	42	STO	059	00	00	092	00	00	
020	18	18	060	67	67	093	00	00	
021	81	RST	061	36	PGM	094	57	57	
022	76	LBL	062	15	15	095	43	RCL	
023	19	D'	063	13	C	096	19	19	
024	99	PRT	064	61	GTO	097	68	NOP	
025	42	STO	065	00	00	098	68	NOP	
026	09	09	066	70	70	099	99	PRT	
027	81	RST	067	36	PGM	100	43	RCL	
028	76	LBL	068	15	15	101	17	17	
029	10	E'	069	18	C'	102	32	X:T	
030	99	PRT	070	59	INT	103	43	RCL	
031	42	STO	071	32	X:T	104	16	16	
032	17	17	072	00	0	105	77	GE	
033	81	RST	073	68	NOP	106	00	00	
034	76	LBL	074	77	GE	107	00	00	
035	14	D	075	00	00	108	01	1	
036	86	STF	076	89	89	109	44	SUM	
037	00	00	077	43	RCL	110	16	16	
038	61	GTO	078	19	19	111	61	GTO	
039	00	00	079	22	INV	112	00	00	
040	46	46	080	77	GE	113	46	46	

F.3 PARTITIONING

Normal, bank one.

F.4 SOLID STATE SOFTWARE MODULE

ML-15.

F.5 NOMENCLATURE

N Number of random numbers in a set.

M Number of sets of random numbers.

UL The highest integer of the required uniform distribution.

LL The lowest integer of the required uniform distribution.

σ The standard deviation of the normal distribution.

μ The mean of the normal distribution seed determines start of random number sequence.

F.6 DATA ENTRY

Enter N, press C.

Enter M, press E'.

Enter *seed*, press D'.

Enter LL or μ, press A.

Enter $UL + 1$ or σ, press B.

F.7 SOLUTIONS

Uniform, press E.

Normal, press D.

After M sets are complete, J additional sets may be generated by entering $M + J$ and pressing E', followed by pressing D or E as appropriate.

Index